The Doolittle Raid

Other Books by the Author

Round-the-World Flights
The Compact History of the United States Air Force
From the Wright Brothers to the Astronauts
Air Rescues! (with Wendell F. Moseley)
Helicopter Rescues
Lighter-Than-Air Flight
Polar Aviation
Minutemen of the Air
The Modern U.S. Air Force
The Saga of the Air Mail
The DC-3: The Story of a Fabulous Airplane
Grand Old Lady: The Story of the DC-3 (with Wendell F. Moseley)
The Legendary DC-3
Our Family Affairs
The Complete Guide for the Serviceman's Wife (with Elizabeth Land)
Doolittle's Tokyo Raiders
Four Came Home
The Wright Brothers: Pioneers of Power Flight
The First Book of the Moon
Jimmy Doolittle: Master of the Calculated Risk

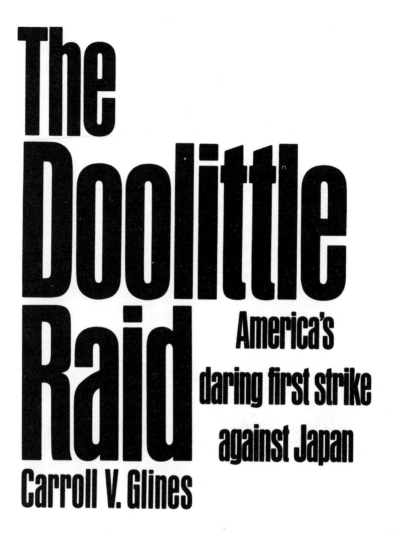

The Doolittle Raid

America's daring first strike against Japan

Carroll V. Glines

ORION BOOKS · NEW YORK

Published by Orion Books, a division of Crown Publishers, Inc., 225 Park Avenue South, New York, New York 10003 and represented in Canada by the Canadian MANDA Group

ORION and colophon are trademarks of Crown Publishers, Inc.

Manufactured in the United States of America

Library of Congress Cataloging-in-Publication Data

Glines, Carroll V., 1920–
The Doolittle Raid: America's daring first strike against Japan
by Carroll V. Glines.
p. cm.
Includes index.
1. World War, 1939–1945—Aerial operations, American. 2. World War, 1939–1945—Campaigns—Japan. 3. Doolittle, James Harold, 1896– . I. Title.
D790.G56 1988
940.54'25—dc19 88-1822
CIP

ISBN 0-517-56748-2

Design by Jake Victor Thomas

10 9 8 7 6 5 4 3 2 1

First Edition

Dedicated to
General James H. "Jimmy" Doolittle
Master of the Calculated Risk

Contents

Foreword

The B-25 raid against Japan has gone down in the annals of World War II as a classic example of the courage and ingenuity of American airmen in combat. Led by the incomparable Jimmy Doolittle, the raid came at a time when the Japanese were advancing steadily across the Pacific. Guam, Wake Island, Hong Kong, and Singapore had fallen. In the Philippines, Gen. Jonathan Wainwright and the remnants of his force were making a brave but hopeless last stand on Corregidor.

The appearance of sixteen B-25s over Japan on April 18, 1942, lifted the gloom that had descended upon America and her Pacific allies. The bomb damage that resulted was not great, compared with that inflicted later in the war, but the raid had some far-reaching effects. For the defense of the home islands, the Japanese were forced to retain fighter units that had been intended for the Solomons, and they felt compelled to expand their Pacific perimeter beyond the area where it could be defended adequately. The full impact of the raid on the minds of the Japanese military leaders and its consequent influence on the course of the war in the Pacific were not realized until long after that conflict.

For America and her allies the raid was a badly needed morale booster. Besides being the first offensive air action undertaken against the Japanese home islands, the Tokyo raid accomplished some other "firsts" that augured well for the future. It was the first war action in which the United States Army Air Forces and the United States Navy teamed up in a full-scale operation against the enemy. The Doolittle Raiders were the first (and last) to fly land-based bombers from a carrier deck on a combat mission and first to use new cruise control techniques in attacking a distant target. The incendiary bombs they carried were the forerunners of those used later in the war. The special camera recording apparatus developed at Lieutenant Colonel Doolittle's request was adopted by the AAF and the crew recommendations concerning armaments, tactics, and equipment were used as the basis for later improvements.

It was twenty-six months before American bombers went

back to Japan. During those months of bitter fighting America was slowly building her land, sea, and air forces and with them driving the enemy, island by island, back across the Pacific. In 1944 and 1945 mighty fleets of B-29s penetrated the skies over Japan and finished the job begun by Jimmy Doolittle and his raiders in 1942.

Curtis E. LeMay

General, USAF (Ret.)

Former Chief of Staff

Introduction

Each year around April 18, a group of World War II air force veterans who flew together on a historic war mission meet for a three-day reunion in a large city somewhere in the United States. While most of the program for the three days is light-hearted, part of one day is set aside for a business meeting and luncheon. The good-natured kidding stops. Guests are ushered from the room. The men sit down to serious discussion of group affairs.

After the meeting the group is served a luncheon. Before each man is set a silver goblet with his name engraved on its side twice—right side up and upside down. Waiters pour brandy for each man and then they, too, are asked to leave.

The chairman for the reunion rises and the group follows his cue. He lifts his goblet high and proposes a toast, "to those who have gone." The solemn men, all in their golden years, lift their goblets in response and answer, "To those who have gone." They drink to conclude the toast, each man knowing that before another reunion is held, he may be included among "those who have gone." If a man has died during the previous year, a member of his air crew proceeds to the goblet case and turns his goblet over.

The roster of their departed comrades is called and one of the members present who served on the crew with one of the departed responds for him.

The men who pay this annual tribute to their departed comrades are members of an exclusive military fraternity that no one else can join. Of the original eighty only a few more than half survive. Some day, like the Civil War veterans of yester-year, they too will hold their last reunion and the group will be no more.

While the men may slowly fade away, the deed that brings them together each year will remain forever engraved on the pages of American military and aviation history. They performed a miracle by bombing an enemy capital at a time when the nation's morale had reached the lowest level ever recorded. They began the reverse of the tide of Japanese conquest and brought the first good news for America and her Allies in the beginning months of the most devastating war in history.

The story of the 1942 Doolittle raid against Japan and its tragic aftermath is told in the following pages as often as possible by the participants themselves. Since the research spans more than a quarter century, some who were interviewed and provided personal information are now deceased but, fortunately, their words and thoughts have been preserved.

This is the true story of eighty very brave men who deserve a permanent place in our hearts and memories.

The Doolittle Raid

1

The Day of Infamy

Twenty minutes after noon on December 8, 1941, ten shiny black limousines entered the grounds of the U.S. Capitol in Washington, D.C. They stopped at the south entrance, and President Franklin D. Roosevelt slowly emerged from the lead car, surrounded by Secret Service agents and assisted by his son James in the uniform of a Marine captain. The president, badly crippled from polio many years before, eased into a wheelchair and proceeded to the chamber of the House of Representatives where he was greeted with prolonged applause from the nation's legislators, Supreme Court justices, civilian guests, and members of the press. He waved briefly but did not smile. The address he was about to make to the emergency joint session of Congress would be the most momentous of his presidency.

The large clock on the wall behind Speaker of the House Sam Rayburn showed 12:29 P.M. Rayburn rapped his gavel and motioned for the audience to be seated while the president opened a black notebook. Then, in the measured tones that the world had grown used to hearing, Roosevelt began to speak:

> Yesterday, December 7, 1941—a date which will live in infamy—the United States of America was suddenly and deliberately attacked by naval and air forces of the Empire of Japan.

The president recounted the attack on Pearl Harbor, Hawaii, and other Japanese offensive moves of the previous twenty-four hours and directed that all measures be taken for the nation's defense. "No matter how long it may take us to overcome this premeditated invasion," he said, "the American people in their righteous might will win through to absolute victory."

He concluded: "I ask that the Congress declare that since the unprovoked and dastardly attack by Japan on Sunday, December 7th, 1941, a state of war has existed between the United States and the Japanese Empire." Within the hour, a nation's resolve was expressed. War was formally declared and the United States began the painful and seemingly impossible task of building military forces capable of eventually defeating the overwhelming combined air, ground, and naval power of Japan, Germany, and Italy.

Far out in the Pacific aboard his aircraft carrier, Commander Mitsuo Fuchida, leader of the air units that carried out the "unprovoked and dastardly attack" against the United States, was basking in the praise of his superiors. He had faithfully and successfully completed his mission of surprise and destruction. He had no regrets.

The concept of attacking America by decimating its Pacific naval forces based in Hawaii was not an idea hatched a short time before the "infamous" attack of December 7, 1941. Having fought on the side of the victorious Allies in World War I, Japan had emerged strong and imagined itself a rival for primacy in the Pacific against the United States. The Imperial Defense Policy adopted in 1918 designated the United States as potential enemy number one.

The anti-United States policy can also be traced to a nonfiction book entitled *Sea Power in the Pacific* by Hector E. Bywater and published by the London *Daily Telegraph* in 1921. The author was the paper's Far East correspondent who reported on Japan's naval activities after World War I. In 1925, Bywater wrote a novel entitled *The Great Pacific War*, which was based in part on his original book. In it, he described a Japanese surprise attack on the U.S. Asiatic Fleet at Pearl Harbor, with simultaneous attacks being launched against Guam and the Philippines. Both books were translated at Japan's Naval War College, distributed to students, and discussed at length in class seminars during the following years. One of those who assiduously studied the possibilities of grand conquest for Japan was Isoroku Yamamoto, future mastermind behind his country's grand strategy to "own" the Pacific.

Encouraged by Yamamoto, who was promoted to admiral and placed in command of the Combined Japanese Fleet in 1939, other Japanese militarists became obsessed with the thought of defeating a powerful enemy like America. All Japanese high-ranking officers who occupied leading positions in the navy for two decades avidly and openly discussed the possibility of war against America. It was inevitable that the idea would eventually leak into the open. Dr. Ricardo Rivera Schreiber, the Peruvian envoy in Tokyo, learned that the Japanese were indeed planning to make a "surprise mass attack on Pearl Harbor" and reported it on January 27, 1941, to a top staff member at the American embassy. Passed through State Department channels, the report ended up in U.S. Navy headquarters in Washington. Naval intelligence analysts replied formally to the State Department that "based on known data regarding the present disposition and employment of Japanese naval and army forces, no move against Pearl Harbor appears imminent or planned for the foreseeable future."[1]

By this time, however, Admiral Yamamoto was making detailed plans for the upcoming attack. Having lived in America as a student at Harvard and as a naval attaché in Washington, he felt he knew America's strengths and weaknesses. He made two basic assumptions: (1) that a major part of the U.S. Navy's fleet in the Pacific would be at Pearl Harbor at any given time, especially on the weekends; and (2) that he could move a large naval task force undetected across the Pacific to a rendezvous point north of Hawaii.

On November 4, 1941, Yamamoto approved Combined Fleet Top Secret Order Number 1, a bulky 151-page document detailing Operation Z, the basic plan for the Pearl Harbor attack, as well as simultaneous assaults on Malaya, the Philippines, Guam, Wake Island, and Hong Kong. Two days later, he set December 8 (December 7 in Hawaii) as "Y-Day" and named Vice Adm. Chuichi Nagumo overall commander of the thirty-one-ship Pearl Harbor Carrier Striking Force consisting of six aircraft carriers, two battleships, two heavy cruisers, a light cruiser, nine destroyers, three submarines, and eight tankers. One by one, the ships assigned to the force slipped quietly out of their respective berths and headed for a rendezvous in Tankan Bay off Etoforu Island, a remote area north of the four main islands of Japan. Another force of about twenty-five submarines began staging to converge south of Oahu, including five with midget submarines riding piggyback on top.

With the militarists firmly in control in Japan, the logistics of the plan had been well under way by the time Yamamoto issued his basic order. Supplies to support this large effort had been carefully and secretly accumulated. The strike force would proceed to a point about 1,000 miles north of Hawaii off the usual shipping lanes between North America and the Far East and beyond the range of the U.S. Navy's PBY patrol planes. The day before the attack, the large ships would refuel for the last time and proceed southward in darkness toward Hawaii. The planes from the carriers would begin takeoffs in two waves from about 250 miles out from Oahu beginning at daybreak.

The air portion of the plan needed an experienced leader. The man chosen was Cmdr. Mitsuo Fuchida, thirty-nine, a pilot with over three thousand hours flying time who had served in combat during the China War. He had graduated from the Japanese Naval Academy in 1924 and the Naval War College in 1937 and had been thoroughly indoctrinated with the ultimate scheme of neutralizing America's influence in the Pacific. In September 1941, he was assigned to the aircraft carrier *Akagi* as commander of all air groups of the First Air Fleet and told of the forthcoming attack he was to lead. He recalled his concerns:

> From ordinary fleet practice we had to shift our energies to specific training for this all-important mission calling for vast and intensive preparations; and, what is more, everything had to be done in haste. It was already late September, and the attack plan called for execution in December![2]

Pilots and crew members flew hundreds of bombing and gunnery training missions. One handicap to their efforts, according to Fuchida, was that the pilots could not yet be told about the planned attack for security reasons. In mid-November, the planes were taken on board their respective carriers, which then headed for the rendezvous point traveling singly and taking separate courses to avoid detection.

On November 25, 1941, Admiral Yamamoto issued an operations order from his flagship *Nagato* at Hiroshima to Vice Admiral Nagumo in charge of the attack force:

> The Task Force will leave Tankan Bay on 26 November and, making every effort to conceal movement, advance to the stand-by point, where fueling will be quickly completed.

As the force steamed eastward and all hands were told of their mission, discussions between the United States and Japan steadily deteriorated in Washington, according to the Japanese plan. Despite the growing evidence contained in intercepted messages that Japan was intent on beginning hostilities, no American was convinced that war was so imminent. Coded messages from Japan to Ambassador Saburo Kurusu in Washington were intercepted regularly by army and navy communications analysts and cryptographers who had previously broken the Japanese top-secret PURPLE code. However, the possibility of war still seemed remote even though naval intelligence lost track of the two Japanese carrier divisions steaming eastward because message traffic had diminished to almost nothing.

On December 2, Tokyo time, an electrifying coded message was sent to the task force:

> NIITAKA YAMA NOBORE

("Climb Mount Niitaka"), which meant "Proceed with attack." The message had no meaning to the U.S. cryptographers who intercepted it.

Meanwhile, a Japanese spy had been reporting daily on the ships at Pearl Harbor. By 0600 (Hawaii time) on Sunday December 7, there were eight battleships, three airplane tenders, seventeen destroyers, and other smaller ships at anchor, but no aircraft carriers, a big disappointment to Fuchida and his planning staff. At that moment, the strike force was 230 miles north of Oahu; the carriers were turned into the wind and brought to full speed. Fuchida gave the signal and the huge armada of planes lifted from the carriers' decks, formed into battle formations in two waves, and headed south.

The strength of the Japanese aerial attack force was enormous. There were 135 dive bombers, 40 torpedo bombers, 104 high-level bombers, and 81 fighters. Fuchida, flying in a high-level bomber marked with red and yellow stripes to distinguish it as the commander's, was along as an observer. When airborne, he tuned in Honolulu's most popular station, KGMB, on his radio compass and was given a gratis weather report. The weather was only partly cloudy, so the attack could proceed as planned. One of two reconnaissance planes launched earlier confirmed the number and types of ships at Pearl Harbor.

"Now I knew for sure that there were no carriers in the harbor," Fuchida wrote later. "The sky cleared as we moved in on the target and Pearl Harbor was plainly visible from the northwest valley of the island. I studied our objective through binoculars. 'Notify all planes to launch attacks,' I ordered my radio man who immediately began tapping the key. The order went in plain code: 'To, to, to, to . . .'. The time was 0749."[3]

At 7:55 A.M. on that quiet Sunday morning, the first wave of Japanese planes attacked Hickam Field to keep the Army Air Corps from rising to the island's defense. At the same time, strikes were made on Bellows and Wheeler Fields. The Naval Air Station at Ford Island, the ships anchored in the harbor, and the Marine Air Station at Ewa were also blasted. At 0757 torpedo planes started their runs on the battleships: at 0805 the level bombers dropped their loads on the ships lying helpless below. Surprise had been assured.

Knowing that Admirals Nagumo and Yamamoto and the General Staff were anxious to hear about the attack, Fuchida ordered the coded message for a successful surprise raid sent to the fleet:

TORA. TORA. TORA.

[The use of this code word came from a Japanese saying, "A tora (tiger) goes out 1,000 *ri* (2,000 miles) and returns without fail."]

At 8 A.M., the U.S. Navy's Pacific fleet headquarters radioed the message to Washington that shocked the world:

AIR RAID. PEARL HARBOR. THIS IS NO DRILL.

For the next thirty minutes the first of the two waves of

Japanese planes rained blow after blow on the American military installations. In that time the bulk of Hawaiian-based air power was destroyed. To make sure, the second wave renewed the assault. The entire attack lasted one hour and forty-five minutes. In that brief span of time, the empire of Japan became the dominant naval and air power in the Pacific. The score for the Japanese:

- A total of 18 American ships, including 7 battleships, were sunk or seriously damaged.
- U.S. naval installations were severely crippled. Of 169 U.S. naval planes in Hawaii, 92 were destroyed, 39 badly damaged.
- Three Army Air Forces installations were badly damaged. Of the 231 planes assigned to the Hawaiian Air Force, 96 were completely destroyed. Only 79 could subsequently be used for combat.
- On the attack, 2,403 American military personnel and civilians were killed.

It was only during the last half hour of the attack that American forces could mount any resistance. About thirty Army Air Corps fighters were able to get airborne but no navy planes. Eleven Japanese planes were claimed shot down. Two U.S. pilots flying P-40s, Lts. George Welch and Kenneth Taylor, were credited with seven between them.

Fuchida lingered over the area, taking photographs after the second wave of attackers had started back to their carriers. When he returned to *Akagi*, the other planes had been refueled and rearmed, ready for a second attack, but were held waiting for Fuchida's report. He told Admiral Nagumo that, although there had been great damage, it should not be assumed that everything had been destroyed. "There are still many targets to be hit," he said, "therefore, I recommend that another attack be launched."

Nagumo did not agree. In retrospect, Fuchida said later, "I had done all I could to urge another attack, but the decision rested entirely with Admiral Nagumo, and he chose to retire without launching the next attack. Immediately flag signals were hoisted ordering the course change, and our ships headed northward at high speed."[4]

The Japanese had lost twenty-nine planes, one large and five midget submarines; fifty-five airmen and nine submariners had died. One of the midget sub pilots, Ensign Sakamaki, was captured when his boat went aground on the north side of Oahu, and he became the first Japanese prisoner of the war.

By 9:30 A.M. air force patrol planes began a fruitless search for the enemy. By nightfall they had made nearly fifty sorties—all without seeing the enemy again.

The Japanese returned home as heroes. Commander Mitsuo Fuchida was ordered to report to the Imperial Palace for an audience with Emperor Hirohito, a rare honor for a junior officer. Fuchida, a name that would be forever linked to the Pearl Harbor attack, would be heard from again, as a result of another surprise raid—this one against Japan—in one of the strange coincidences of World War II.

2

A Concept Is Born

The policeman at the White House gate stepped out of the guard house as the army staff car approached. He held up his hand, indicating he wanted to check the occupants in the rear seat. The officer peered inside and recognized the stony, unsmiling Army Chief of Staff, Gen. George C. Marshall. On Marshall's left with the ever-present grin that had earned him the nickname "Hap," sat Gen. Henry H. Arnold, Chief of Staff of the Army Air Forces. The policeman smiled back at Arnold and waved the car inside the White House grounds.

It was exactly two weeks almost to the hour that the first news of the attack on Pearl Harbor had reached Washington. Upon Marshall, Arnold, and Chief of Naval Operations Adm. Ernest J. King had fallen the unprecedented task of planning and directing the mobilization of the most powerful army, navy, and air force the world had ever known. Since that "infamous" Sunday, President Roosevelt was briefed daily on the problems and plans of the military buildup. On this day, the trio was joined by Harry Hopkins, Roosevelt's special advisor, Adm. Harold R. Stark, Secretary of War Henry Stimson, and Secretary of the Navy Frank Knox.

The group was shown into the president's study, where they were greeted warmly one by one. General Marshall presented his estimate of the global situation, after which the president discussed the developments in Africa and Europe and then focused on the Far East. He said he wanted to strike back at Japan at the earliest possible moment and asked everyone present to consider ways and means to take the war to the Land of the Rising Sun. He asked what had been accomplished thus far.

Marshall briefed the president on plans to "militarize" the

former army and navy pilots flying for the Flying Tigers, the American Volunteer Group in China under Col. Claire Chennault. Roosevelt emphasized that he wanted a bombing raid on the home islands of Japan as soon as possible to bolster the morale of America and the Allies. This request, repeated emphatically over and over again in the weeks following, made an impression on everyone present. The president's sense of urgency was transferred to their respective staffs by Marshall, King, and Arnold when they returned to their offices. Arnold dictated notes of the meeting to his secretary, which resulted in a memorandum to the War Plans Division of the Air Staff directing that plans be drafted for retaliatory air strikes against Japan.

Beginning December 24, Marshall, King, and Arnold met with their British army, navy, and air force counterparts who had come to the States with Prime Minister Winston Churchill. These meetings, known as the Arcadia Conferences, lasted through January 14, 1942. The group met almost daily with the president and followed up with meetings of "working committees" to develop long-range strategy against the three Axis powers.

One of the principal subjects at a meeting on January 4, 1942, was the unsettled French situation in North Africa. The decision was made to invade the area and neutralize any resistance by unfriendly French forces. Admiral King suggested that three U.S. Navy carriers should be used to transport the needed aircraft. He recommended that one carrier should carry about seventy-five to eighty navy fighters aboard and another eighty to one hundred army fighters. The third would be used to transport army bomber and cargo planes, gas, bombs, and ammunition.

Arnold did not dispute King's suggestion about the army bombers and cargo aircraft but he knew there would be some problems to solve. That night, in his office in the Munitions Building, he transcribed his notes and drafted a memo to the War Plans staff. "By transporting these army bombers on a carrier," he wrote, "it will be necessary for us to take off from the carrier, which brings up the question of what kind of plane—B-18 bomber and DC-3 for cargo?

"We will have to try bomber take-offs from carriers. It has

never been done before but we must try out and check on how long it takes."[1]

The Army Air Forces War Plans Division staff studied this unusual memo from their chief and began the work to check all aspects of the North African invasion plan. Army fighters could be launched from the deck of a carrier without difficulty, but could a loaded B-18 medium bomber or a DC-3 cargo plane? It would take some research to find out.

Thus, the seed of an idea of using a navy carrier to transport army bombers to an area of operations had been planted by Admiral King, but he never envisioned medium bombers or cargo transports actually flying from a carrier's deck. It was Arnold who took the possibility one step further. However, he did not realize just how good his idea was. He did not know then that his directive to "try out and check on how long it takes" would eventually result in different army aircraft being launched from a navy carrier against the enemy in another theater of war.

The first month of war found the defensive structure of the Allied nations crumbling on every front. In the Pacific, one Japanese victory followed another with shocking speed. American forces in the Philippines had retreated onto the Bataan Peninsula. The British army, after surrendering the base at Penang, retreated southward as the Japanese continued their advance upon Singapore. In the oil-rich Dutch East Indies, enemy forces had landed on Borneo, Timor, Celebes, and New Guinea.

The rapid pace of these successes was not countered by any showing of Allied power. Wake Island fell on December 23, which confirmed the worst fears of Americans that the U.S. Navy's power had been destroyed at Pearl Harbor. In the Philippines, President Manuel Quezon, confined to a wheelchair, was sworn in on December 30 for a second term at the entrance to Malinta Tunnel on Corregidor while Japanese guns boomed in the distance.

In an attempt to bolster the morale of the Filipinos and the Americans holding out on Bataan, Roosevelt sent a message: "I give to the people of the Philippines my solemn pledge that their freedom will be redeemed and their independence established and protected. The entire resources in men and materials of the United States stand behind that pledge."

The president's message gave the fifteen thousand Americans and sixty-five thousand Filipinos on Bataan renewed courage and hope. They were supposed to hold out for six months, if possible, and await the coming of massive fleets of ships and planes from America. These massive fleets did not exist but the men fighting for their lives did not know this. They had no choice but to keep on fighting as long as possible.

Amon G. Carter, publisher of the Fort Worth, Texas, *Star Telegram* and aviation enthusiast, wrote to his old friend Maj. Gen. Edwin M. "Pa" Watson, military secretary to the president, on December 18. Like hundreds of other well-meaning Americans, Carter thought he had an original idea that would help win the war. He naively suggested that five hundred long-range bombers loaded with four thousand pounds of bombs could bomb Tokyo with airline pilots at the controls.

Watson forwarded Carter's letter to General Arnold on December 30 for comment. On January 7, Arnold replied to Watson that "the fundamental idea is sound but the problem of execution is something more than that expressed by Mr. Carter. However, we will have a solution in the near future which we hope will get the results desired."[2]

Adm. Ernest J. King, after one of the January meetings with the president, motored to the Washington Navy Yard to meet with his staff aboard a former German yacht, the *Vixen*, then serving as his flagship and second office. Several key members of his staff lived and worked aboard. King would brief them on his meetings with the president and continually reiterate Roosevelt's desire to strike back at Japan.

On January 10, after King had retired to his cabin, Capt. Francis S. Low, a submariner on King's staff, knocked on King's door and asked if he could speak to his chief alone. Not an easy man to talk to because of his stern demeanor, King made his staff uncomfortable when in his presence.[3]

King invited Low inside, wondering about this unusual visit. "Yes, Low, what's on your mind?"

"Sir, I've got an idea for bombing Japan I'd like to discuss with you."

King was immediately interested. Like Arnold, he had sent memos to his staff after each meeting with the president noting that their commander-in-chief continually asked when the military was going to "do something" to retaliate against the Japanese.

Low continued, "I flew down to Norfolk today to check on the readiness of our new carrier, the *Hornet*, and saw something that started me thinking."

Low paused when he saw the quizzical look on his boss's face, then continued. "The enemy knows that the radius of action of our carrier airplanes is limited to about three hundred miles. Today, as we were taking off from Norfolk, I saw the outline of a carrier deck painted on an airfield which is used to give our pilots practice taking off from a short distance . . ."

King was patient with Low, but so far he hadn't been told anything new. "I don't understand what you're getting at, Low."

"Well, Sir, I saw some army twin-engine planes making bombing passes at this simulated carrier deck at the same time. If the army has some planes with longer range than our carrier planes and if they could take off in the length of a carrier deck, then it seems to me a few of them could be loaded on a carrier and used to bomb Japan. It would be a mighty big surprise to the Japanese and would certainly build up the morale of the American people."

King leaned back and said nothing for a moment. Low felt uneasy and expected a curt rebuff because he was a submariner, not a pilot, and knew little about airplanes or carrier operations.

"Low, you may have something there. Talk to Duncan about it in the morning."

As Low turned to go, King cautioned, "One thing, Low. Don't tell anyone else about this."

Low immediately phoned Capt. Donald B. "Wu" Duncan at his Washington apartment and asked to see him first thing the next morning. Duncan, a 1917 graduate of the Naval Academy, was King's air operations officer and highly respected for his planning ability and knowledge of carrier aviation.

When they met, Low explained his idea and how he had

conceived it the day before ("fortuitous association," he later told the author). "As I see it," Low told Duncan, "there are two big questions to be answered: first, can such a plane—a land-based twin-engine medium bomber—land aboard a carrier? And second, can such a plane, stripped down to its bare essentials and loaded with bombs and gasoline, take off from a carrier deck? If either one or both of these questions can be answered affirmatively, we may have a whole new concept of operation to go on."

"The answer to your first questions is a definite negative," Duncan replied. "In the first place, a carrier deck is too short to land an Army medium bomber safely. Even if one could stop in time, there would be no place to stow it because it wouldn't fit on an elevator to be taken below and make way for the next plane. The newest bombers, the North American B-25 Mitchell and Martin B-26 Marauder have tricycle landing gear. This design means increased landing speed and the tails are so high off the deck that there is no way to install a landing hook. Besides, the tail structures are too weak to take the shock of hard, sudden-stop landings."

"And my second question?"

"That will take some figuring. I'll get to work and let you know."

"All right," Low said, "but the Boss said not to tell another soul what you're doing."

Wu Duncan found a vacant office and buried himself in the details of his study. He made discreet inquiries of the army concerning its medium bombers, especially the B-25 and B-26, asking for such information as landing speeds, dimensions, range, and load capabilities. He checked with navy sources for deck space data, experience with heavily loaded takeoffs, and Pacific weather patterns to determine the best time for raids against Japan.

At the end of five days, Duncan emerged with a thirty-page handwritten analysis. He settled on the North American B-25 as the only plane that could possibly be used. The Martin B-26s were too "hot" to get off from a carrier's restricted deck space. The B-25 could carry two thousand pounds of bombs and make a two-thousand-mile flight only if extra gas tanks were installed.

Duncan felt that the carrier *Hornet* would be the ideal ship to carry the B-25s to a launch point. Commissioned in October 1941, she was due to sail from Norfolk to the Pacific in February. She could steam at twenty-five knots or better, and the modified B-25s could take off from her deck safely with only a light wind. Using a screening force of another carrier, cruisers, and destroyers, the *Hornet* could be brought within about five hundred miles of Japan so the bombers could be launched. After bombing Japan, the bombers could escape to China and the navy task force could withdraw to safer waters. Since army pilots were not trained to take off in the length of a carrier's deck, they must be taught and the navy would have to conduct the training. To prove that the B-25s could indeed fly from a carrier, it should be tried as soon as possible.

When Duncan told Low he had finished his study, they both went to see Admiral King. Unsmiling as usual, King leafed through Duncan's handwritten report while the two subordinates stood by uneasily. When he finished reading, King said, "Go see General Arnold about this and if he agrees with you, ask him to get in touch with me. But don't mention this to another soul!"

As the two officers turned to go, King called them back. "Duncan, if this plan gets the green light from Arnold, I want you to handle the navy end of it," he said firmly, and then dismissed the pair with a wave of his hand. They immediately made an appointment to see General Arnold the next day, January 17, 1942.

3

The B-25B Special Project

When Low and Duncan presented their idea to Hap Arnold, Low recalled that Arnold "was most enthusiastic" about a carrier-based raid against Japan. He did not tell them that he had already asked his own staff to check into the feasibility of just such a plan in connection with the forthcoming invasion of North Africa. Staff members had not yet made their recommendations to him because of the workload imposed on them by the Arcadia Conference, which was just ending.

Arnold immediately got in touch with King and told him he liked the idea. After they decided on the fundamental division of responsibility between them, King said that Wu Duncan would coordinate all the navy planning. Whoever Arnold chose to carry out the Army Air Force's side of the task would oversee the modification of whatever planes were chosen, the training of the crews, and the transfer to the West Coast for loading on the carrier.

The man Arnold needed for this kind of dangerous mission had to be someone who was used to doing the impossible with an airplane. He should not only be an experienced pilot but someone who could inspire others by example and who knew airplanes not only as a pilot knows them but as an aeronautical engineer. Arnold sent down the hall for Lt. Col. James H. "Jimmy" Doolittle.

"The selection of Doolittle to lead this nearly suicidal mission was a natural one," Arnold later explained. "He was fearless, technically brilliant, a leader who not only could be counted upon to do a task himself if it were humanly possible, but could impart that spirit to others."[1]

Arnold, saddled with the gigantic task of forming an air force of unprecedented size, needed strong, capable air leaders. Good men with flying experience—and guts—were hard to find. "Our reservoir of skilled and experienced officers was so shallow," Arnold wrote later in his memoirs, "that every time we lost one he was almost irreplaceable."[2]

Jimmy Doolittle was one of those "irreplaceable" officers. Called "master of the calculated risk," he had won nearly every aviation trophy there was. Racing and test pilot, aeronautical engineer, and holder of many aviation speed records and firsts, Doolittle was a man whose fast-paced activities belied his name. Not only was he the first to fly coast to coast in less than twenty-four hours, he was also first to do it in less than twelve. He was first to fly an outside loop but, most significantly for the future of aviation, he was the first to take off, fly a set course, and land an airplane without ever seeing the ground—thus pioneering what was then called "blind flying." He had earned masters and doctoral degrees from the Massachusetts Institute of Technology and had become world-renowned for his aeronautical knowledge as well as his varied flying skills.

Doolittle missed seeing service during World War I. He entered army flight training in November 1917, and became a flying instructor. In 1921, he participated in the battleship bombings off the Virginia coast led by Gen. Billy Mitchell, famous air power advocate. Between then and 1930, Jimmy stayed in the air corps until he could no longer afford to support his wife, his mother, his wife's mother, and his two sons on a lieutenant's pay. He resigned his commission and took a position with Shell Oil Company in charge of their aviation department. He accepted a reserve commission as a major, however, and maintained an active association with the struggling peacetime Army Air Corps.

When war began in Europe in September 1939, Doolittle was sure the conflict would eventually involve America. After a trip to Europe where he saw the growing German *Luftwaffe* firsthand, he got in touch with his old friend Hap Arnold, briefed him on what he had seen and volunteered to return to active duty.

On July 1, 1940, orders were issued assigning Doolittle in his reserve grade of major to Indianapolis as assistant district supervisor of the Air Corps' Central Procurement District. Four months later Doolittle was transferred to Detroit, where the automobile industry had difficulty changing from production of civilian goods to tanks, aircraft components, and other military needs. These two assignments were not designed to keep Doolittle, then forty-three, out of the cockpit and behind a desk. Roosevelt's plans to make America "the arsenal of democracy" meant that the nation's industries had to be converted from making peacetime goods to war materiel for the Allies. Retooling and reorganizing almost every industry was a mammoth, almost impossible task. Arnold knew that Doolittle not only had the necessary engineering background but the tact, finesse, and experience needed to deal with industry as well.

By December 7, 1941, the entire automotive industry had agreed on their "terminal quotas" of automobiles for the civilian market. Throughout the time that Doolittle had been in Indianapolis and Detroit, he had kept in close touch with Arnold. Although not on Arnold's staff and far beneath him in rank, no one ever tried to stop Jimmy from going out of the usual military channels to contact Arnold directly if he had a problem. He never abused the privilege that their friendship had given him and always used it in the best interests of getting his assigned job accomplished.

On December 24, Arnold telephoned Doolittle in Detroit.

"Jim, I'd like to have you on my staff here in Washington," Arnold said. "How soon can you come?"

"I can be there in four hours," Doolittle replied.

When Doolittle officially transferred to Washington on January 2, 1942, he was promoted to lieutenant colonel and became a troubleshooter for Arnold to help solve serious technical problems. He was authorized to cut across command lines and report directly to his chief.

One of the problems was the high accident rate of the Martin B-26 Marauder medium bomber, which pilots had renamed "Murderer." In his memoirs, Arnold wrote: "Our new pilots were afraid of the B-26 and we had one accident after another. Seemingly, all that was necessary was for one engine to go sour on a B-26 while in flight, and it would crash."[3]

"It was an unforgiving airplane," Doolittle recalled. "It was killing pilots because it never gave them a chance to make mistakes. Hap asked me to check into the problem and recommend to him whether or not it should continue to be built. I checked it over, flew it, and liked it. There wasn't anything about it that good piloting skill couldn't overcome. I recommended it continue to be built and it was."[4]

Arnold asked Doolittle to go to a B-26 transition school and show pilots who were apprehensive about flying it that it could be flown safely. The school commander had all the pilots lined up along the ramp when Doolittle arrived. As they waited, a B-26 landed on one engine, a feat that had been rumored "impossible." Doolittle spoke to the group, asked what they had heard the airplane could *not* do, and proceeded to demonstrate that what they had heard was pure bunk. He took off, quickly feathered one engine, turned into the dead engine, another feat considered impossible, flew around the pattern in tight turns, and made several more single-engine landings. When he departed, there wasn't a single doubter left.

Continually conscious of the president's request to strike back at the Japanese and having heard the basic idea of a carrier-based raid by army bombers, Arnold's next problem was to confirm whether or not it could be done. Arnold called Doolittle in after Duncan and Low left and asked, "Jim, what bomber do we have that will get off in five hundred feet with a two-thousand-pound bomb load and fly two thousand miles?"[5]

Doolittle pondered the question a moment. The air force had bombers that could take off in five hundred feet but none that could do that and fly two thousand miles with a ton of bombs. Still, maybe the Douglas B-18 or B-23 or the North American B-25 could do it. The Martin B-26 needed too much takeoff distance and the heavy four-engine Boeing B-17s and Consolidated B-24s coming into the inventory could never get off in a mere five hundred feet.

"General, I'll need a little time and I'll get the answer to you in a day or two."

Next day, Doolittle reported to Arnold that the choice narrowed down to the B-18 and the B-25 but both would have to be modified with extra gas tanks to fly the required distance.

"One more fact that I must tell you," Arnold said. "The plane must take off from a narrow area not over seventy-five feet wide."

"Well, then, the only answer is the B-25 because the B-18's

wing span is too great for a safe takeoff. Now, what's behind all this?"

Arnold quickly described the mission against Japan to Doolittle, who immediately realized its significance if successful. Doolittle was enthusiastic and volunteered to take over the project, get the planes modified, and train the crews. It was the kind of problem solving Doolittle liked.

Arnold talked briefly with Admiral King, who told Arnold, "We'll get your men within striking distance of Japan, then it's up to them. We'll shoot for a West Coast departure of about April first. I'll send Duncan to Pearl Harbor to work out details with Admiral Nimitz and I'll let you know when we're ready for you. As I see it, the biggest problem will be security. The fewer who know what we're doing, the better."[6]

Arnold agreed. Not only would the lives of the bomber crews depend on secrecy but also the hundreds of men in the naval task force. If the Japanese were aware of an approaching naval force that had escaped the Pearl Harbor attack, they would marshall their forces in great strength to finish the job they had begun in Hawaii. Duncan and Doolittle went their independent ways knowing what they had to do.

"I was given the greatest gift you can be given in the service to get a job done—top priority," Doolittle recalled. "I had top priority on everything right from Hap. I could have anything I wanted. It was the only reason we got everything we wanted when we wanted it. It was a hell of a lever."[7]

At 2:00 P.M. on January 28, 1942, General Arnold met again with the president, secretary of war, Admiral King, General Marshall, and others in the White House. Discussions of strategy centered around the situation in the Pacific and the Far East. In his report of that meeting, Arnold noted that the president asked again about the progress being made on plans for bombing Japan.

"At that time, the Doolittle project was underway," Arnold recalled, "but all those present did not yet know about it and we didn't want it to be common knowledge so I steered clear of it and talked about bombing Japan from China and Russia."[8]

While Arnold concerned himself with broad strategy on two fronts a world apart, Doolittle was sorting out the pieces of the puzzle for which he was responsible—choosing the units from which the aircraft and the crews would come, making arrangements for modifications, and setting up a training schedule.

Meanwhile, Captain Duncan was setting the navy's wheels in motion. One of his first actions was to request a submarine be dispatched to send back weather data from the waters off Japan. Lt. Cmdr. William L. Anderson, skipper of the *Thresher*, was ordered to proceed via Midway Island, make frequent weather observations, observe enemy shipping, and attack targets of opportunity. Weather would play an important part in such a mission. Not only the aircraft but the task force would be endangered if it was caught in a typhoon or severe storm.

The mission of the *Thresher* was only the beginning. A force of ships to escort and protect one or two carriers had to be made up of destroyers, cruisers, oilers, and submarines. Gathering such a force would put a severe strain on the Pacific fleet still trying to recover from the devastation at Pearl Harbor. The risk of carrying the war to the Japanese side of the Pacific was great.

But there was still a basic question to be answered. Both Duncan and Doolittle, experienced airmen, had calculated that it would be possible to take a loaded B-25 off a carrier's deck, but could they be wrong? Duncan decided to find out.

The USS *Hornet*, the navy's newest carrier, was due in Norfolk on January 31 to be readied for her first war mission. It offered an excellent chance to find out if the B-25s could get off safely. Besides, the *Hornet* was scheduled to go to the Pacific. It might be the one selected for the raid. Duncan made arrangements with Arnold's office to have three B-25s waiting at dockside when the *Hornet* arrived at Hampton Roads. He radioed Capt. Marc A. Mitscher, the carrier's skipper, that he would come aboard to discuss urgent business.

Meanwhile, three army air force crews had been selected for the takeoff trials. Lt. John E. Fitzgerald, a 1940 flying school graduate, had about four hundred hours in B-25s when war was declared. He received orders to fly to Norfolk where he was put in charge of two other crews assigned to the mission. The three crews made about thirty practice short-field takeoff runs at one of the navy's auxiliary fields. However, one of the B-25s had an engine malfunction and did not participate thereafter.

On the afternoon of February 2, Duncan reported to Mitscher and discussed the experiment without telling Mitscher the real purpose of the trials. Early next day, the two B-25s were loaded aboard and the huge carrier left the dock and steamed off the coast about one hundred miles.

The carrier faced into the wind and the pilots manned their planes. Fitzgerald's plane, lightly loaded, was maneuvered into position by the navy deck crewmen and the engines started. The launching officer signaled to Fitzgerald to rev up his engines to the maximum. At the proper instant, the "go" signal was given. The Mitchell raced down the gently sloping deck and lifted easily into the air with space to spare.

"When they spotted the planes for takeoff," Fitzgerald recalled,[9]

> I was surprised to see that we had almost five hundred feet of usable deck space and that the plane's airspeed indicator showed about forty-five miles per hour just sitting there. That meant that we had to accelerate only about twenty-three miles per hour.
>
> When I got the "go" signal, I let the brakes off and was almost immediately airborne—well ahead of my estimate. One thing that worried me though was the "island" out over the flight deck on which the skipper stood so he could have a clear view of the deck operations. The wing of my plane rose so rapidly that I thought we were going to strike this projection. I pushed the control column forward and the wing just barely passed underneath. I climbed and circled back to watch Lieutenant McCarthy take off.

Lt. James F. McCarthy's plane, also lightly loaded, was jockeyed into position and roared skyward. It, too, was airborne before reaching the end of the deck. The two B-25s joined up and disappeared over the horizon, their crews unaware of the significance of their experiment.

Duncan was now satisfied that his calculations were correct. The wind had been about twenty knots down the deck and the speed of the *Hornet* had been only ten knots. At a top speed of twenty-five knots and an average wind, it seemed certain that a fully loaded B-25 bomber could make a successful carrier takeoff.

While Duncan was busy working out the navy's share of the

coming operation, Doolittle coordinated the air force share. Modification of the planes had to be accomplished as soon as possible. New gas tanks had to be designed, drawings made, a contractor found, the planes scheduled into the modification center, and tests made of the installations. To get the job done by April 1, Doolittle had to invoke his top priority from Hap Arnold continually. "I was extremely unpopular everywhere I went," he said, "but with that top priority straight from the top, I got what I needed and I got it quickly."

On January 22, Doolittle requested that eighteen B-25s be made available to Mid-Continent Airlines at Minneapolis, Minnesota, "for alteration as required." He flew to Wright Field, Ohio, and conferred with Brig. Gen. George C. Kenney and his staff to tell them what he needed in the way of assistance for the "B-25B Special Project" but did not tell them why. In addition to the new gas tanks, new bomb shackles and other special equipment would be needed. Several planes were to be equipped with small electrically operated cameras that would take sixty pictures at half-second intervals, starting automatically when the first bomb was dropped. The others were to carry 16-mm motion picture cameras similarly mounted. Landing flares were to be relocated forward of the rear armored bulkhead to protect the crew against fires if the aircraft were hit by enemy fighters or anti-aircraft fire.

Doolittle also set other wheels in motion. He asked Arnold's intelligence staff to select the best targets in Japan for the mission. On January 31, Brig. Gen. Carl Spaatz replied with maps and a list of industrial targets located in Tokyo, Kobe, Nagoya, Yokohama, and six other major cities. The list included iron, steel, magnesium, and aluminum industries, in addition to aircraft plants, petroleum refineries, and naval objectives.

When Doolittle had coordinated the different modification phases of the project, he returned to his office in Room 4414 of the Munitions Building. He sat down at his desk, pulled out a lined tablet, and reviewed the concept in his mind. Was there anything else that had to be done in regard to the modification of the planes? The blueprints were being made, armament was being prepared, targets were being selected. What other tasks needed to be accomplished? To clarify the whole project in his mind, he began to write:[10]

Subject: B-25 Special Project
To: Commanding General, Army Air Forces

The purpose of this special project is to bomb and fire the industrial center of Japan.

It is anticipated that this will not only cause confusion and impede production but will undoubtedly facilitate operation against Japan in other theaters due to their probable withdrawal of troops for the purpose of defending the home country.

An action of this kind is most desirable now due to the psychological effect on the American public, our allies and our enemies.

The method contemplated is to bring carrier-borne bombers to within 400 to 500 miles (all distances mentioned will be in statute miles) of the coast of Japan, preferably to the south southeast. They will then take off from the carrier deck and proceed directly to selected objectives. These objectives will be military and industrial targets in the Tokyo-Yokohama, Nagoya and Osaka-Kobe areas.

Simultaneous bombings of these areas is contemplated with the bombers coming in up waterways from the southeast and, after dropping their bombs, returning in the same direction. After clearing the Japanese outside coastline a sufficient distance, a general westerly course will be set for one or more of the following airports in China: Chuchow, Chuchow (Lishui), Yushan and/or Chienou. Chuchow is about 70 miles inland and two hundred miles to the south southwest of Shanghai.

After refueling, the airplanes will proceed to the strong Chinese air base at Chungking, about 800 miles distant, and from there to such ultimate objective as may, at that time, be indicated.

The greatest non-stop distance that any airplane will have to fly is 2,000 miles.

Eighteen B-25B (North American medium bomber) airplanes will be employed in this raid. Each will carry about 1,100 gallons of gasoline which assures a range of 2,400 miles at 5,000 feet altitude in still air.

Each bomber will carry two 500 lb. demolition bombs and as near as possible to 1,000 lbs. of incendiaries. The demolition bombs will be dropped first and then the incendiaries.

The extra gasoline will be carried in a 275-gallon auxiliary leakproof tank in the top of the bomb bay and a 175-gallon flexible rubber tank in the passageway above the bomb bay. It is anticipated that the gasoline from this top tank will be used up and the tank flattened out or rolled up and removed prior to entering the combat zone. This assures that the airplane will be fully operational and minimizes the fire and explosion hazard characteristic of a near empty tank.

In all other respects the airplanes are conventional. The work of installing the required additional tankage is being done by Mid-Continent Airlines at Minneapolis. All production and installation work is progressing according to schedule and the 24 airplanes (6 spares) should be completely converted by March 15th.

Extensive range and performance tests will be conducted on #1 article while the others are being converted. A short period will be required to assemble and give special training to the crews. The training will include teamwork in bombing, gunnery, navigation, flying, short take-off and at least one carrier take-off for each pilot.

If the crews are selected promptly from men familiar with their jobs and the B-25B airplane, the complete unit should be ready for loading on the carrier by April 1st.

General operational instructions will be issued just before take-off from the carrier.

Due to the greater accuracy of daylight bombing, a daylight raid is contemplated. The present concept of the project calls for a night takeoff from the carrier and arrival over objectives at dawn. Rapid refueling at the landing points will permit arrival at Chungking before dark.

A night raid will be made if, due to last minute information received from our intelligence section or other source, a daylight raid is definitely inadvisable. The night raid should be made on a clear night, moonlight if Japan is blacked out; moonless if it is not.

All available pertinent information regarding targets and defenses will be obtained from A-2, G-2 and other existent sources.

The Navy has already supervised takeoff tests made at Norfolk, Va. using three B-25B bombers carrying loads of 23,000 lbs., 26,000 lbs. and 29,000 lbs. These tests indicate that no difficulty need be anticipated in taking off from the carrier deck with a gross load of around 31,000 lbs.

The Navy will be charged with providing a carrier (probably the *Hornet*), loading and storing the airplanes and with delivering them to the take-off position.

The Chemical Warfare Service is designing and preparing special incendiary bomb clusters in order to assure that the maximum amount that limited space permits, up to 1,000 lbs. per airplane may be carried. 48 of these clusters will be ready for shipment from Edgewood Arsenal by March 15th.

1st Lt. Harry W. Howze, now with the Air Service Command and formerly with the Standard Oil Company of New Jersey, will be charged with making arrangements for the fuel caches in China. He will work with A-2 and A-4 and with Col. Claire Chennault, a former Air Corps officer and now aviation advisor to the Chinese government. Col. Chennault should assign a responsible American or a Chinese who speaks English to physically check and assure that the supplies are in place. This man should also be available to assist the crews in servicing the airplanes. That the supplies are in place can be indicated by suitable radio code signal. Work on placing supplies *must* start at once.

Shortly before the airplanes arrive, the proper Chinese agencies should be advised that the airplanes are coming soon but the inference will be that they are flying up from the south in order to stage a raid on Japan from which they plan to return to the same base.

Radio signals from the bombing planes immediately after they drop their bombs may be used to indicate arrival at gasing points some six or seven hours later.

Care must be exercised to see that the Chinese are advised just in time as any information given to the Chinese may be expected to fall into Japanese hands and a premature notification would be fatal to the project.

An initial study of meteorological conditions indicates that the sooner the raid is made the better will be the prevailing weather conditions. The weather will become increasingly unfavorable after the end of April. Weather was considered largely from the point of view of avoiding morning fog over Tokyo and other targets, low overcast over Chuchow and Chungking, icing and strong westerly winds.

If possible, daily weather predictions or anticipated weather conditions at Chungking and the coast should be

> sent, at a specified time, in suitable code, in order to assist the meteorologist on the carrier in analyzing his forecasts.
>
> Lt. Col. J. H. Doolittle, Air Corps, will be in charge of the preparations for and will be in personal command of the project. Other flight personnel will, due to the considerable hazard incident to such a mission, be volunteers.
>
> Each airplane will carry its normal complement of five crew members: pilot, co-pilot, bombardier-navigator, radio operator and gunner-mechanic.
>
> One crew member will be a competent meteorologist and one an experienced navigator. All navigators will be trained in celestial navigation.
>
> Two ground liaison officers will be assigned. One will remain on the mainland and the other on the carrier.
>
> At least three crew members will speak Chinese—one in each of the target units.
>
> Should the Russians be willing to accept delivery of 18 B-25B airplanes, on lease lend, at Vladivostok, our problems would be greatly simplified and conflict with the Halverson project avoided.

Doolittle now knew what else had to be done. Each element of the plan had to be started and followed up. There would no doubt be some compromises and changes but if any of the important details were overlooked or not completed on time, the success of the mission would be in jeopardy. Most worrisome of all was the installation of the extra gas tanks because gas capacity could mean the difference between landing in enemy territory, ditching in the sea, or getting to friendly territory—between death and survival. The only element more important to the crews than fuel would be their defensive guns. Gas and gun problems were almost to doom the entire mission.

4

"Tell Jimmy to Get on His Horse"

The choice of the type and the number of aircraft to be used for the mission against Japan determined that they would be furnished from the three squadrons (Thirty-fourth, Thirty-seventh, and Ninety-fifth) of the Seventeenth Bombardment Group, and its associated Eighty-ninth Reconnaissance Squadron, located at Pendleton, Oregon. The group had been flying antisubmarine patrol missions off the Oregon and Washington coasts in B-25 Mitchell bombers since the war began and most of the crews were fully qualified.

On February 3, Lt. Col. William C. Mills, commanding officer of the Seventeenth, received orders to transfer the group to the Columbia Army Air Base, Columbia, South Carolina. While the unit was getting ready to move its ground and air echelons, Mills was instructed to pass the word among his squadrons and the Eighty-ninth, commanded by Maj. John A. Hilger, that volunteers were needed for an extremely hazardous mission that would require the highest degree of skill and would be of great value to the war effort. By the time the four squadrons were in place at Columbia, the response was overwhelming. Every man who had heard the call volunteered.

On Mills's recommendation Doolittle selected Hilger as his deputy and explained that he would be responsible for taking twenty-four qualified crews and required ground personnel to Eglin Field, Florida, to get started on a training program. Doolittle told Hilger that he and the men selected should prepare themselves for a mission that would require a takeoff from a carrier, bombing of an enemy target, and a landing in China where the planes would be delivered to the Chinese air force. However, Hilger was to tell the crews only that the mission was risky, would require exceptionally short takeoffs, and would involve an attack against the enemy. Doolittle would commute between Washington and Eglin to coordinate the planning and thus avoid use of the telephone, which could be tapped. Hilger would remain at Eglin in charge of the group in Doolittle's absence.

Lt. Col. Mills had delegated to the three squadron commanders—Capt. Edward J. "Ski" York, Capt. Al Rutherford, and Capt. Karl Baumeister—the task of choosing the men for the mysterious mission. All three volunteered as their men had, but Mills would permit only York, a West Point graduate, to go. Hilger, York, Rutherford, and Baumeister drew up rosters of an approximately equal number of men to make up twenty-four complete aircraft crews. Mechanics, armorers, radio men, and other ground support personnel were also designated and ordered to proceed to Eglin from Columbia as fast as planes could be made available to transport them.

Hilger and the major part of the B-25B Special Project arrived at the Florida base between February 27 and March 3. No one except Hilger knew anything about the project, and Doolittle cautioned all those selected not to speak to anyone or speculate on what they were going to do. They were assigned barracks and an operations building on a separate part of the Eglin base. The base commanding officer had been told only that the unit was to undergo "special training" and that he should provide such facilities and supplies as they required on request without questioning why.

Before Doolittle left Columbia for Washington, Hilger suggested that it would be a good idea if a navy flying instructor were assigned to the project to teach the pilots how to make carrier takeoffs, which would require a special technique. Army air force pilots were not trained to take heavily loaded bombers off in the short space of a carrier's deck, while navy pilots had to demonstrate their proficiency in carrier takeoff and landing procedures before graduation from flying school. Doolittle agreed and requested the navy to assign an instructor. Lt. Henry L. Miller, USN, received orders to proceed to Eglin from Pensacola. Years later, he recalled his impressions:[1]

> I reported to the field's commanding officer and learned that Lt. Col. Jimmy Doolittle was the commanding officer of the detachment. I figured something big was happening.

When I arrived, I met Capts. "Ski" York, Davey Jones, and Ross Greening. I told them why I was reporting aboard. They seemed surprised. I didn't know that the whole operation was still a mystery to them.

After we chatted a while they asked me if I had flown a B-25 before. I had to be honest. I had never even *seen* a B-25 before. They took me outside and I got my first look. Man, how I wanted to get my hands on that airplane!

After looking at the performance data and pilots' handbooks, we all climbed into the plane, proceeded to an auxiliary field that had been set aside for their group and made two practice takeoffs. I acted as co-pilot for Davey Jones and Ski York while Ross Greening observed. I gave them instructions and they followed them to the letter. On the first takeoff, the indicated airspeed was 50 miles an hour. The three Army pilots were skeptical and would not believe that we could take that plane off with a gross weight of 27,000 pounds at 50 miles an hour. They agreed that the airspeed indicator must be off.

On the second takeoff, with Davey Jones at the controls, we got off at an indicated 60 miles an hour because Jones held it on the ground a bit longer than York had done. Even so, the three of them were convinced. They didn't know it then but before they were finished, they would be able to take off from 350 feet in a 40-knot wind with the plane loaded to 31,000 pounds—2,000 pounds over its designed maximum load.

On March 3, Doolittle arrived at Eglin and the entire group of about 140 men was assembled to hear him. It was a typical Doolittle pitch—short and to the point:[2]

"My name's Doolittle. I've been put in charge of the project that you men have volunteered for. It's a tough one and it will be the most dangerous thing any of you have ever done. Any man can drop out and nothing will ever be said about it. The operation must be made up entirely of volunteers. If anyone wants to bow out, he can do so right now."

Doolittle paused and the room was quiet. Several hands went up and Doolittle nodded toward a young lieutenant.

"Sir, can you give us any more information about the mission?" he asked.

"No. I'm sorry. I can't right now." Doolittle replied. "But

I'm sure you will start getting some ideas about it when we get down to work. Now, that brings up the most important point and you're going to hear this over and over again. This entire mission must be kept top secret. I not only don't want you to tell your wives or buddies about it, I don't even want you to discuss it among yourselves."

Doolittle paused again to let his words sink in. "The lives of many men are going to depend on how well you keep this project to yourselves. Not only your lives but the lives of hundreds of others will be endangered because there are a lot of people working on this thing. Don't start any rumors and don't pass any along. If anybody outside this project gets nosy, get his name and give it to me. The FBI will find out all about him.

"Our training will stress teamwork. I want every man to do his assigned job. We've got a lot of work to do on those planes to get them in shape. There's a lot of training in store for navigators, bombardiers, and engineer–gunners. The main job for the pilots is to learn how to get the B-25 off the ground in the shortest possible distance with heavy loads. We've got about three weeks, maybe less. Remember, if anyone wants to drop out, he can. No questions asked. That's all for now."

Doolittle set up the unit on typical squadron lines: Maj. Jack Hilger was appointed executive officer; Maj. Harvey Johnson, adjutant; Capt. Edward J. "Ski" York, operations officer; Capt. David M. Jones, navigation and intelligence officer; Capt. C. Ross Greening, gunnery and bombing officer; 1st Lt. William M. Bower, engineering officer; and 1st Lt. Travis Hoover, supply officer.

During the first few days at Eglin, Doolittle took these men aside and told them the general nature of the project, why the B-25 was chosen, the main objective of the raid, and how the planes were to be carried within reach of the targets but without specifically telling them what the targets would be. He told them they would learn their destination only when aboard the carrier. "I did this," Doolittle told the author, "because I knew that these factors would affect the training program." Secrecy was stressed again. It was uppermost in Doolittle's mind and he wanted to be sure it was in everyone else's as well.

From the first day of training of the air crews, it was understood that all twenty-four crews would take the training and go aboard the carrier, even though only fifteen planes were planned for the mission at that time. This was done to assure that no word would leak out from the disappointed crew members who would not go, and that there would be plenty of spare crew members if anyone became ill or decided to drop out at the last minute.

As the training of the pilots progressed, it proved to be a harrowing experience for most of them. Army pilots were not taught to take off in extremely short distances at bare minimum airspeed; they were taught to have plenty of airspeed before lifting off. Their training had always been from airports with long runways. Taking a medium bomber off with the tail almost striking the ground was unnatural and scary to them. But under Lieutenant Miller's careful instruction, they all soon learned.

"All pilots, with the exception of a few conservatives, caught on quickly," Miller recalled. "Doolittle, Gray, and Jones were particularly outstanding. But it was found that constant practice was necessary because most were prone to switch back to a conventional takeoff if not reminded."[3]

In addition to takeoff practice, other training missions were scheduled. It had been hoped that each crew would receive fifty hours of flying time to be divided into day and night navigation, gunnery, bombing, and formation flying. But maintenance problems with the gas tank installations and the gun turrets kept the planes on the ground much of the time. As a result, most crews were able to get only about twenty-five hours of their planned training in the air.

Before navigation practice was begun, Doolittle required all engine and flight instruments to be calibrated and fuel consumption carefully checked. Since each plane would be required to fly at least nineteen hundred miles on about eleven hundred gallons of gas, the engines had to operate at maximum efficiency using long-range cruise techniques. However, the gas tank modifications were a constant source of trouble. The 265-gallon steel tanks leaked so profusely that they were replaced by 225-gallon self-sealing tanks, but leaks in the connections and other mechanical problems persisted.

Since the aircraft were to fly at low level until reaching the target areas, Doolittle approved the removal of the bottom gun turret and the installation of a 60-gallon fuel tank in its place. The rear gunner would refill this tank from ten 5-gallon cans of gasoline as the fuel level went down.

De-icing boots were installed on the leading edges of the wings and tail surfaces along with anti-icing equipment for the propellers. Since it had not yet been decided definitely whether China or Russia would be the destination, icing could be a problem if the latter were chosen.

The heavy 230-pound liaison radios normally installed were removed at Doolittle's request because radio silence was required during the mission. In addition, the coils were removed from the command transmitters and stowed elsewhere in each plane so that broadcasts would not be made through unintentional use of a plane's interphone.

These modifications were important but probably most important from a survival standpoint were the guns used to defend the planes in combat. The B-25Bs of that era were woefully deficient in their armament. Each was equipped with one upper and one lower turret and while the twin .50 caliber guns were fairly reliable, the turret power mechanism failed repeatedly so that the gunners could not rotate them to aim at enemy fighters boring in. The tail had no guns and a single .30 caliber flexible machine gun was carried in the nose, which had to be placed in a gun port, aimed, and fired by the bombardier.

Capt. Ross Greening, as armament officer, was responsible for trying to solve the continuing gun problems. With Doolittle's approval, he had two long broomsticks painted black and installed in the tail of each plane to deceive enemy pilots attacking from the rear. Greening was relieved when the lower turret was ordered removed. When Doolittle made the decision, he remarked, "A man could learn to play the violin good enough to play in Carnegie Hall before he could learn to fire that thing."

While Greening was trying to solve the gun problems, a question arose. Should the top secret Norden bombsight be used on this mission? It was designed for high-altitude precision bombing and this mission required bombing from a low altitude, so low that the Norden would be practically useless. Greening designed a simplified bombsight he called the "Mark

Twain." Constructed in the Eglin shops out of two pieces of aluminum that cost about twenty cents, it proved surprisingly accurate. Greening reported that "actual low altitude bombing tests carried out at 1,500 feet showed a greater degree of accuracy with this simplified sight than was obtained with the Norden by the same bombardiers. This not only permitted greater accuracy in bombing but obviated the possibility of the highly classified Norden sight from falling into enemy hands."[4] He had the "twenty-cent bombsights" installed in each B-25.

Surprisingly, most of the gunners who volunteered for the project had never fired a .50 caliber machine gun nor operated a power turret before. They had used .30 caliber machine guns in their training. Unfortunately, gunnery practice with the twin .50s was delayed for all of them because of the turret problems. By the end of the training period, most gunners had been able only to ground-fire their guns on the test range, bore-sight them, and fire a few bursts in flight. One gunner, Sgt. Doug Radney, reflected later on his lack of experience with the guns he was to use. He said, "I suppose I should have been concerned at the time but I don't remember being worried about anything much in those days. I knew that if the Boss thought things were OK, then we'd come out of it all right."[5]

One of the gunners had other duties. He was Dr. (1st Lt.) T. Robert White, a physician attached to the Eighty-ninth Reconnaissance Squadron. As soon as "Doc" White had heard of the call for volunteers for a special mission while en route to Columbia, he wired Major Hilger and asked him to "squeeze me in somewhere." Hilger, glad to have the popular doctor want to go along, had no choice but to turn him down. "The only way you could go, Doc," Hilger told him, "would be to train as a gunner."[6]

"That's fine with me, Major," White said. "I've always wanted to be a gunner." And that's what he was. He took training with all the other gunners and scored second highest on the ground targets with the twin .50s. He was assigned to a crew. But there was more for Doc White to do. Between firing practice sessions, he checked the immunization records of all flight crew members and gave innoculations for pneumonia, typhus, tetanus, bubonic plague, yellow fever, and smallpox. "I got a lot of static from the fellows," White recalled. "For some of them whose shot records showed they hadn't had them, it meant as many as eleven shots over a three-week period."[7]

During the second week at Eglin, Doolittle flew to Washington and reported to Arnold what his problems were and how he was solving them. His real purpose, however, was to nail down a point that had been bothering him. "It occurred to me, General," he said, "that I'm the guy who knows more about this whole project than anyone else. You asked me to get the planes modified and the crews trained and this is being done. They're the finest bunch of boys I've ever worked with. I'd like your permission to lead this mission myself."[8]

Arnold stared at Doolittle a moment. His ever-present grin faded, then he said, "I'm sorry, Jim. I need you right here on my staff. I can't afford to let you fly every combat mission you might help plan."

Doolittle recalled the incident with a chuckle:[9]

> I launched into my sales pitch, and finally Hap shrugged his shoulders and said, "OK, Jim, it will be all right with me if it's all right with Miff Harmon." When he said that, I quit talking and got out before he changed his mind.
>
> Miff Harmon—Gen. Millard Harmon who was later killed in the war—was Hap's chief of staff and had his office just down the hall from Arnold's. I thought I smelled a rat so I ran down the hallway and burst into Miff's office. "Miff," I said, "I've just been in to see Hap and gave him a report on the project I've been working on. I told him I wanted to lead the mission. He said it was OK with him if it's OK with you."
>
> Miff was caught flatfooted which is what I had hoped. "Sure, Jim," he answered. "Whatever is all right with Hap is all right with me. Go ahead."
>
> I thanked him and just as I closed the door, I heard Miff's intercom buzz. It was Hap and I heard Miff say plaintively, "But Hap, I just gave him my permission since he said it was OK with you."
>
> I didn't wait to hear any more. I beat it back to Eglin and hoped Hap wouldn't later order me to stay home. He never did.

Whenever Doolittle returned to Eglin he followed his personal training program in earnest. "Naturally, I wanted to fly the mission as first pilot," he said, "but I wanted to go only on the basis that I could do as well as or better than the other pilots who had already started on the training program. So I took Hank Miller's course and was graded along with the others. I made it, but if I hadn't I would have gone along as a co-pilot and let one of the younger, more proficient pilots sit in the left seat."[10]

All the crews flew as teams, which was very important in Doolittle's view. When five men fly together day after day and get to know one another's techniques and mannerisms, that crew will develop high morale and will tackle anything assigned to it. If personality differences appeared or individual proficiency was lacking, crew assignments were adjusted accordingly.

On one of his training flights, Doolittle flew with Lt. Richard E. Cole, co-pilot; Lt. Henry A. Potter, navigator; Sgt. Fred A. Braemer, bombardier; and Sgt. Paul J. Leonard, engineer–gunner. The original pilot, Capt. Vernon L. Stinzi, had become ill and Doolittle filled in for him as pilot. He liked the way this crew worked together and was satisfied with their proficiency from the first day he flew with them. When Stinzi did not return to duty, these men became Doolittle's crew.

Doolittle depended on his officers to coordinate the project at Elgin while he flew back and forth to Washington or wherever he needed to go to follow up on arrangements. He kept no written records and did all of his coordinating on a man-to-man basis without any of his contacts knowing what he was up to. Armed with Hap Arnold's "top priority," which had become common knowledge but without the reason being known, Doolittle knew that time was growing short and he continued to needle anyone who got in his way to get aircraft parts, armaments, maps, information, or anything else required.

By the middle of March, the *Hornet*, by now destined to be the ship that would deliver the B-25s to the takeoff point, passed through the Panama Canal en route to San Francisco and the Alameda Naval Air Station. Capt. Wu Duncan had made all the necessary arrangements with Admiral Nimitz's headquarters in Honolulu and had passed the word to General Arnold that his side of the arrangements for a sixteen-ship task force would soon be complete.

At the end of the third week in March, Duncan wired Admiral King in Washington from Honolulu:

TELL JIMMY TO GET ON HIS HORSE.

King called Arnold, who immediately passed the message to Doolittle at Eglin. That simple coded sentence was launching eighty airmen and ten thousand naval personnel on an adventure that would change the course of the war in the Pacific.

5

"This Force Is Bound for Tokyo"

In the weeks between the middle of January and the day Jimmy Doolittle got the signal to take his crews west to McClellan Field near Sacramento and then to Alameda Naval Air Station for loading aboard the carrier, the war news had gone from bad to worse. The situation in the Philippines was hopeless. Manila had been declared an open city on the day after Christmas. During the first week in January, American and Filipino troops fought delaying actions as they backed down the Bataan Peninsula. Lacking everything but courage, the fatigued troops were reduced to eating dogs, iguanas, monkeys, and snakes to stay alive.

On February 22, Gen. Douglas MacArthur was ordered to leave Luzon and go to Australia to take command of Allied troops when those forces were provided. He finally left on March 22 and, when he arrived in Darwin, announced: "The President of the United States ordered me to break through the Japanese lines and proceed from Corregidor to Australia for the purpose, as I understand it, of organizing the American offensive against Japan, a primary purpose of which is the relief of the Philippines. I came through and I shall return."[1]

Meanwhile, the Japanese had taken Hong Kong and Singapore with overwhelming air, ground, and naval power. Burma fell on March 7, then Sumatra. Java was blocked off from rescue by Allied forces, and on March 9 the Netherlands East Indies surrendered its ninety-eight thousand troops.

While the Japanese consolidated their gains in Southeast Asia, they next turned their attention toward Australia. Darwin was attacked in February, followed by occupation of New Britain, New Ireland, part of New Guinea, the Admiralty Islands, and the Gilberts. In just four months, the Japanese had made incredible conquests. By the end of March, the entire

Pacific Ocean west of a line drawn from the Aleutian Islands in Alaska to Hawaii to Australia was dominated by the Japanese. Linkup with the German forces battling in North Africa now seemed possible. If the Germans were to push eastward through the Middle East to India, the combined Japanese and German forces could then consolidate their gains and be halfway toward their goal of world conquest.

When Capt. Wu Duncan arrived in Honolulu, his task was to confer with Adm. Chester W. Nimitz, commander-in-chief of the Pacific Fleet, and convey the plan to bomb Japan using a Navy task force to transport the army bombers to the launch point. Nimitz was a man "of cheerful yesterdays and confident tomorrows," according to his Naval Academy yearbook. He welcomed the requirement to prepare for a bold attack on Japan. He had sent Adm. William F. Halsey to make surprise attacks with the carrier *Enterprise* in February and March against enemy-held Wake Island and then Marcus Island located about one thousand miles southeast of Tokyo. These raids were successful in that they proved the U.S. Navy was able to counterattack but the damage was minimal and hardly seemed worth the effort. However, the purpose was to divert the enemy's attention and persuade him to pull his forces up from the south and thus release the pressure on the Philippines. However, the Japanese were not impressed and kept to their basic strategy of moving against Australia.

Nimitz liked the plan Duncan explained and called Halsey in to meet Duncan, now promoted to rear admiral. Halsey recalled the meeting:

> Wu Duncan told us that something big was in the air, something top secret; Lt. Col. James H. Doolittle, with Navy cooperation, had trained sixteen Army crews to take B-25s off a carrier's deck, and the Navy had promised to launch them for Tokyo. They might not inflict much damage, Wu said, but they would certainly give Hirohito plenty to think about.
>
> Chester Nimitz asked me, "Do you believe it would work, Bill?"
>
> I said, "They'll need a lot of luck."
>
> "Are you willing to take them out there?"

"Yes, I am."

"Good," he said. "It's all yours!'

I suggested that the operation would run more smoothly if Miles and I could discuss it man-to-man with Doolittle, whom I had never met. Chester agreed and gave us orders to proceed to San Francisco.[2]

Duncan worked with the CINCPAC planning staff on the details for a sixteen-ship task force. It was decided that seven ships would accompany the *Hornet* from Alameda and meet up with an eight-ship force that included Halsey's flagship, the carrier *Enterprise*. The joinup would take place near the one-hundred-eightieth meridian.

Duncan left Pearl Harbor for San Diego to meet Capt. Marc A. Mitscher, skipper of the *Hornet*, who had just arrived after transiting the Panama Canal. Mitscher had not yet been told about the mission and was delighted to have a part in it. He had been aboard when the two B-25s had flown off the carrier at Norfolk, so he knew the planes could be launched without much difficulty. Duncan then flew to San Francisco to await the arrival of Doolittle from Florida and Halsey from Hawaii.

On March 23, the morning that Doolittle received Hap Arnold's call to "get on his horse," he gave a short talk to the crews:

> Today's the day we move out. I'm going to tell you one more time what I've been harping on ever since we came to Eglin. Don't tell *any*one what we were doing down here. Even if you think you've guessed what our mission is, just keep in mind that the lives of your buddies depend on your not breathing a word about this to another soul.[3]

Doolittle dismissed all but the crews of the twenty-two planes chosen for the trip (two planes had been damaged in practice takeoffs). He told them to fly their planes to the maintenance depot at McClellan Field for an inspection and final modifications.

Doolittle arrived at McClellan and conferred with the depot commander and his staff, who were not told the details of the pending mission. He insisted that no one was to tamper with any equipment or remove anything—the planes were simply to be inspected. He explained that a number of modifications had already been made but that more were required. New propellers were needed, the sixty-gallon rubber gas tanks in the rear compartments were to be installed, and new hydraulic valves were needed for the ever-troubling gun turrets. The seat-type parachutes were to be replaced with back-type chutes. The liaison radio was to be removed from each plane and new glass navigational windows were to replace the original Plexiglass.

Doolittle was told that not all the material for this work had been received. He tried to instill a sense of urgency in the civilian workers but he could see he wasn't making much of an impression. The maintenance workers went about their work leisurely while Doolittle fumed. He advised his crews to stay with their planes and observe all the work being done. They were to report anything they didn't like to him or Ski York. It wasn't long before he heard complaints. Ted Lawson described his experience in his book *Thirty Seconds over Tokyo*:[4]

> I had to stand by and watch one of the mechanics rev my engines so fast that the new blades picked up dirt which pock-marked their tips. I caught another one trying to sandpaper the imperfections away and yelled at him until he got some oil and rubbed it on the places which he had sandpapered. I knew that salt air would make those prop tips pulpy when they had to be scraped.
>
> The way they revved our motors made us wince. All of us were so afraid that they'd hurt the ships, the way they were handling them, yet we couldn't tell them why we wanted them to be so careful. I guess we must have acted like the biggest bunch of soreheads those mechanics ever saw, but we kept beefing until Doolittle got on the long-distance phone, called Washington and had the work done the way we wanted it done.

Doolittle had indeed called Washington and refused to speak to anyone except Hap Arnold. "Things are going too slowly out here," he told his chief. "I'd appreciate it if you would light a fire under these people. They're treating this whole project as 'routine' and that won't get the job done in time."[5]

Arnold reacted immediately. The B-25B Special Project suddenly became the most important project on the base. The civilian workers took an intense interest in these B-25s with the broomsticks instead of guns sticking out the tails. And no liaison radios? Why did they need shiny new propellers, which were promptly painted as soon as they were installed? Instead of the Norden bombsight, there was this strange-looking crude aluminum gimmick in its place. And there were those rubber gas tanks in the crawlway above the bomb bay.

The crews were a strange bunch, come to think of it. They griped every day about what the civilian mechanics were doing and kept looking over the shoulders of anyone working on their planes. If crew members were asked what the fuss was all about, the answer was always, "Mind your own business." They were a clannish group who did not associate with anyone on the base and, without regard for rank differences, stuck together off duty as well as on.

While there was slight improvement in the pace of the work being accomplished, the quality of the work was below par and the crews complained to Doolittle continually. The situation reached a climax one afternoon when Doolittle was talking with several pilots in McClellan's base operations. Outside, a civilian mechanic was trying to start one of the B-25s when it backfired violently and black smoke poured out of the exhausts. Doolittle stopped talking and rushed out of the building on a dead run, shouting to the man in the cockpit to shut the engine down. The mechanic paid no attention and the backfiring continued. Doolittle ripped open the forward hatch, leaped up into the cockpit and almost yanked the man from the pilot's seat. As Jack Hilger later told the author, "I don't know what he told that fellow but the air inside that cockpit turned blue!"

The reason for Doolittle's anger was obvious to his pilots. The carburetors on all the planes had been carefully bench-checked and fine-tuned to get the maximum mileage while cruising at low altitude. The engines had to be started carefully with a precise starting procedure. Backfiring would throw them out of adjustment and increase fuel consumption. Doolittle knew better than anyone else that their lives would depend on getting the most miles out of the fuel as possible.

When Doolittle's anger subsided, the mechanic explained

that he was merely going to run up the engines as he was required to do after carburetors were adjusted.

"What? Do you mean somebody fooled around with these carburetors without my OK?" Doolittle shouted, incredulously.

"All I know is that they were both checked, found way out of adjustment, and set the way they're supposed to be."[6]

This was the last straw for Doolittle. He ordered his men to check everything being done on their planes and report anything that was wrong to him. Doolittle called Arnold and told him what had happened. Arnold demanded a reply through channels. The day after the B-25s left McClellan for Alameda, the reply was put in Arnold's in-basket. The base commander defended his mechanics and pointed out that pilots often tended to worry about the condition of their planes as the departure date for going overseas approached. He did admit, however, that good help was hard to find as the war effort got more intense.

On March 30, Doolittle went to San Francisco to meet his wife, Joe, who was coming in from Los Angeles where she had been visiting her ill father. The evening before, he had received a call from Arnold in Washington saying that he was to meet Admiral Halsey the following evening. After getting Joe settled in a hotel, he went to a quiet, out-of-the-way restaurant where he met with Halsey, Capt. Miles Browning, his chief of staff, and Duncan. The latter explained that the *Hornet*, in company with the cruisers *Nashville* and *Vincennes*, the oiler *Cimarron*, and the destroyers *Gwin*, *Meredith*, *Monssen*, and *Grayson*, to be known as task Force 16.2, were to leave San Francisco April 2. Halsey, on the *Enterprise* in charge of Task Force 16.1, would leave Hawaii on April 7, accompanied by the cruisers *Northampton* and *Salt Lake City*, the oiler *Sabine*, and destroyers *Balch*, *Benham*, *Ellet*, and *Fanning*. The rendezvous of the two forces would become Task Force 16 and would take place on Sunday, April 12 at latitude 38°00′ north, 180°00′ longitude. The armada would then proceed westward and refuel from the *Cimarron* and *Sabine* eight hundred miles off the coast of Japan. The oilers would then detach themselves while the rest of the force dashed toward the launch point.

Halsey later reported that, "Our talk boiled down to this: we would carry Jimmy within four hundred miles of Tokyo, if we could sneak in that close; but if we were discovered sooner, we would have to launch him anyway, provided he was in reach of either Tokyo or Midway.

"That suited Jimmy. We shook hands and I wished him luck."[7]

What Halsey had not discussed was the tremendous risk that the navy was taking. If marauding Japanese submarines discovered this sixteen-ship force steaming westward, it would be an unprecedented opportunity to cripple what was left of the U.S. Navy's strength in the Pacific. Coupled with Japanese attacks by land-based bombers or a heavy enemy carrier force, it could mean the end of American naval strength in the Pacific for many months to come.

Doolittle knew full well that if Halsey's ships were under fire, and they were not within reach of Japan with the B-25s, his planes would be kicked over the side so that the *Hornet*'s fighters could be brought up and launched to protect the fleet. All he could hope for was that the secret had been kept and that no information had gotten to the enemy.

After the meeting, Doolittle called Jack Hilger and told him to have all aircraft flown to Alameda the next day for loading aboard the *Hornet*. That night Hilger rounded up the crews and told them to report to the flight line the next morning ready to go: "When we get to Alameda, we'll want to know if there's anything wrong with your ships. Give them a good test flight and put at least an hour's time on them."[8]

But giving the order to fly did not mean that it was going to be easy to get the planes out of the hands of the civilian mechanics. Since all the work called for had not been completed, regulations forbade the release of any planes to their crews. Hilger had his orders and he was going to obey them. After heated arguments, he finally got the planes on their way one by one.

Doolittle arrived and made out his flight plan. He was handed a report form that regulations required pilots to sign asking for an opinion of the work performed on the planes while at McClellan. He took one look at the form and wrote diagonally across it in large print: LOUSY!

The base operations officer looked shocked and shook his

head. "Just a minute, Colonel. You'll have to give me a detailed report. This simply won't do!"

"I haven't got time," Doolittle snorted as he headed for his B-25.

"I won't sign your clearance, then," the young officer called out. He stared in disbelief as Doolittle climbed into his plane, started engines and took off.

The operations officer turned to Jack Hilger and said, "Who does that guy think he is? He's headed for a lot of trouble!"

Hilger had watched the incident with a sly smile. "He sure is," he drawled. "He sure is!"[9]

As the planes landed at Alameda Naval Air Station, Doolittle and Ski York greeted each pilot. "Anything wrong with your ship?" they asked. If a pilot admitted some malfunction with an engine or vital equipment, he was directed to a nearby hangar instead of the wharf. When sixteen planes had been sent to the dock for loading, Doolittle told York, "These planes will go. Tell all the crews to get aboard the carrier whether or not their plane is on the dock."[10]

Navy crewmen swarmed over the B-25s as soon as their crews shut down the engines. Gas was drained from the tanks. A navy "donkey" hooked a tow bar to the nose gear of each B-25 and towed it down to the pier, the crews walking solemnly behind. A huge dockside crane reached down and hauled the bombers aboard. Lt. Hank Miller was waiting for the crews on deck.

"I was proud of those fellows that day," Miller recalled. "As each man came aboard, he saluted the National Ensign and then the Officer of the Deck and said, 'Sergeant or Lieutenant or Captain so-and-so reporting aboard for duty, Sir.' They were a smart-looking outfit and I was mighty proud of the way they had responded to my teaching."

The navy crews were curious about the B-25s but asked no questions. Several, knowing that Miller had been born and reared in Alaska, suspected that the *Hornet* was going in that direction but he gave them no clues.

On one of his trips to Washington from Eglin, Doolittle had talked at length with Hap Arnold about the arrangements being made in China to receive the aircraft after the raid. It was decided that secrecy could not be maintained when dealing with Generalissimo Chiang Kai Shek's staff in Chungking because of leaks on other projects, so Arnold did not relay any detailed information on the B-25 project to China. However, Gen. Joseph E. "Vinegar Joe" Stilwell had been told the bare essentials of the project before he left the States in February to take over the China-Burma-India Command. He was told of the necessity to prepare five airfields to receive the "First Special Aviation Project" but was not told from where the planes were to come.

When no word had been received from Stilwell about the progress of preparation of the airfields by March 16, Arnold sent Stilwell an urgent telegram, which was not answered. Two days later, he sent another:[11]

> REFERENCE SPECIAL AIR PROJECT DISCUSSED WITH YOU BEFORE DEPARTURE, TIME GETTING SHORT FOR SPOTTING GAS AT AGREED POINTS.

On March 22, Stilwell wired Arnold that Standard Oil Co. of Calcutta had thirty thousand gallons of one-hundred-octane gasoline and five hundred gallons of grade 120 oil in five-gallon tins on hand. He asked why it was needed and requested authority to order it moved to China.

Stilwell's lack of a sense of urgency was understandable. He was not a pilot and had no sympathy for aviation problems. Because of the extreme secrecy surrounding the B-25 project, communications about it were limited to what essential arrangements were needed but not why. However, it was necessary to get Chiang's approval before the bombers could land in China so he was informed reluctantly but the Generalissimo feared a violent reaction from the Japanese occupying China if American planes landed there after bombing Japan's capital city. However, he was, in effect, overruled because the project was not to be stopped. General Marshall, army chief of staff, later apologized to the generalissimo for failing to consult him.

By March 25, Arnold was getting more concerned that arrangements were not shaping up in China. He sent another message to Stilwell specifying the amount of fuel needed, where it was to be located, and what arrangements were required for the crews. On the twenty-ninth, Stilwell replied that he recommended the use of Chinese gasoline instead of flying gas in from India "due to lack of communications, time shortage, and impossibility of secrecy."[12] He advised that two fields—Kweilin and Chuchow—were the only fields safe for heavy bomber operations. He reported that Chiang Kai Shek had disapproved the use of fields at Yushan, Kian, and Lishui unless an inspection was made by an American officer.

Arnold relayed this information to Doolittle via navy channels and then prepared a wire for Stilwell:[13]

> SPECIAL PROJECT WILL ARRIVE DESTINATION ON APRIL TWENTIETH. SHOULD A CHANGE IN ARRIVAL DATE ARISE AN ATTEMPT WILL BE MADE TO NOTIFY YOU. YOU MUST HOWEVER BE PREPARED FOR VARIATION WITHOUT NOTICE.

As the planes were being hoisted aboard the *Hornet*, Doolittle conferred with Captain Mitscher. When the fifteenth plane was tied down, Doolittle said, "I think we'll take one more. Since none of the lads have actually made a carrier takeoff or even seen one, it would give them a lot of confidence to see it done. About a hundred miles out, we could send that sixteenth plane back. Hank Miller could be the co-pilot."[14]

Mitscher rubbed his leathery face a moment, fixed his bright blue eyes on Doolittle, and said thoughtfully, "All right, Jimmy, it's your show." He ordered the sixteenth B-25 hoisted aboard and tied down. He told Miller to find himself a bunk.[15]

At 3:00 P.M. on April 1, the *Hornet* moved to the middle of San Francisco Bay and anchored. The B-25 crews had been assigned quarters throughout the ship and settled in. Doolittle called them together, gave them another brief lecture about secrecy, and, much to their surprise, let them go ashore for the evening.

The unexpected freedom gave the crews an opportunity for a last fling in San Francisco and most took advantage of it. Several pilots went to the "Top of the Mark" Hopkins Hotel to view the sights. Lt. Dick Knobloch, co-pilot on Lt. Edgar McElroy's crew, had guessed where they were bound and remembered his concern. There in the bay in plain sight was the *Hornet* with their B-25s easily visible on the deck. He leaned over to Ross Greening and whispered, "I hope they rounded up all the Japanese spies. If they didn't I hope they think those planes are just being transported to Hawaii."[16]

Greening nodded and grinned. "What's the matter, Knobby, don't you know you can't take a B-25 off a carrier?" he asked mockingly. Knobloch grinned in reply. He hoped it *was* possible but they had only been told it had been done. None of them, not even Doolittle, had actually done it or seen it done.

On the morning of April 2, after spending the night in a San Francisco hotel with his wife, Doolittle packed his B-4 aviator's bag, and said, casually, "Joe, I'm going to be out of the country for a while. Call you when I get back."[17]

Joe Doolittle nodded and smiled. After many years of hellos and good-byes, she had almost, but not quite, grown used to Jimmy's comings and goings. He was always casual about his trips, which he tried to keep as short as possible. She never asked the "whys" of his goings because she knew that if he wanted her to know, he would tell her. She usually did not know until afterward that he had risked his neck in some way, set a new speed record, or achieved another aviation "first." Since he had returned to active duty and was working directly for Hap Arnold, the top flying officer in the rapidly growing Army Air Forces, she realized that she had no need to know. Her job was to stay in contact with their two sons, keep busy, and wait for his return.

Back on the *Hornet*, Doolittle went to Mitscher's cabin and the two of them discussed the departure plans to see if anything had been left undone. Some B-25 parts that had not been received at McClellan were still missing but were to be delivered by navy blimp to the carrier after it had cleared San Francisco Bay.

It was confirmed between the two of them that the sixteenth plane would take off after the *Hornet* was about one hundred miles at sea to prove to any doubting crew members that it could be done. Just as they concluded that all had been done that could be done, they were interrupted by the intelligence officer, who had classified messages for Doolittle from Washington. One message, relayed from General Stilwell in China, confirmed that the placement of gas and oil and marking of the airports in China was being accomplished. There were two other messages, both dated March 31, 1942:[18]

> MAY GOOD LUCK AND SUCCESS BE WITH YOU AND EACH MEMBER OF YOUR COMMAND ON THE MISSION YOU ARE ABOUT TO UNDERTAKE. ARNOLD

> AS YOU EMBARK ON YOUR EXPEDITION PLEASE GIVE EACH MEMBER OF YOUR COMMAND MY DEEP APPRECIATION OF THEIR SERVICES AND COMPLETE CONFIDENCE IN THEIR ABILITY AND COURAGE UNDER YOUR LEADERSHIP TO STRIKE A MIGHTY BLOW. YOU WILL BE CONSTANTLY IN MY MIND AND MAY THE GOOD LORD WATCH OVER YOU. MARSHALL

Mitscher received a message from Admiral King, which read: "I hope—and expect—that the first war operation of the *Hornet* will be a success. I am confident that it will be insofar as her officers and crew—under your able leadership—can make it so. Good luck and good hunting."[19]

As Mitscher and Doolittle talked, the seven accompanying ships in Task Force 16.2 got underway and slowly passed up the Bay and under Golden Gate Bridge to stand by for the *Hornet* to clear the harbor. The sun was bright although visibility was poor. Just before the *Hornet* started to get underway, Doolittle was ordered ashore in the captain's gig to answer an urgent telephone call from Washington. Doolittle recalled:

> I thought it was going to be either Hap Arnold or General Marshall telling me I couldn't go. My heart sank because I wanted to go on that mission more than anything since I had planned it and worked on it from the beginning. I might have tried to argue with Hap but not Marshall. I was sure the jig was up.
>
> It was General Marshall. "Doolittle?" he said. "Yes, General," I replied. "I just called to personally wish you the best of luck," he said. "Our thoughts and our prayers will be with you. Good-bye, good luck, and come home safely." All I could think to say was, "Thank you, Sir, thank you." I returned to the *Hornet* feeling much better.[20]

At 11:48, the *Hornet* entered the channel and passed under the Golden Gate bridge with the B-25 Mitchell bombers in full sight of hundreds of San Franciscans going about their daily chores. It seemed to Doolittle's men that the navy was deliberately placing their mission in jeopardy, whatever it was to be, after they had been so careful about security. Although the navy has never explained why such a risk was taken, Capt. Frederick L. Riefkohl, skipper of the *Vincennes*, commented:[21] "I was rather skeptical about our crew at the time, as many of my old-time men who had been on her almost a year had left and we sailed from there with a crew that was practically fifty percent recruits." With so many ships and lives at stake, it is perhaps for this reason that a night departure was not considered safe.

Mitscher's force gathered into formation and steamed westward. Mitscher's orders were to steer a meandering, circuitous course to the rendezvous with Halsey's force on April 12. However, Halsey had been delayed returning to Pearl Harbor on Pan American's Clipper plane and had to notify Mitscher to delay the rendezvous with Task Force 16.1 for twenty-four hours.

That afternoon, Mitscher decided to tell his men in the task force where they were going. He told his chief signal officer to notify the rest of the ships by semaphore that "this force is bound for Tokyo." He told all hands on the *Hornet* the same thing by loudspeaker, and reaction from the crew was immediate. "Cheers from every section of the ship greeted the announcement," he said, "and morale reached a new high, there to remain until after the attack was launched and the ship was well clear of combat areas."[22]

At dusk, Mitscher called the first of many battle drills. As sailors rushed to their assigned battle stations, the B-25 crews raced to their respective planes and simulated getting them airborne but without starting engines. Each rear gunner practiced unlimbering his turret guns. If an emergency arose, the B-25 crews were to be ready either to fly their planes off or to push them over the side.

At about noon on April 3, Hank Miller was on the flight deck talking with Lt. Dick Joyce, who had been designated as the pilot to fly the sixteenth plane back to the mainland. Doolittle approached and said, "Talk to you a minute, Hank?"

"Yes, Sir," Miller replied.

The two walked to Joyce's plane and looked down the deck. Doolittle then climbed up into the cockpit and eased into the left seat. Miller followed, wondering what Doolittle was thinking.

Motioning toward the gently plunging bow, Doolittle said, "That looks mighty short to me, Hank."

"Colonel Doolittle, it won't be a problem," Miller replied. "You see that tool kit way up the deck there? That's where I used to take off in fighters. With the carrier turned into the wind and going at top speed, you won't have any trouble getting off."

Doolittle was quiet a moment, then smiled at Miller and said, "Hank, what do they call 'baloney' in the navy?"[23]

The two chatted briefly and went their separate ways. Doolittle climbed to the bridge to see Captain Mitscher. Miller went below to the pilot's wardroom for lunch, confident that he would soon be on his way back to Florida. As he finished dessert, the ship's loudspeaker blared: "Lieutenant Miller, report to the captain on the bridge."

When Miller got to the bridge, Doolittle was just leaving. When Doolittle was out of sight, Mitscher asked Miller how he felt about the takeoff. "We probably can't give you forty knots of wind over the deck today, Miller. Still want to try it?"

Miller assured him that he did. "We won't need forty knots, Captain, because we have about 460 feet of deck space and we won't be fully loaded. We can make it easily with what speed you can crank up in the *Hornet*."

Mitscher looked at Miller thoughtfully for a moment and asked, "Do you have all of your clothes aboard?"

"Yes, Sir, I brought everything along because we're going to take that B-25 back to Columbia, South Carolina."

"Well, if you say there will be no problem getting off, we'll take that extra plane with us," Mitscher said.

Miller was surprised. "That's fine, Sir, but would you drop me off at the next mail buoy, please? I've been traveling from Florida on the authorization of only a phone call. When I get back to Pensacola, they'll probably make me an ensign again."

Mitscher grinned. If the B-25s got off successfully and the *Hornet* survived the dangerous intrusion into Japanese-infested waters, the navy would see that this lieutenant's career would suffer no ill effects.

A short time after this discussion, Navy blimp *L-8* arrived over the *Hornet*. Maneuvering carefully, the *L-8* lowered to the carrier's deck two boxes containing the navigators' windows Doolittle had ordered. Meanwhile, air patrol coverage was being provided by PBY Catalina flying boats since the *Hornet*'s fighters could not be brought up on the deck crowded with B-25s. Below, the B-25 crews were settling into their assigned quarters, many of which had been given up by the navy crewmen. Doolittle had told his men previously what their mission was, the five target cities (Tokyo, Yokohama, Nagoya, Osaka, and Kobe), how close to the Japanese coast the navy was going to try to get them, and the escape route to China. "After we hit our targets," he said, "we'll head for the small airfields in China that will be marked on your maps, gas up as quickly as we can, and then fly on to Chungking. I've been told everything is set there. After arrival, we will all await further orders."

Doolittle again made his offer for anyone to withdraw, but again no one did. Members of the spare crews tried to persuade some of the assigned crew members to withdraw but got no takers.[24]

"Although some of us may have guessed correctly where we were going and a few like Hilger, Greening, Jones, and York knew, the rest of us were relieved to find out officially," Bob Emmens, co-pilot on York's crew, recalled. "The takeoff practice, the over-water navigation flights, the cruise control techniques we practiced, all added up. We now had a clear purpose for everything we had done."[25]

The burden of concern for the outcome for each crew fell on the pilots. All of them, at one time or another during the ensuing days, paced off the distance between the lead airplane lashed to the deck and the bow. Not one had taken his B-25 off in that short a distance at Eglin and there were lingering doubts. Hank Miller had told them it would be no problem, but he had never done it in the B-25. Doolittle had told them that B-25s had been launched from the *Hornet*, but he hadn't *seen* anybody do it. And Doolittle himself had never done it.

There was only one thing they could do: put their faith in "the Boss." He would be piloting the first plane off and would have the shortest length of deck. If he could do it, so could they. Looking back on being told what their mission was, one pilot reflected, "I guess I should have started worrying when we got the big picture but I had full confidence in the boss. He had that knack of giving everyone confidence in their own abilities and that we could all perform as he wanted us to. We were sure we'd all complete the mission as planned."[26]

On April 3, Doolittle called his crews together and introduced two naval officers—Cmdr. Apollo Soucek and Lt. Cmdr. Stephen Jurika. Soucek was the *Hornet*'s air officer and described the basics of carrier operations, methods used to position the aircraft, the duties performed by the deck hands, and the signals used to launch planes. Jurika, the *Hornet*'s intelligence officer, briefed them on the target areas.

Jurika's connection with the upcoming raid could be said to date back to 1939. "I was assigned as assistant naval attaché and naval attaché for air to the American embassy in Tokyo," he recalled.[27] "We did not have bombing maps of Japan and one of my principal jobs was to make them. I spent most of my time locating and pinpointing industries, industrial areas, and all manner of bomb target information.

"One of my greatest sources of information at this time was the Soviet naval attaché, who had a wealth of information on Japanese industry. He used liberal quantities of vodka in an attempt to elicit information from me. But I was able to pour a great many of his drinks into his potted palms without his knowing it. He attempted to get information from me about our forces in the Far East but he was a great source of information on Japanese industry.

"Among other ways we had of obtaining information was sailing in the bay from Tokyo to Yokohama, journeying on American ships from Yokohama to Kobe, and photographing the ports and shipyards we passed en route. At the end of my two-year tour, we had quite a dossier on Japanese industry."

Jurika spoke to the crews almost every day, telling them of Japanese customs, political ideologies, and history. "During the briefings," Jurika said, "I covered the locations of the Japanese industries, anti-aircraft batteries, and such wonderful aiming points as the Diet Building towers and the three radio towers near the navy ministry in downtown Tokyo. I showed them where the Imperial Palace was and how to avoid that. In general, I covered all the escape and evasion tactics which could be used to get in and out in one piece."[28]

Jurika recalled that not many of the crew members paid much attention to his talks. "I felt that most of the pilots, with the exception of Colonel Doolittle, were far more interested in getting their aircraft off the flight deck of the *Hornet* than they were in any possible troubles they might encounter over Japan. There were very few questions during these briefings."

Doolittle arranged for other lectures to keep his men occupied and prepare them mentally for any eventuality, now that there was no question about the mission or the ultimate destination. Doc White of Lt. Don Smith's crew, gave talks on first aid. He cautioned them to take immediate care of any scratch or cut. "The Chinese use 'night soil' for fertilizer," he said. "Everything is tremendously infected with very potent organisms. The Chinese themselves are immune to it or they die in infancy. The tiniest scratch can develop into a raging infection within only a few hours. Whatever you do, take any little cut or scratch seriously, as if your life depended on it, because it will."[29]

The *Hornet*'s navigator, Cmdr. Frank Akers, gave the pilots a refresher course in navigation but he thought his words were not taken seriously. "The pilots were a carefree bunch," he said "and seemed little concerned as to the danger of the mission or what might happen to them if they were shot down over Japan.

"A great many of them grew beards and our suggestions that this was giving the Japanese an additional torture device in case they wished to pluck them out had no effect."[30]

While the pilots were being given lectures in the pilots' ready room, the gunners practiced firing at kites let out behind the carrier. Since most of them were also mechanics, they fussed with their planes at all hours of the day and night.

Doolittle made it a practice to meet with his crews two or three times a day. After Jurika had given them a review of the target cities, he let the pilots of each plane choose their target city and the airfield in China where they wanted to land. When their choices were mutually agreed upon, he passed out target folders.

"I want every crew to get this clear," he said. "You are to bomb only military targets. I don't want any of you to get any ideas about bombing the Temple of Heaven—the Imperial Palace. And avoid hospitals, schools, and other nonmilitary targets.

"Most planes will carry three five-hundred-pound demolition bombs and one five-hundred-pound incendiary. You will drop the demolitions in the shortest space possible, preferably in a straight line, where they will do the most damage. You will drop the incendiaries as near to the others as possible in an area that looks like it will burn. If you can start a couple of good fires in a Japanese city, their buildings are so inflammable they'll never put them out. Avoid all stone, concrete, and steel targets because you can't do much damage to them."

One pilot, thinking that Doolittle meant for them to look for residential areas to drop the incendiaries, asked if that was so.

"Definitely not!" Doolittle shot back. "You are to look for and aim at military targets only, such as war industries, shipbuilding facilities, power plants, and the like. And remember what I said about the Emperor's Palace. It isn't worth a plane factory, a shipyard, or an oil refinery, so leave it alone!"[31] This was an admonition he repeated many times.

While the task force was working its way westward, Doolittle and his men were unaware what was happening in China. On the day the B-25s were being loaded at Alameda, Japanese bombers and fighters began a series of attacks on the Chinese fields where the Doolittle raiders were to refuel. Fortunately, little damage was done at first but the attacks presaged a general movement of Japanese ground forces through the area. It would not be long before the fields would be overrun and used by the Japanese air force or destroyed so the Americans could not use them.

On April 2, as Task Force 16.2 was leaving San Francisco Bay, Arnold had inquired of Chungking about the homing beacons that were to be placed at the Chinese airfields and requested that transmitter frequencies between two hundred and sixteen hundred kilocycles be made available for the project. However, the reason for the request was still a mystery and no one knew why the requests for preparations had to be made before the night of April 19. On April 5, Chungking reported that all but one of the five fields could provide adequate homing services. Arnold immediately responded that the numbers "57" were to be used for identification.

Although it seemed that the arrangements were being carried out in China, misunderstandings were developing between Chungking and Washington. Chiang Kai Shek had given permission reluctantly for the use of the Chinese airfields on March 28, but he was deeply concerned because he knew the Japanese reputation for massive and excessive retaliation against his people if there was any indication they had been helping the American cause. Col. Claire L. Chennault, commander of the famous Flying Tigers who were fighting for Chiang, was also kept in the dark because of the necessity for secrecy about the mission. Ironically, if he had been informed, the outcome might have been different, because he had perfected the East China Air Warning Net. Col. Clayton Bissell, Stilwell's air officer, did not know how good that net was or he might also have had an influence on the outcome of the mission.

Several attempts were made to survey the Chinese fields, but a C-39 transport plane sent out to check on arrangements crashed for unknown reasons. Several days later two ancient Curtiss Hawk fighters were dispatched several times to look at the fields, but weather conditions were so bad they were forced to abort each time.

After the C-39 crashed, Chiang Kai Shek began to have misgivings about the project and on April 11 requested Bissell to write Washington and ask that the project, whatever it was, be delayed until the end of May so that Chiang's ground forces could be moved into position to prevent Japanese occupation of the Chuchow area.

Marshall replied on the twelfth that he was unable to recall the mission but, as if to give some measure of hope, affirmed that the planes would pass to Stilwell's control after the one landing for fuel. Arnold also wired Chungking saying the project could not be halted and added, "We are depending upon your assistance as regards flares for landing and guidance and supplies for refueling."[32]

The misunderstanding was getting worse. On the fourteenth,

at Chiang's insistence, Bissell wired Arnold that "the special project requiring only one landing the Generalissimo wishes delayed." He added, "Details on mission cannot be given to Generalissimo since they are not known here."[33]

Frustration was growing in Washington. On April 15, Marshall directed Stilwell to explain the timing and reasons for the upcoming mission to Chiang. Arnold followed next day with a similar message, again stating that "no changes in plans or additional discussion of information feasible re project at this late date."[34]

It was now only a matter of a few hours before the B-25s would be en route to their targets in Japan. Concern was mounting in Washington for the safety of Doolittle's crews and what the Japanese reaction to the bombing would be on the Chinese in the occupied areas of China.

In addition, the task force itself, at great risk in Japanese waters, could well be lost if the surprise attack by land-based bombers were to be deduced as having come from the two-carrier task force. On April 18, Marshall sent a final message to Chungking:[35]

> ATMOSPHERE OF TOTAL MYSTERY WILL SURROUND SPECIAL PROJECT. STILWELL TO DENY ANY CONNECTION WITH PROJECT IN RE TO PUBLIC INFORMATION. NO PUBLICITY DESIRED FOR PROJECT. DESIRE GENERALISSIMO TO OBSERVE SAME POLICY. REPORT ANY INFORMATION ON RESULTS OF PROJECT IMMEDIATELY TO WAR DEPARTMENT.

When Admiral Halsey returned to Pearl Harbor, he related the final details of the task force's mission to his staff; and on April 7, Admiral Nimitz approved Operation Plan No. 20-42, stating that "this force will conduct a bombing raid against the enemy objective specified in Annex C which is being furnished Commander Task Force Sixteen only."[36]

In addition to the sixteen ships in Halsey's force, two submarines, the USS *Trout* and the USS *Thresher*, were to maintain patrol stations beginning on April 15 and report any enemy forces that might threaten Task Force 16. Any surface ships or submarines sighted west of the rendezvous point would be presumed unfriendly. During the month of April, all U.S.

submarines proceeding to and from patrol stations would not be routed north of 0°30′ north latitude.

On April 8, Halsey, with his flag flying from the carrier *Enterprise*, steamed through the submarine nets at Pearl Harbor and headed northwest. The accompanying ships were the cruisers *Northampton* and *Salt Lake City*. The destroyers *Balch*, *Benham*, *Ellet*, and *Fanning* zigzagged protectively among the larger ships, while the oiler *Sabine*, slowest ship in the force, trailed behind the "Big E."

While the Halsey force was proceeding to the rendezvous point, Mitscher's force was having to mark time in bad weather. High winds whipped up heavy sea swells and made refueling impossible. Two men were rescued after being thrown overboard from the *Cimarron* while attempting to refuel the *Hornet*. On the morning of the thirteenth, the two task forces merged at the rendezvous point of 38° north latitude, 180° longitude, and the ships maneuvered into cruising formation. When all were on station, Task Force 16 steamed due west at sixteen knots.

As the hours dragged on, the B-25 crews were having difficulties with their planes. Many minor difficulties developed: generator failures, turret troubles, fouled spark plugs, leaky gas tanks, and hydraulic system problems. The *Hornet*'s maintenance shops were kept busy repairing and substituting parts if none were available among the B-25 replacement kits. The tension mounted among the B-25 mechanics as they sweated out their respective plane problems.

While the sixteen ships plunged westward, the American garrison on Bataan had been fighting its final skirmishes. On April 9, Bataan was surrendered but Gen. Jonathan Wainwright and thirty-five thousand of his troops escaped to Corregidor to continue their last-ditch stand. On April 10, thousands of American and Filipino soldiers, now prisoners on Bataan began their forced march, which would be referred to ever after as the Bataan Death March.

On April 13, Japanese General Yamashita ordered his forces to batter down Corregidor, the last bastion held by Americans. Within a forty-eight-hour period, the island endured twenty-two bombing raids. To their great credit, the beleaguered Americans were able to hold on for three more weeks, but the outcome was preordained. America had never recorded a darker period in its history.

6

The Enemy Is Alerted: The Mission Begins

The war news for the Japanese had not taken a single bad turn in the war thus far, and by April complacency had set in, especially in the home islands. The people were reminded that invasion was impossible because in 1281, Kublai Khan, the notorious Chinese warlord, had sent a mighty armada to invade and conquer Japan but it was destroyed by a great typhoon. From that time on, the Japanese were told that their nation was forever protected by the *Kamikazi* or Divine Wind.

The Japanese military planners were more realistic, however. They did provide some meager air defense units around the large cities. At a meeting of high-level war strategists on November 4, 1941, Premier Tojo, when queried by Admiral Hyakutake about air defenses in the war they knew was coming, had made this reply:

> I do not think the enemy could raid Japan proper from the air immediately after the outbreak of hostilities. Some time would elapse before the enemy could attempt such raids. I believe that enemy air attacks against Japan proper in the early stages of the war would be infrequent and would be carried out by carrier-based planes. If it should become possible for the enemy to raid Japan from bases in the Soviet Union we might face considerable danger, but I think that this is not likely in the early stages of the war.[1]

Tojo, as well as his military advisors, obviously thought that any raids against Japan would have to be by short-range, carrier-based planes, not land-based planes flying from a carrier. Although Japanese intelligence underestimated American ingenuity, it had a strong capability to intercept and analyze radio messages winging around the Pacific. At 6:30 A.M. on April 10, the Combined Fleet radio intelligence unit intercepted messages being flashed between the Halsey and Mitscher forces before they joined up. One Japanese historian described the reaction in the Japanese naval headquarters:

> Under mounting tensions, the Combined Fleet made accurate calculations. If the enemy were to proceed westward, Tokyo would be attacked from the air around the 14th, because even if the carriers came at full speed they would have to approach within 300 miles of the home islands in order to fly the planes they carried. However, our surveillance net was 700 nautical miles off-shore and the enemy, in order to break through this net and penetrate 300 nautical miles inward, would require 15 or 16 hours, so it would be possible for us to attack the enemy at our leisure the day before he launched his planes.[2]

Unfortunately, American naval intelligence did not know about a line of approximately fifty Japanese radio-equipped fishing boats that formed the early warning surveillance network. Despite occasional forays by American submarines into the area, the one-hundred- to three-hundred-ton fishing vessels had escaped their notice or, if seen, were not thought to be part of any early warning system.

Another unknown was the state of Japanese air defenses. Japanese naval and army defense units armed with about three hundred 75-mm antiaircraft guns and backed up by nearly one hundred Type 97 (Nate) single-engine fighters were in place around the country's major cities. Although poorly equipped and trained, if forewarned, they did constitute a formidable threat to the sixteen B-25s soon to be en route to the home islands.

When the first messages between Halsey and Mitscher were intercepted on April 10, Vice Adm. Matome Ugaki, chief of staff of the Combined Fleet, made an assessment of the forces available to meet the Americans estimated to arrive offshore by the fourteenth. Although a large force was returning home from the Indian Ocean after repeated victories, it would not arrive in Japanese waters until the eighteenth, too late to engage the Americans. However, the twenty-sixth Air Flotilla was available to back up the home defenses with sixty-nine bombing and scouting planes.

Ugaki and Vice Adm. Seigo Yamagata, the twenty-sixth's commander, agreed on a plan. When the Americans were within six hundred miles of land, the first bombers would be dispatched. If any carriers were still afloat after the first wave, torpedo bombers would be sent out a few hours later. There would be no escape and the American carrier strength in the Pacific would be wiped out. However, no more intercepts of American radio messages were made, and when the fourteenth came and went without any reports, they were disappointed. Apparently, the Americans were headed somewhere else. It was decided that a state of alert would remain in effect in case more reports were received that indicated the enemy was approaching the Japanese islands.

Halsey's force steamed on. The *Enterprise*, despite deteriorating weather, launched air patrols during daylight hours until the weather got too bad to launch and recover planes safely. Search flights were made at dawn and dusk up to two hundred miles in an arc sixty degrees off the task force's westerly heading. On the afternoon of the fifteenth, Halsey signaled the other ships by semaphore that they would be refueled one thousand miles off Japan. The carriers and cruisers would then proceed to a point five hundred miles from land to launch the army bombers. The destroyers and tankers would remain in the vicinity where the refueling was to take place and rejoin when the launching force came dashing back from the launch point.

The tension aboard all the ships increased. Would they be spotted before they could get close enough to launch the B-25s? The uncertainty was compounded when an English-speaking radio news program originating in Japan repeated a British News Agency bulletin that "three American bombers have dropped bombs on Tokyo." However, the announcer quickly added, "This is a most laughable story. They know it is absolutely impossible for enemy bombers to get within five hundred miles of Tokyo. Instead of worrying about such foolish things, the Japanese people are enjoying the fine spring sunshine and the fragrance of the cherry blossoms."[3]

On the sixteenth, the *Enterprise* sent up more frequent patrols but no contacts were made. On April 17, eighteen scout bombers were launched at dawn. In early afternoon, the tankers refueled the large ships and withdrew with the destroyers. The two carriers and four cruisers increased speeds to twenty knots. As they did so, the winds picked up to gale speeds.

Meanwhile, the B-25s had been spotted on the deck for takeoff. Doolittle had 467 feet of deck in front of his plane. The tail of the last plane hung out over the stern. Two white lines had been painted on the deck—one for the left wheel and one for the nose wheel of the bombers. If the pilots kept their wheels on these lines, they could be assured their right wings would miss the superstructure of the carrier's island by about six feet.

As the B-25s were being positioned, Mitscher called Doolittle to the bridge. He spread out a large map and pointed out the position of the six ships. "Jimmy, we're in the enemy's back yard now. Anything could happen from here on in. I think it's time for our little ceremony."[4]

Mitscher called the B-25 crews to the flight deck over the loudspeaker while Doolittle went below to get the messages he had received from Marshall and Arnold to read to his men. Mitscher had also received mail when Halsey's force had joined his. Enclosed were some medals that had been presented to H. Vormstein, John B. Laurey, and Daniel J. Quigley, ex–navy enlisted men, to commemorate the visit of the U.S. Fleet to Japan in 1908. They had forwarded the medals to Secretary of the Navy Frank Knox with the request that they be returned "via bomb to Tokyo." Knox had forwarded the medals to Nimitz at Pearl Harbor asking that the request be complied with at an appropriate time.

When everyone had assembled around a bomb that had been brought on deck, Mitscher made a short speech about the medals and handed them to Doolittle, who attached them to the bomb. Lt. Jurika stepped forward and added a medal he had been given by the Japanese before he left his attaché post in 1940. Several crew members wrote slogans on the bomb like "I don't want to set the world on fire—just Tokyo" and "You'll get a BANG out of this."

The crews posed for photos taken by a navy photographer

and kidded each other good-naturedly but they all knew that the time for takeoff was growing close. Doc White checked the dog tags of the B-25 crews going on the mission and gave a few of them final inoculations they had missed at Eglin. Survival equipment for each man was checked once more. Each crew member had been issued a Navy gas mask, a .45 automatic pistol, ammunition clips, hunting knife, flashlight, emergency rations, first aid kit, canteen, compass, and life jacket. Besides the clothes they stuffed into their B-4 bags, some added items they thought would be non-existent in China such as razor blades, toothpaste, candy bars, and cigarettes. Lt. Jacob E. "Shorty" Manch, six-foot, four-inch co-pilot on Lt. Bob Gray's crew, wanted to take his wind-up phonograph and records. Lt. Horace E. "Sally" Crouch, bombardier–navigator on Lt. Dick Joyce's crew, remembering the lectures about the lack of sanitation in China, stuffed rolls of toilet paper into his B-4 bag.

Despite the continual checking of each plane by the crews, mechanical problems were still cropping up. The right engine on Lt. Don Smith's plane cracked a blower, which had to be removed and repaired below decks. Almost every plane had gun turret problems; hydraulic systems leaked and spark plugs fouled. Doolittle went from plane to plane, questioned the mechanics, and inspected each B-25 from nose wheel to the broomstick "guns" in the tail. On the afternoon of the seventeenth, he called the flying crews together for a final briefing.

"The time's getting short," he said. "By now every one of you knows exactly what he should do if the alarm is sounded. We were originally supposed to take off on the nineteenth but it looks like it will be tomorrow, the eighteenth, instead. This is your final briefing. Be ready to go at any time.

"We should have plenty of warning if we're intercepted. If all goes as planned, I'll take off tomorrow afternoon so as to arrive over Tokyo at dusk. I'll drop incendiaries. The rest of you will take off later and can use my fires as a homing beacon."[5]

Doolittle repeated what he had been saying since the first meeting, that any man could drop out if he wished. Again, no one took him up on the offer. He cautioned the rear gunners about not dropping the five-gallon gas cans overboard after they were emptied because they might float long enough to leave a trail back to the task force.

There was one question that lurked in the minds of most of the crewmen but no one had yet dared to ask it. Finally, one pilot raised his hand and asked, "Colonel Doolittle, what should we do if we lose an engine or get hit by ack-ack fire and crash-land in Japan?"[6]

Doolittle's answer was quick and firm. "Each pilot is in command of his own plane when we leave the carrier," he said. "He is responsible for the decision he makes for his own plane and his own crew. If you're separated, each one of you will have to decide for yourself what you will do. Personally, I know exactly what I'm going to do."

The room was silent. Doolittle didn't go any further so one of the group asked, "Sir, what *will* you do?"

"I don't intend to be taken prisoner," he answered. "If my plane is crippled beyond any possibility of fighting or escaping, I'm going to bail my crew out and then drive it, full throttle, into any target I can find where the crash will do the most damage. I'm forty-five years old and have lived a full life. Most of you are in your twenties and if I were you, I'm not sure I would make the same decision. In the final analysis, it's up to each pilot and, in turn, each man to decide what he will do."

Doolittle's final caution was to get rid of any letters, diaries, photos, and identification that would link them with the *Hornet*, their former units in the States, or their training. Any such items were to be placed in self-addressed envelopes and turned over to the navy personnel who would safeguard them until security officers decided they could be sent to stateside addresses.

The B-25 crews spent the rest of the seventeenth preparing for their departure. Ammunition and bombs were loaded. Engines were given a last-minute run-up. Doc White, ever mindful of crew morale and well-being, had come aboard the *Hornet* in San Francisco with eighty quarts of bourbon "for medicinal purposes"—one for every crew member. He exchanged these with the navy medical supply officer for pints of medicinal rye, which were easier to carry in the B-4 bags and, in case of bailout, could be stuffed in their flight jackets. He reminded them that it would be especially useful as an antiseptic for any cuts and scratches.

The loading and positioning of the planes was complete by sunset, as the force steamed ahead on a course of 276 degrees. Each man was to have his personnel belongings packed and ready to go. Below decks, as had been the practice among the air force crews each day after work was done, the poker games started. The night of the seventeenth was no exception.

The two carriers and their accompanying ships steamed ahead in total darkness. At 3:00 A.M., Ens. Robert R. Boettcher, on watch as officer of the deck, rceeived a message by light signal from the *Enterprise*:

TWO ENEMY SURFACE CRAFT REPORTED.

The big E's radar had spotted two small ships off the bow at a distance of twenty-one thousand yards. A light appeared briefly on the horizon.

The *Enterprise*'s short-range, high-frequency radio broadcast a crisp command to all ships to turn right to a course of 350 degrees to avoid detection. General quarters was sounded and all hands went to their assigned battle stations. The B-25 crews dressed and waited. The two fishing boats, part of the early warning net, faded from the radar screen; the "all clear" was sounded at 3:41. At 4:11, the task force turned westward again. The B-25 crews returned to their quarters to resume their interrupted sleep.

At 5:08, the *Enterprise* sent off the dawn patrols consisting of eight Grumman F4F fighters and three Douglas SBD scout bombers to search at a maximum distance of two hundred miles. Three more scout bombers were sent aloft for combat patrol above the task force.

The weather was turning sour. Moderately rough during the night, the wind increased and low clouds hung ominously over the area. Rain squalls smashed across the decks and the sea began to swell into thirty-foot waves. The wind sliced off the tops of the waves and drenched the deck crews.

At 5:58, Lt. O. B. Wiseman, one of the SBD pilots, sighted a small fishing vessel. He jotted down the following message on his knee pad:

"Enemy surface ship—latitude 36-04N, Long. 153-10E, bearing 276 degrees true—42 miles. Believed seen by enemy."

Wiseman passed the paper to the gunner in the rear seat, making a throwing motion with his hand. The gunner pulled a small bean bag from his pocket, stuffed the message inside and peered over the side as Wiseman headed for the Big E.

When the SBD was directly over the carrier, the gunner threw the bag on the deck, where it was scooped up by a sailor and rushed to Halsey on the bridge. Halsey immediately ordered all ships to turn left to a course of 220 degrees. Had Wiseman's plane been seen? It wasn't likely at forty-two miles, but at 7:38 another patrol vessel was sighted by a lookout on the *Hornet* only twenty thousand yards away. If the vessel could be seen by the *Hornet*, it had to be assumed that the task force had been sighted and that it had radioed the sighting to Japan.

The sighting became a certainty when the *Hornet's* radio operator intercepted a message in Japanese that had originated close by. At 7:45, Ens. J. Q. Roberts sighted the vessel, now only twelve thousand yards away.

Halsey had no option but to order the *Nashville* to sink the enemy boat. He then flashed a message to Mitscher:

LAUNCH PLANES X TO COL DOOLITTLE AND GALLANT COMMAND GOOD LUCK AND GOD BLESS YOU

Doolittle, on the bridge when the order came, shook hands with Mitscher, leaped down the ladder to his cabin, shouting to everybody he saw, "OK fellas, this is it. Let's go!" At the same time, the blood-chilling klaxon horn sounded, followed by the announcement: "Army pilots, man your planes!"

The B-25 crews had not been fully aware of the drama taking place around them. Some had finished breakfast and were lounging in their cabins; others were shaving; some were still asleep until the klaxon sounded. A few had their bags packed but most still had some packing to do.

Lt. Shorty Manch, determined to take his phonograph, his .45 caliber automatic, and a carbine, had no room for the records he had put in a cake tin. He asked his buddy, Lt. Bob Clever, navigator on Ted Lawson's *Ruptured Duck*, to put them under the navigator's seat on his plane. Clever reluctantly agreed.

Doc White hurriedly passed out two pints of rye to each man as they rushed past. Lt. Dick Knobloch ran from plane to plane with bags of sandwiches he had gotten from the galley. There was confusion as army and navy men ran back and forth on their respective missions. Mechanics ripped off engine covers and stuffed them up into the rear hatches. Tie-down ropes were unfastened and wheel chocks pulled away. A navy "donkey" attached a tow bar to nose wheels and pushed and pulled the planes into takeoff position. Gas tanks were topped off and the crews rocked the planes back and forth to get rid of any air bubbles in the tanks that would prevent a few more gallons of precious fuel from being pumped in. Sailors filled the five-gallon cans with fuel and passed them hand-to-hand to the rear gunner in each B-25.

On the bridge, Mitscher ordered the *Hornet* to full speed into the wind and her bow plunged into towering waves that smashed across the deck. The *Hornet*'s air officer on the bridge brought out a large blackboard and noted the carrier's compass heading and the wind speed so the pilots would have some idea how much airspeed they had to gain for takeoff. Hank Miller rushed from plane to plane to shake hands and wish the crews good luck. "I'll be on the right side holding up a blackboard to give you any last-minute instructions before you go," he shouted. "Look at me just before you release your brakes."[7]

Doolittle, in the lead plane, started his engines and warmed them up. Near the bow on the left side, Lt. Edgar G. Osborne, the signal officer, stood by holding a checkered flag. When Doolittle was satisfied that his engine instruments were "in the green," the checklist complete, and crew ready, he gave a "thumbs up" to Osborne. Osborne responded by swinging the flag in a circle as a signal for Doolittle to ease the throttles forward. Osborne swung the flag in faster and faster circles, keeping one eye on the bow. At the instant the deck was beginning its upward movement, chocks were pulled from under Doolittle's wheels and Osborne gave him the "go" signal. Doolittle released the brakes and the B-25 inched forward,

slowly at first, then faster. As the plane passed the ship's island, the nose wheel rose first, followed by the main wheels, and Doolittle was airborne with plenty of deck to spare.

All the remaining pilots, now getting ready to be jockeyed into position, had watched Doolittle's plane apprehensively. They knew that if he had had trouble and didn't make it, they couldn't. They breathed sighs of relief as Doolittle brought up his gear and flaps, circled to the left, came back over the deck to check his compass against the carrier's course and faded off into the distance.

The log of the *Hornet* noted that Doolittle was airborne at 8:20 ship time. Instead of following three hours later as originally planned, Lt. Travis Hoover, was maneuvered into takeoff position, started his engines, and took off five minutes after Doolittle.

"Hoover kept his nose in the up position too long and nearly stalled out," Lt. Hank Miller recalled.[8] "After the third plane took off, I wrote 'STABILIZER IN NEUTRAL' on the blackboard. I think the rest of them saw and took my advice.

"Succeeding takeoffs were all good except one—Ted Lawson's—because he either forgot his flaps or inadvertently put them back into the 'up' position instead of 'neutral.' But he got away with it.

"The flaps on three other planes were up as they maneuvered into position, but the flight deck crew caught them before takeoff. The only casualty to the planes was a cracked nose glass on Lt. Don Smith's plane when it was rammed into the tail cone of the one ahead of it. There wasn't enough damage to worry about so he took off in order."

Each plane had gotten off without apparent difficulty, but the last plane, piloted by Lt. Bill Farrow, had a mishap on the deck that forecast the kind of luck this crew was going to experience before the day was over. Since its tail was sticking out over the stern section, the loading of the plane's rear compartment could not be completed until the plane ahead of it was moved forward. Six deck handlers held down the nose wheel while Farrow taxied slowly forward on the seesawing deck. Just as the plane ahead revved up its engines and the sailors moved away from Farrow's nose wheel, Seaman Robert W. Wall, one of the six, lost his footing and slipped into the spinning pro-

peller. There was nothing Farrow could do as he watched horrified. The left prop chewed into Wall's left arm and threw him aside. His crewmates rushed to his side and carried him to sick bay where his arm was amputated a short time later.

Farrow's plane was logged off at 9:20 A.M. an hour after Doolittle's. Doolittle had 620 miles to go to Tokyo, his target area. Farrow's distance was calculated as an even six hundred miles to Inubo Saki, the nearest point of land.

At 7:52 an order had been signaled to the *Nashville* to "attack vessel and sink same," according to the ship's log. She opened fire at nine thousand yards and after a salvo, shifted to rapid fire but the vessel could not be seen in the raging sea. Meanwhile, the *Enterprise* sent its dive bombers aloft, and when the *Nashville* stopped firing, they made several attacks. The crew of the vessel fired back at the planes with machine guns and a light cannon. The enemy ship headed for the *Nashville* and the planes continued their strafing runs. At 8:21, the log noted "Enemy vessel on fire," followed by "Enemy vessel sunk" two minutes later. The *Nashville* maneuvered to pick up survivors. "Attempts to rescue one man sighted proved unsuccessful," the log noted.

As soon as the last B-25 left the deck, the entire task force reversed course and headed east at full speed. Now divested of the army bombers, the *Hornet*'s planes were brought up on deck and prepared to share the scouting and patrol duties. Since it was now certain that an alert message had been sent to Japan from the picket boat, it was a sure bet that Japanese fighting vessels or aircraft anywhere near the area would be searching for the intruders. The assumption was well-founded; the *Enterprise*'s radar operator spotted a patrol aircraft en route toward the task force but it turned back under the low clouds and poor visibility without getting closer than thirty miles.

At 11:30, Ens.'s R. M. Elder, R. K, Campbell, and J. C. Butler of Bomber Squadron Three were launched from the *Enterprise* to make single-plane searches to the southwest. Lt. R. W. Arndt, leading a three-plane flight took off a few minutes later to attack vessels reported fifty-eight miles away. Campbell reported at 11:50 that he had sighted a patrol boat

painted dark gray, with a tall radio antenna towering above its deck. He made two diving attacks but scored no hits with his bombs. He returned firing his machine guns but could see only minor damage inflicted.

Lieutenant Arndt and his two wingmen attacked another picket vessel and dropped their bombs, but without success. In reporting on Arndt's mission, the squadron's war diary noted: "No apparent damage from bombs except for one 100-lb. bomb near miss which evidently stopped the fire on one small caliber AA gun located aft. The enemy used radical maneuver and returned AA fire with what appeared to be a 1″ gun."

Ensign Butler, searching another sector, sighted a third picket boat towing a smaller boat. He made three bomb runs, dropping one bomb each time. The two one-hundred-pound bombs were duds but the five-hundred-pound bomb landed near the port side, causing some minor damage to the larger boat. Butler strafed the vessel after his bombs were gone and returned to the carrier thinking that he had sunk the small boat and damaged the larger one. He reported that his plane received three hits from enemy fire.

The other planes, also unable to make successful runs on the enemy vessel bobbing in the heavy seas, withdrew after their bombs were gone. The *Nashville* opened fire with its five- and six-inch guns for the next twenty minutes and finally got results. Overwhelmed by the quantity of lead being thrown their way, the Japanese crew raised a white flag and the *Nashville* ceased firing. While it circled, the enemy boat slowly sank. Five survivors were sighted in the water and picked up. All were suffering from shock, immersion, and fright. Despite the heavy firing by the planes and the cruiser, only S2c. Nakamura Suekichi was injured slightly, with a bullet wound in the neck.

There had been eleven crewmen aboard the picket boat, the *Nitto Maru*. Suekichi wrote to the author in a letter years later that, "The waves were high that day and I could not help worrying that our 70-ton *Nitto Maru* would capsize at any moment." He told navy interrogators that he had seen some planes while he had been on watch and went below to arouse his skipper, CPO Gisaku Maeda. Maeda assumed they were the usual morning patrol planes from Japan and stayed in his bunk. A short time later, Suekichi went below and told his captain, "Sir, there are two of our beautiful carriers now dead ahead."[9]

Maeda burst out of his bunk and leaped up the ladder to the deck. No Japanese carriers were supposed to be in his patrol area. He studied the large gray hulks through his binoculars and said sadly, "Yes, Suekichi, they are beautiful but they are not ours." He handed the binoculars to Suekichi and went below. He reached into his sea bag, pulled out a revolver, cocked it, put it to his head, and pulled the trigger.

"At that time," Suekichi said, "we radioed thc *Kiso*, the flagship of the Fifth Fleet, that the enemy had been sighted. When the American cruiser fired on us, I could actually see the approaching shells. The airborne attack by the enemy became more severe, but we really doubted whether they could hit us, so we pointed our gun at the enemy. Looking back on our actions now, we acted foolishly. But, after all, we thought we were fighting for the great spirit of Nippon. Since we had communicated the discovery of the enemy ships and planes, we were positive that no damage could occur in Japan."

While the *Nashville* was completing its after-action chores, the planes returned to the *Enterprise* to rearm. One of them, piloted by Lt. L. A. Smith, couldn't make it. His SBD engine had been hit by small-arms fire, causing the oil pressure to drop to zero. He and his gunner, AMM2C H. H. Caruthers, ditched and were rescued by the *Nashville* shortly thereafter.

Danger still hounded the American task force. A small enemy submarine was sighted and attacked, but it hurriedly slipped beneath the waves undamaged. Other Japanese patrol vessels and planes were sighted on the task force's radar but were not attacked. That evening, when the day's activities were reviewed, Halsey and his staff were surprised at the number of enemy vessels reported. Halsey wrote in his war diary that

> in addition to the radar contact with two craft made at 0310, actual contact showed one submarine, 14 PY's [patrol vessels] and 3 AK's [probably "mother ships"] concentrated in an area about 130 miles by 180 miles. A similar concentration was reported by a submarine just returned from patrol in the East China Sea which stated that 65 sampans had been

> sighted in an area just about the same size as that mentioned above. These are indications of the degree to which the Japanese are using these small craft for patrols and screens around their vital areas.[10]

Halsey apparently did not know at that time that enemy long-range patrol planes had also been dispatched after the alarm had been sent to Japan. If these planes, larger and capable of making sustained bombing attacks, had sighted the task force, the outcome might have been different.

Halsey kept the task force steaming eastward at full speed through the night and at dawn on the nineteenth sent up air patrols from both carriers. No more enemy ships were sighted but a scout bomber from the *Hornet*, piloted by Lt. G. D. Randall with radioman T. A. Gallagher aboard, ran out of fuel only seven miles from the carrier. The airplane glided into the high seas and sank immediately. Neither man was recovered.

Task Force 16 returned to Pearl Harbor one week almost to the hour after the B-25s had departed. Halsey sent a "well done" to each of the ships in the force and declared the mission a success. "The Japs chased us all the way home, of course," he wrote later. "Whenever we tracked their search planes with our radar, I was tempted to unleash our fighters, but I knew it was more important not to reveal our position than to shoot down a couple of scouts. They sent a task force after us; their submarines tried to intercept us; and . . . even some of their carriers joined the hunt; but with the help of foul weather and a devious course, we eluded them."[11]

The mission over, Halsey touted up the score. The army bombers had been launched successfully, three enemy patrol boats had been sunk or damaged severely, and the task force had escaped without a scratch. The *Thresher* and *Trout*, on their special mission to observe Japanese ship movements, report the weather, and attack targets of opportunity, had exceptionally good hunting. The *Thresher* had sunk the *Sado Maru*, a three-thousand-ton freighter at the entrance to Yokohama Harbor. The *Trout* had damaged a fifteen-thousand-ton freighter, had beached or sunk a seven-thousand-ton freighter and a one-thousand-ton patrol vessel.

There was a minus side to this first joint army–navy combat venture in history, however. Halsey lost three of his planes and three more were damaged in landing accidents. Two lives had been lost, and one seaman had been seriously injured.

In reflecting later on the Doolittle raid, Halsey wrote, "In my opinion, their flight was one of the most courageous deeds in military history."[12]

A sad fact that has never been dealt with previously by the navy or the army air forces is that Halsey was supposed to have sent a signal to Washington that was to be relayed to Chungking. The message was to report the time that Doolittle and his sixteen planes had departed the carrier and were en route to China via their targets. Arnold and Marshall in Washington were then to notify Stilwell, Chennault, and Chiang Kai Shek that the "special project" planes were expected to arrive soon so that the air defense net could be notified and the airfields' homing beacons turned on. This message was especially vital to Doolittle's men because their departure from the carrier was a day earlier than originally planned. For reasons the navy has never explained, the message was not sent.

When questioned about this, Doolittle told the author that he did not know why the message was not sent but believed it possible that the threat to the task force was so great at the time that Halsey did not want to risk his sixteen ships, which represented a large part of the navy's fighting capability in the Pacific. Doolittle and the string of B-25s winging their way at low altitude toward their targets fully expected the Chinese airfields to be ready for them if they survived the flight over their Japanese targets.[13]

The stationing of a long line of radio-equipped picket boats six to seven hundred miles off the coast of Japan was a clever early warning net that surprised the Americans. Japanese radar was primitive and the U.S. Fleet was the only enemy force they had to fear. The picket boats that had sighted the Halsey force and the others stretched out in a long line were assigned to Vice Adm. Jushiro Hosogaya, commander of the Fifth Fleet.

On April 1, the three squadrons of the Twenty-sixth Air Flotilla under Vice Adm. Seigo Yamagata had been deployed to Kisarazu, Misawa, and Minami Torishima bases for patrol duty. When the naval radio intelligence unit intercepted the lively message exchanges between ships of the American fleet on April 10, surveillance was increased. Although the anticipated arrival and interception of the Americans did not take place on the fourteenth as estimated, the Japanese still maintained a listening watch. However, the strict radio silence observed by the Halsey force after it linked up with Mitscher's ships paid off. The report from the *Nitto Maru*, the picket boat that sighted and reported the U.S. task force, was the first firm indication that the Americans were headed directly for Japan.

As soon as this first report was received in Japan, a confirmation was requested but there was no answer. Vice Adm. Matome Ugaki, commander-in-chief of the Combined Forces at Hashirajima, wrote in his diary that day that "we became tense over the report from *No. 23 Nitto Maru* and I immediately issued Order No. 3 against the American fleet."[14]

Ugaki studied the resources that were immediately available to meet the threat. Thirty-five land attack planes of the twenty-first Air Flotilla, fresh from battle in the Philippines, had just arrived, along with sixty-three carrier planes from the carrier *Kaga* berthed at Tateyama. Vice Adm. Nobutake Kondo, commander of the Second Fleet, had returned victoriously from operations in the Indian Ocean with a large task force. The total number of planes that could be dispatched to intercept the Americans consisted of ninety carrier fighters, eighty medium bombers, thirty-six carrier bombers, and two flying boats.

Kondo was ordered to take charge of the interception operation and left Yokosuka with ten destroyers and the heavy cruisers *Aito*, *Takao*, *Maya*, *Nachi*, *Haguro*, and *Myoko*. Vice Adm. Tadakazu Nagumo, commander of the First Air Fleet, was instructed to proceed to the estimated interception point, with the carriers *Akagi*, *Soryu*, *Hiryu*, *Suikaku*, and *Shokaku*.

Added to this formidable opposition force were six submarines of the Eighth Submarine Fleet and three submarines of the Third Submarine Fleet, which were ordered to swing about from their current missions and pursue the Americans. Thus, the entire Japanese fleet that was within a day's run of intercepting the enemy were instantly turned toward the Halsey force. If the B-25 takeoffs had been delayed until the carriers were within 450 miles of the Japanese coast as planned, only a miracle could have saved the task force and the B-25s might not have gotten off at all. By the time the orders to the Japanese commanders were sent and the various units were gearing up to comply, Doolittle's sixteen planes were winging their way to Japan a few feet above the waves.

As far as can be determined, the first person to sense something amiss from the fragmentary information available from the picket ships was Vice Adm. Yamagata at Kisarazu. At 10:30, one hour after the last B-25 had left the *Hornet*, the regularly scheduled morning patrol plane should have reached a point about 650 miles at sea, but no position report was received. When another hour went by without a report, Yamagata sent three patrol bombers to a point five hundred miles out. Fifteen minutes later, he ordered twenty-four fighters and twenty-five torpedo bombers into the air.

The weather over the Japanese islands was clear but the frontal system with low clouds and rain squalls that had surrounded the Halsey force lay between the Americans and the Japanese air units. Visibility was down to three miles or less. Frustrated, the Japanese pilots gave up one by one. At this time, Doolittle was approaching the Boso Peninsula. The planes behind him were spread out in an arc about fifty miles wide because of the changing winds and compasses that had been thrown off by two weeks aboard the carrier. The low clouds prevented the navigators from taking any sun shots with their sextants. The B-25s were heading toward their targets but would not be able to determine their positions until they made landfall. Meanwhile, the Japanese were ready for something but they knew not what. Jimmy Doolittle and his raiders were about to achieve the surprise they had hoped for. It would be a psychological touché—a surprise air attack launched from a carrier, precisely as the Japanese had accomplished at Pearl Harbor.

On the morning of April 18, a curious set of circumstances was developing in the capital city of Tokyo. From the time of the attack on Pearl Harbor, Japanese propaganda assured the people that an air attack against Japan by the enemy was impossible. However, Tokyo itself had a model civil defense organization, which had been set up several years before the outbreak of war. Each block had an air raid warden, and air raid drills had become frequent enough that they had become routine and caused little disruption to the city's normal functions.

On the sixteenth, the Tokyo papers announced that there would be an air raid drill on Saturday, April 18. This information was conveyed to the American and British embassies, where the staffs were restricted on the night of the seventeenth by city police. The "first alarm" simulation was sounded shortly after 9:00 A.M. Tokyo time, on the eighteenth, just as the last few B-25s were leaving the *Hornet*. In this condition, no sirens were sounded and the population did not seek shelter, but air raid wardens were notified to report to their posts and Tokyo fire-fighting brigades brought their equipment out on the streets.[15]

Throughout the morning air activity over the capital increased, with army planes practicing for ceremonies for the emperor's birthday and the dedication of the Yasukuni Shrine for the Japanese war dead on April 25. A group of Type 97 Nate fighters engaged in mock dog fights over the city. Barrage balloons were raised and lowered for practice along the Tokyo waterfront. Although the Japanese navy seemed aware of the developing threat offshore, the army air defense commander for the Tokyo area was apparently not fully informed. Just before noon, however, three air defense fighters were ordered aloft and others were put on runway alert.

By noon, the practice air raid defense activities were drawing to a close. The barrage balloons were lowered for the last time and about a dozen defense fighters were airborne, along with some training planes. A few fire-fighting teams were still in the streets assembling their equipment for return to their firehouses.

The traffic on Tokyo's streets reached its usual high volume for a Saturday afternoon. Hundreds of people were on their way to baseball games, flower festivals, and shopping areas. For those working in the war industries, it was the lunch hour. The weather was warm and sunny with gentle spring breezes.

As Jimmy Doolittle's plane crossed the Japanese coast, Lt. Hank Potter, the navigator, located their position on his map as eighty miles north of the city and told Doolittle to turn left.

When the city came into view, Doolittle pulled the B-25 up to twelve hundred feet and lined up on a factory area. He told Sgt. Fred Braemer, the bombardier, to open the bomb bay doors. Braemer, using the "twenty-cent Mark Twain" bomb sight that Ross Greening had designed, flicked a toggle switch on and drew a bead on the factory complex ahead. At exactly 12:20 Tokyo time, the first American bombs of World War II fell on the Japanese home islands.

7

"Believe All Planes Wrecked"

Jimmy Doolittle, known internationally for his racing, stunting, and aeronautical accomplishments and called "master of the calculated risk," took one more calculated risk in a life that had been full of them. He roared down the *Hornet*'s pitching deck, lifted off smoothly, pulled up the gear and flaps, and started a gentle left turn. He flew over the *Hornet*'s deck to check his compass with the carrier's heading and pointed the B-25 on a westerly course. "The takeoff was easy," he reported later. "A night takeoff would have been possible and practicable."[1]

About a half-hour after departure, Doolittle's plane was joined by the B-25 flown by Lt. Travis Hoover, the second to leave the *Hornet*. Flying about two hundred feet above the water, Doolittle sighted a camouflaged Japanese naval vessel thought to be a light cruiser. Two hours later, a twin-engine land plane flew about three thousand feet overhead headed toward the task force but apparently did not see the B-25.

"We were somewhat north of the desired course," Doolittle recalled, "but I decided to take advantage of the error and approach Tokyo from a northerly direction, thus avoiding what we anticipated would be strong opposition to the west."[2] As his B-25 crossed the coastline about eighty miles north of Japan's capital city, Doolittle turned left. His official report of the mission from his viewpoint was typically terse:[3]

> Many flying fields and the air full of planes north of Tokyo. Mostly small biplanes apparently primary or basic trainers.
>
> Encountered nine fighters in three flights of three. This was about ten miles north of the outskirts of Tokyo proper.
>
> All this time had been flying as low as the terrain would permit.

Continued low flying due south over the outskirts of and toward the east center of Tokyo.

Pulled up to 1,200 feet, changed course to the southwest and incendiary-bombed inflammable section. Dropped first bomb at 1:30 (ship time).

Anti-aircraft fire very active but only one near hit.

Lowered away to housetops and slid over western outskirts into low haze and smoke.

Passed over small aircraft factory with a dozen or so newly completed planes on the line. No bombs left. Decided not to machine gun for reasons of personal security.

Passed on out to sea flying low.

Navigator plotted perfect course to pass north of Yaki Shima. Saw three large naval vessels just before passing west end of Japan.

Made landfall somewhat north of course on China coast.

Ceiling lowered on coast until low islands and hills were in it at about 600 feet. Just getting dark and couldn't live under overcast so pulled up to 6,000 and then 8,000 ft. in it. On instruments from then on though occasionally saw dim lights on ground through almost solid overcast. These lights seemed more often on our right and pulled us still farther off course.

Decided to abandon ship. Sgt. Braemer, Lt. Potter, Sgt. Leonard and Lt. Cole jumped in order. Left ship on A.F.C.E. [auto pilot], shut off both gas cocks and I left. Should have put flaps down. This would have slowed down landing speed, reduced impact and shortened glide.

All hands collected and ship located by late afternoon of 19th.

Requested General Ho Yang Ling, director of the Branch Government of Western Chekiang Province to have a lookout kept along the seacoast from Hangchow Bay to Wen Chow Bay and also have all sampans and junks along the coast keep a lookout for planes that went down at sea, or just reached shore.

Early morning of 20th four planes and crews, in addition to ours, had been located and I wired General Arnold, through the embassy at Chungking:

TOKYO SUCCESSFULLY BOMBED. DUE BAD WEATHER ON CHINA COAST BELIEVE ALL AIRPLANES WRECKED. FIVE CREWS FOUND SAFE IN CHINA SO FAR.

Bad luck:

(1) Early takeoff due to naval contact with surface and aircraft.

(2) Clear over Tokyo.

(3) Foul over China.

Good luck:

(1) A 25 mph tail wind over most of the last 1,200 miles.

Lt. Richard E. Cole, Doolittle's co-pilot, recalled his own experience:[4]

After takeoff and when everything was squared away, the boss and I took turns at flying. When I wasn't flying, Hank Potter, Braemer, Leonard, and I were continually checking the gas or other things about the ship. No one slept or got sick. Everyone prayed but did so in an inward way. I guess we all wondered more than anything—trying to imagine what was in store for us. If anyone was scared it didn't show. I believe I can honestly say that no one was really scared. I don't say this in a bragging way, it's just that at least we had never faced danger and didn't have sense enough to be scared.

One thing I remember clearly is that the tune "Wabash Cannonball" kept running through my mind. One time I was singing and stamping my foot with such gusto that the boss looked at me in a very questioning manner like he thought I was going batty.

We flew low and kept a sharp lookout for surface ships and other aircraft. We veered once or twice to miss some ships and flew directly under a Japanese flying boat, which didn't see us. Aside from this our trip from the *Hornet* to Japan was uneventful.

Since we had a load of incendiaries, our target was the populated areas of the west and northwest parts of Tokyo. Over the target I kept Paul Leonard advised of enemy aircraft and at one time counted more than eighty. We were not bothered by fighters; however, flak shook us up a little and left some holes in the tail. We made landfall on the Chiba Peninsula east and northeast of Tokyo. Japan looked very pretty and picturesque from what I could see. We flew at treetop level until our target area then pulled up to twelve hundred feet, dropped our bombs, and lowered to treetop level again. People on the ground waved to us. It was about

12:15 Tokyo time, the weather was clear but a little hazy, which limited forward vision. We could see the moat, the Imperial Palace, and downtown Tokyo. Hoover flew on our wing practically all the way to the target, then he turned off and headed for his target, which was an electrical plant. I saw his bombs hit and explode, throwing much debris into the air.

Hank Potter did a fine job of navigating. After we left the target area we headed for open sea, taking a southwest course to the southernmost tip of Japan. As we headed out over the China Sea, Hank estimated we would run out of gas 135 miles from the Chinese coast. Because of this we began making preparations for ditching. Without our knowledge the good Lord had fixed us up with a brisk tailwind. We flew at low level and occasionally could see sharks basking in the sun—which made the ditching very unappealing.

We made landfall on the Chinese coast about 8:45 P.M. as it was just getting dark. Shortly after we climbed to eight thousand feet and we all bailed out when the fuel warning light came on. I dove out head first facing the rear of the ship. This caused me to scrape or drag on the sides of the hatch. Fortunately, it didn't affect the operation of the chute. I remember I had my flashlight in my right hand and after bailing out changed it to my left so I could pull the ripcord. The descent seemed like ages. The clouds, rain, and fog were so thick nothing could be seen so I just waited. Suddenly a tree limb brushed my feet and I came to a stop. My chute had drifted over the top of a thirty-foot pine tree. I couldn't have landed easier if I had planned it. Except for a black eye, I was all in one scared piece and I do mean scared.

I climbed to the top of the tree and untangled my chute, then got down for a look around. I had landed on the top of a very steep mountain and from what I could see with my flashlight, it looked treacherous. I decided to make a hammock from my chute and spend the night in the tree. This I did. It was quite comfortable and kept me dry but I didn't sleep except for short dozes.

My only visitor was a cottontail rabbit, which I could see with my flashlight. Daylight came about 5:30 so I gathered up my chute and started walking. Using my compass I walked due west keeping to the ridges and avoiding traveled footpaths. I ran across several wood gatherers, farmers, and

Crew No. 1 (Plane No. 40-2344): *from left to right*, Lt. Henry A. Potter (Navigator); Lt. Col. James H. Doolittle (Pilot); S. Sgt. Fred A. Braemer (Bombardier); Lt. Richard E. Cole (Co-Pilot); S. Sgt. Paul J. Leonard (Engineer–Gunner). (Air Force Photo)

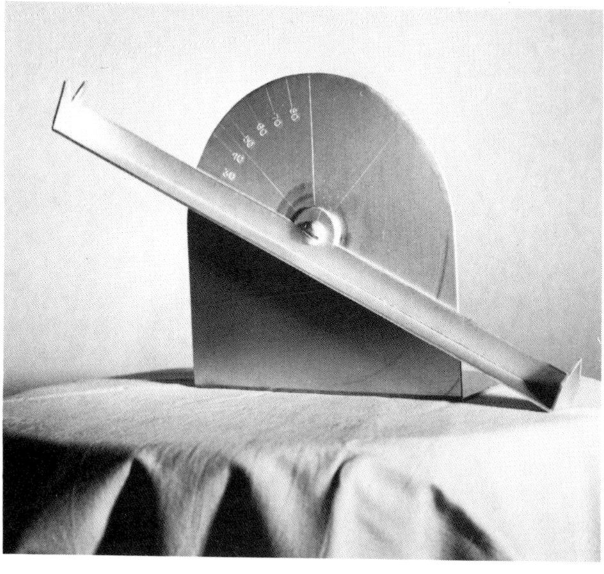

Replica of the Mark Twain bombsight used by all planes on the raid. Designed by Capt. Charles R. Greening, they were constructed in the Eglin Field shops at a cost of twenty cents each. Knowing airspeed and altitude, a bombardier could compute the angle at which the sighting bar should be set. When the target passed the line of sight, bombs were released. At low altitudes, this sight was more effective than the top secret, expensive Norden bombsight. (Sight reproduced by Lt. Col. Horace E. Crouch; photo by Francis N. Satterlee)

Crew No. 2 (Plane No. 40-2292): *from left to right*, Lt. Carl R. Wildner (Navigator); Lt. Travis Hoover (Pilot); Lt. Richard E. Miller (Bombardier); Lt. William N. Fitzhugh (Co-Pilot); Sgt. Douglas V. Radney (Engineer–Gunner). (Air Force Photo)

Two B-25s were damaged during takeoff practice at Eglin Field, Florida. Shown here is the plane piloted by Lt. Warren A. Beth; no one was injured. Lt. Henry L. Miller, USN, who was training the pilots in short-field takeoffs, was aboard. (Photo by Lt. J. Royden Stork)

The *Hornet* steams westward from San Francisco with the B-25s lashed to the deck. The bombers' engines were run up daily; en route crews were briefed on navigation, Japanese and Chinese customs, first aid, target information, and emergency procedures. (Navy Photo)

Crew No. 3 (Plane No. 40-2270): *from left to right*, Lt. Charles J. Ozuk (Navigator); Lt. Robert M. Gray (Pilot); Sgt. Aden E. Jones (Bombardier); Lt. Jacob E. Manch (Co-Pilot); Cpl. Leland D. Faktor (Engineer–Gunner). (Air Force Photo)

Crew No. 4 (Plane No. 40-2282): *from left to right*, Lt. Harry C. McCool (Navigator); Cpl. Bert M. Jordan (Engineer–Gunner); Lt. Everett W. Holstrom (Pilot); Sgt. Robert J. Stephens (Bombardier); Lt. Lucian N. Youngblood (Co-Pilot). (Air Force Photo)

The first B-25 to take off from the carrier *Hornet* was piloted by Lt. Col. James H. "Jimmy" Doolittle. Observing the plane from his position on the carrier's "island" is its skipper, Capt. Marc A. Mitscher. (Navy Photo)

Doolittle's takeoff as seen from the carrier *Enterprise.* Since the *Hornet*'s planes could not take off for patrols while the B-25s were on her deck, the *Enterprise* accompanied the sixteen-ship task force to provide protection. (Navy Photo)

Crew No. 5 (Plane No. 40-2283): *from left to right*, Lt. Eugene F. McGurl (Navigator); Capt. David M. Jones (Pilot); Lt. Denver V. Truelove (Bombardier); Lt. Ross R. Wilder (Co-Pilot); Sgt. Joseph W. Manske (Engineer–Gunner). (Air Force Photo)

Crew No. 6 (Plane No. 40-2298): *from left to right*, Lt. Chase J. Nielsen (Navigator); Lt. Dean E. Hallmark (Pilot); Sgt. Donald E. Fitzmaurice (Engineer–Gunner); Lt. Robert J. Meder (Co-Pilot); Sgt. William J. Dieter (Bombardier). (Air Force Photo)

Although most crew members had cameras with them on the raid, only one returned with photographs taken in the air over Japan. This photo of the naval base at Yokosuka was taken by Lt. Clayton J. Campbell, navigator on Crew No. 13, with the camera belonging to Lt. Richard A. Knobloch.

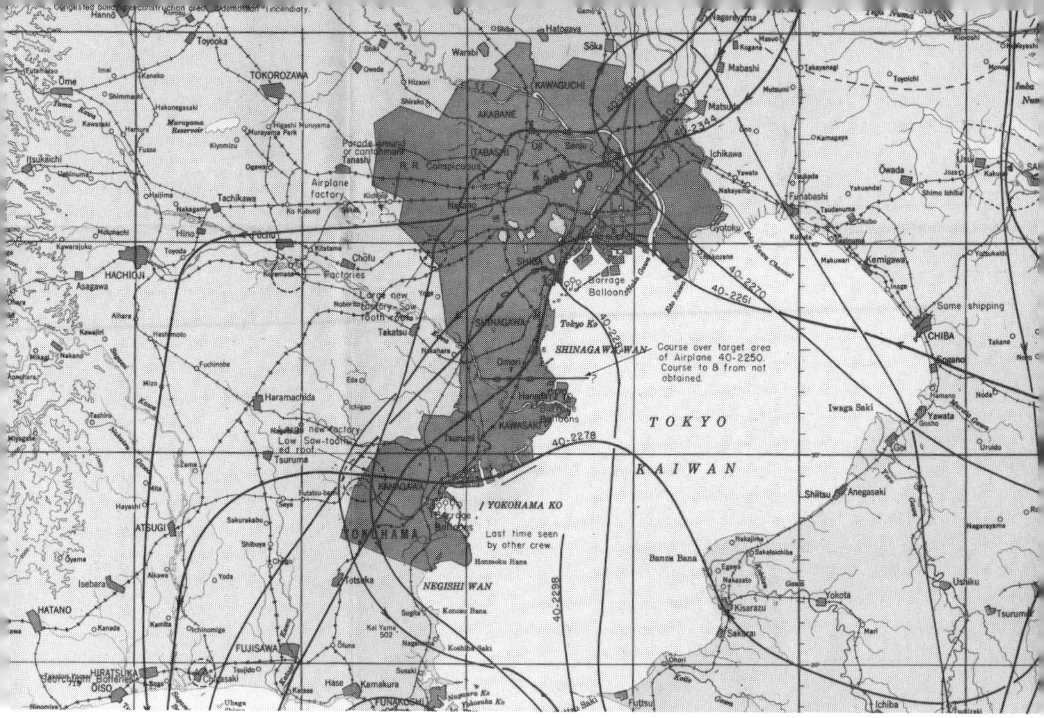

The map above traces the various routes used in the attack on Tokyo and Yokohama. The arrival of planes from so many different directions confused the Japanese so that the takeoff point and the exact number of attacking planes could not be determined. Other planes bombed Osaka, Kobe, and Nagoya. (Air Force Photo)

Crew No. 7 (Plane No. 40-2261): *from left to right*, Lt. Charles L. McClure (Navigator); Lt. Ted W. Lawson (Pilot); Lt. Robert S. Clever (Bombardier); Lt. Dean Davenport (Co-Pilot); Sgt. David J. Thatcher (Engineer–Gunner). Thatcher was awarded the Silver Star for gallantry for protecting and assisting the injured. (Air Force Photo)

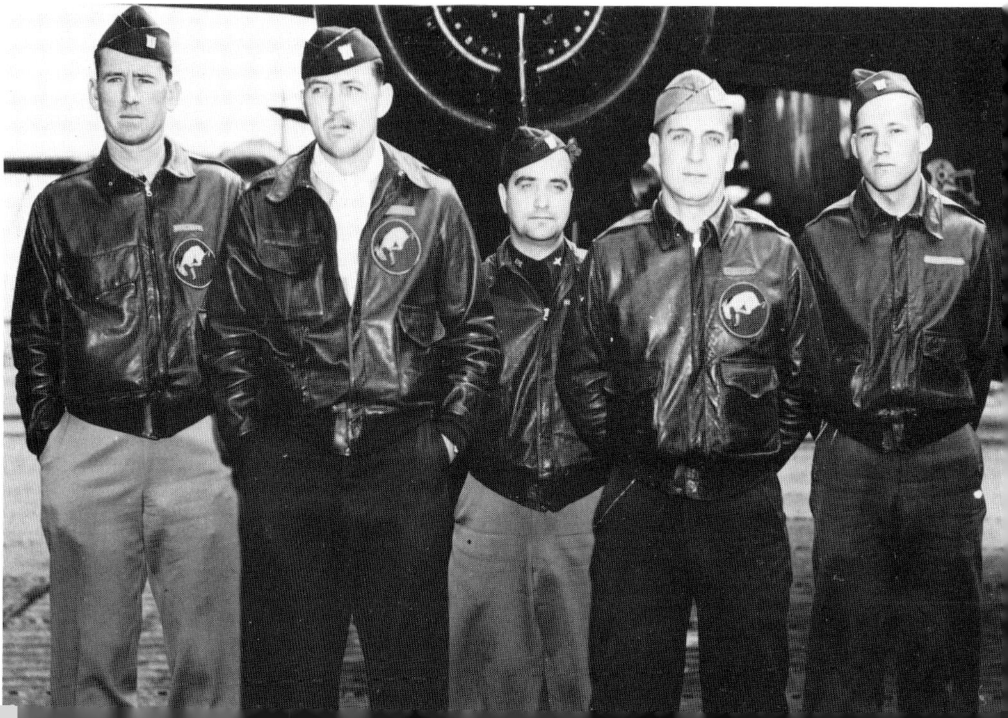

Crew No. 8 (Plane No. 40-2242): *from left to right*, Lt. Nolan A. Herndon (Navigator–Bombardier); Capt. Edward J. York (Pilot); S. Sgt. Theodore H. Laban (Engineer); Lt. Robert G. Emmens (Co-Pilot); Sgt. David W. Pohl (Gunner). (Air Force Photo)

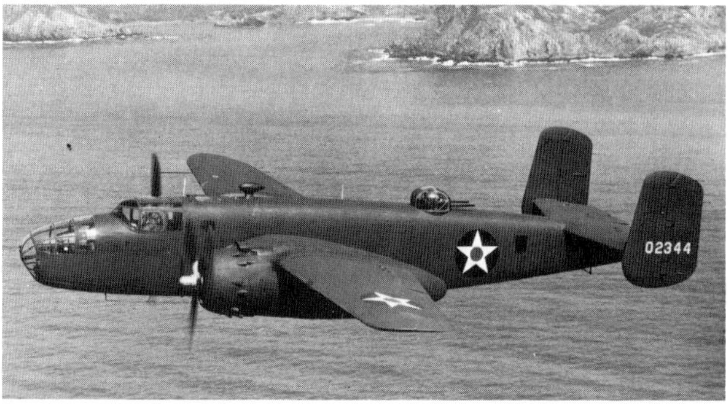

This B-25 is an exact replica of the plane piloted by Lt. Col. Jimmy Doolittle on the mission against Tokyo. The plane has a wingspan of 67′ 7″; length 53′ 5¾″; height 16′ 5″; empty weight 20,300 lb. This plane, presented to the Doolittle raiders in 1958 by North American Aviation, the manufacturer, can be seen at the Air Force Museum, Dayton, Ohio. (North American Photo)

Friendly Chinese were anxious to help Doolittle's raiders after their arrival in China. Receptions and parades were arranged in every village through which they passed en route to Chungking. Shown here is Crew No. 15: *from left to right*, S. Sgt. Edward J. Saylor and Lts. Howard A. Sessler, Donald G. Smith, Griffith P. Williams, and (Dr.) Thomas R. White. Dr. White assisted the injured of Crew No. 7 and amputated the leg of Lt. Ted W. Lawson to save Lawson's life. White received the Silver Star for his gallantry.

even one hunter. They paid no attention to me nor I to them.

Since most of the walking was up and down, I figure I walked only ten or fifteen miles. About sundown I came to a well-traveled path which circled a high peak. I could not avoid this path so I started walking it. Shortly, I ran into an Oriental gentleman who was too nosy to suit me so I pulled my .45 and chased him away. As I walked, he followed me at a good safe distance. At the top of the mountains below my path I could see a small settlement or compound. It looked peaceful enough so I decided to try my hand at meeting the Chinese. As I neared the buildings I could see a Chinese Nationalist flag flying from one. Approaching this a small boy ran out to meet me yelling something in Chinese. A Chinese soldier appeared and beckoned me to come inside. He showed me some drawings of an airplane with five chutes drifting down. After a time he and his fellow soldiers understood that I wanted to be taken to the place where the artist had drawn the pictures and the artist was the old man I had seen previously. He turned out to be a loyal Chinese who later served as our guide and stayed with us until we passed out of occupied territory.

Shortly after this I was taken to the place where the boss was located. He appeared none the worse for his experience except that he had landed in the middle of a rice paddy and was still damp. Later, Potter, Leonard, and Braemer were brought in. They had been picked up by a roving band of renegade guerrillas who robbed them and tied them up. This band was fortunately interrupted by a band of friendly guerrillas who rescued the boys and returned their belongings.

We were holed up in occupied territory at a place called Tien Mu Shen which is between fifty and one hundred miles southwest of Hangchow. This was our base of operations while the boss visited the wreck of our ship. After they decided to move us, we walked, rode small horses, and were even carried in seat chairs to a secret place where we were kept until dark. At about 9:00 P.M. we boarded a Chinese riverboat. The scheme was to move us down the river to a point where another river joined, thence up the second river and out of occupied territory. We got underway about midnight and as we moved down the river we could see the searchlights of Japanese patrol boats. Fortunately, we were not stopped and completed the journey without difficulty.

We arrived at Chosin where we were greeted by all who arrived before us.

As most of the members of other crews were to do, Doolittle bailed out into the rainy darkness not knowing what fate awaited him below. It was his third parachute jump to save his life.[5] He was worried about his ankles, which he had broken in South America during the twenties, so he decided to land with knees bent and fall into a sitting position. He did—up to his neck in a rice paddy fertilized with "night soil." He shucked the parachute and stumbled toward a small farmhouse and banged on the door. No one answered so he headed for a nearby building, which turned out to be the local morgue, occupied by one elderly but very dead Chinese. Chilled to the bone, he stayed there until dawn and then followed a well-worn path toward what he hoped was a village. He came upon a Chinese farmer who spoke no English. Doolittle took out a piece of paper and drew a picture of a train. The farmer nodded and led Doolittle to a local military headquarters where a Chinese major waited with hand outstretched for Doolittle's .45 caliber automatic. Since the major understood a little English, Doolittle explained that he was an American, had parachuted out of his plane during the night, and would not hand over his gun. As he spoke, armed Chinese soldiers surrounded him. "I'll take you to where my parachute is," Doolittle said, plaintively. The major, suspicious that this dirty, smelly foreigner could be what he said he was, agreed to follow, but when Doolittle returned to the rice paddy he had landed in, the parachute was gone.

The major and his soldiers shook their heads. Doolittle decided that the people in the nearby farmhouse would verify his story of banging on the door in the middle of the night and should have heard his plane go over. However, when the farmer, his wife, and two children were routed out to answer the major's questions, they denied knowing anything. "They say they heard no noise during the night," the major said, turning to Doolittle. "They say they heard no plane during the night. They say they saw no parachute. They say you are lying."[6]

Doolittle began to perspire as the major made a move toward him. Doolittle protested vigorously and was saved when two soldiers who had gone inside the house emerged with broad smiles and the parachute. The major, now convinced, extended his hand in friendship and led Doolittle back to his headquarters for a warm meal and a bath. He sent out search parties for the rest of Doolittle's crew and the plane's wreckage.

Doolittle's official report did not mention his personal experience after the bailout and did not reveal the extent of his concern for the crews who were spread over a large area of China. In his mind, his first combat mission was a complete failure. All aircraft were lost to the Allied cause and he was told that at least one crew member had died and others were feared captured by the Japanese. He was relieved that his own crew members were safe and uninjured, although Potter had sprained an ankle in the bailout. After they had joined together, Doolittle made his way to the scene of his crashed B-25 with Sgt. Paul Leonard. When the two arrived at the crash site, Doolittle's morale was the lowest it had been in his life. His once beautiful B-25 was spread over two acres of mountaintop.

The two men picked through the wreckage and Doolittle found his army blouse. It was oil-soaked and someone had already removed all the brass buttons. He sat down dejectedly near the wing of the plane. He described his feelings to the author:

> As I sat there, I was very, very depressed. Paul Leonard took my picture and then, seeing how badly I felt, tried to cheer me up. He said, "What do you think will happen when you go home, Colonel?"
>
> I answered, "Well, I guess they'll send me to Leavenworth."
>
> Paul smiled and said, "No, Sir, I'll tell you what will happen. They're going to make you a general."
>
> I smiled weakly and he tried again. "And they're going to give you the Congressional Medal of Honor."
>
> I smiled again and he made a final effort. "Colonel," he said, "I know they're going to give you another airplane and when they do, I'd like to be your crew chief."
>
> It was then that tears came to my eyes, and I told him that if I ever had another airplane and he wanted to be my crew chief, he surely could.[7]

Doolittle proceeded to Chungking to await his crews and learn what had happened to those captured or missing. There he learned that he had been promoted to brigadier general, thus skipping the rank of colonel. On April 30, all the men present were awarded Distinguished Flying Crosses. Next day, they were invited to lunch with Generalissimo and Madame Chiang Kai Chek.

"I'll bet it was the motliest bunch of men who ever dined with the ruler of any country," Bill Bower, pilot of the twelfth plane off the carrier, wrote in his diary:

> Coveralls, leather jackets, several ties, and everything containing a varied assortment of spots and mud. The Madame is a very wonderful person and made us feel quite at ease. During the meal the Gissimo [sic] came in, spoke to us and offered his apologies. As he speaks no English, a true impression of his greatness is difficult [to assess]. After dinner we gave the Madame General Bissel's wings and a 17th Group insignia.
>
> After supper that evening they called us down to the reception room and every American in Chungking was there. The Madame came in and we were lined up for pictures. Instead, she decorated us with the Chinese Medal of Honor for Meritorious Service.[8]

Since their aircraft had been lost, many of the crew members were ordered back to the States for reassignment to other units. Doolittle and others proceeded to Calcutta to await priority air passage. On May 8, Doolittle threw a small party for those present before he left. Bower's diary states: "At 8:00 everyone gathered in our room [at the Great Eastern Hotel] and it turned out to be a pretty sad sort of a party. We gave Jimmy an enameled pot in fond remembrance of our most serious difficulties, 'the screamers.' I kind of think he hated to leave us as much as we hated losing him. If there were only more leaders of his caliber, war would be much easier. His ability to instill confidence through proper and thorough training was wonderful."[9]

8

Takeoff into History

Lt. Travis Hoover, pilot of the second plane with Lt. William N. Fitzhugh as co-pilot, lined up and began the takeoff run with the B-25's left wheel on the wide white line and nose wheel on the narrow line. "There seemed to be a strong upward sweep of air over the bow, which carried us into a rather sharp zoom," Hoover recalled. "No trouble in making the correction, however."[1]

Fitzhugh noted, "We saw a freighter soon after takeoff and it seemed to be firing at Doolittle's ship, as white puffs of smoke could be seen coming from her deck."

Hoover stayed in sight of Doolittle's aircraft all the way to the Japanese coast. He veered around several small fishing boats en route and zigzagged slightly to follow Doolittle's lead. Several training planes were sighted but no fighters. When Carl Wildner, the navigator, confirmed their position, Hoover veered right looking for his target area.

"There was no good target in the exact area as indicated on the target map," Hoover told interrogators later, "so we selected two factory buildings and storehouses. There was not sufficient time to climb to fifteen hundred feet, so we leveled off at nine hundred feet, and Dick Miller, our bombardier, toggled off the bombs manually in succession at 215 mph. The concussion from the bombs could be felt quite plainly. We turned before Miller could see where they hit. We then dove back down to the rooftops and followed a zigzag course along the west side of Tokyo and Yokohama."[2]

Doug Radney, operating the gun turret in the rear until the electrical motor burned out, reported over the interphone that he could see the target area covered with black smoke. Ahead, Doolittle's plane was visible, so Hoover followed him west toward the Chinese coast as the weather worsened.

"The weather was definitely bad," Hoover recalled. "Visibility was very poor and the clouds came right down to the sea. It was zero-zero in rain showers at the coastline and now getting dark. I turned south and intended to go up into the overcast and head west toward Chuhsien but the left engine cut out as I climbed. I let back down out of the overcast and turned the booster pumps on. Three more times I tried to climb but the engines cut out each time so I started to look for a place to land along the coastline. I planned to land along the beach or on a mountainside but saw a series of small rice paddies and made a wheels-up landing. Just before landing, the gas gauge read ten gallons in each of the front tanks and forty gallons in the two rear tanks."[3]

The landing was a good one, and Radney in the rear reported, "There wasn't much of a jar. After landing I went back and threw out the baggage to the other men."[4]

Hoover decided that the plane should be burned, so Radney went back in the rear compartment, put the incendiary pallet on the turret tank, and tried to set it off, but it wouldn't catch. He returned and set off two landing flares, but they died out. Hoover then set fire to the engines with a gas-soaked tarpaulin. "[The plane] burned quite well and [the fire] spread to various parts of the airplane," Hoover reported.[5]

The five men of Hoover's crew took their equipment and rations and headed westward, not knowing if they were in Japanese-held territory. "We climbed to the top of a mountain and spent the remainder of the night in a trench," Hoover said. "We stayed hidden in an old pillbox all the following day and then hiked westward for the next two days. We met a farmer and, using sign language and our map, learned we were in Chinese territory. We followed a main trail between villages until we were taken in custody by about thirty Chinese guerrilla soldiers. They fed us well and gave us beds."[6]

Dick Miller, the bombardier, reported this encounter differently. "About an hour after leaving the farmer we ran into a group of armed guerrillas who immediately robbed us of everything except our clothes. They took us into a small village. On the trip, another group of guerrillas fired at us from the hills by mistake. At the guerrilla headquarters, we were able to make them understand who we were by sign language, pictures, and some English, which they understood. They returned just about all our personal equipment except our pistols, which they promised to return later."[7]

On April 22, the crew was taken by boat to the village of Ning Hai and then to Sungyao, where they met Tung-Sheng Liu, a Chinese aeronautical engineering student, who had just come through Japanese lines from Shanghai disguised as a merchant. Liu could speak English and acted as interpreter as he guided them by ricksha, bus, train, boat, and on foot to Chuhsien.[8] En route, they met Gen. Yu Chi Ming, commander of the guerrilla forces in that section of China, who told them that one of the crews had crashed near the coast, and that two had been killed and three captured by the Japanese. Joined now by Capt. Davy Jones and Lt. Brick Holstrom who had been left there to intercept gathering crews, the group traveled to Hengyang on May 3 and were taken by DC-3 to Chungking on May 14.

In their official intelligence reports filed in Chungking, all five crew members praised the hospitality of the Chinese people, who were grateful that these Americans had bombed "the land of the dwarfs." Dick Miller reported, "We were very warmly received at each city. They entertained us with banquets and songs and presented us with gifts."[9] The crew gave special recognition to Tung-Sheng Liu for interpreting and helping them to safety. They had to leave him at Hengyang because regulations forbade a foreign national from flying on an Army Air Forces aircraft without permission. In his mission report, Hoover noted: "Liu planned to try to be employed in some way with our forces in this country [China]. I feel no reservation in stating that I feel that he would be of great value if he could be used in some manner."[10]

When the crew said their reluctant good-byes to Liu in Hengyang, none thought they would ever see him again. But not only would Hoover and the survivors of his crew meet him years later, they would find that Liu was a graduate aeronautical engineer, a U.S. citizen, and an air force civilian employee who had a hand in the design of C-5A, the air force's largest cargo aircraft.

After Hoover had left the *Hornet*'s deck, Lt. Bob Gray maneuvered *Whiskey Pete* (named after his pinto back home in Texas) into position and took off. Also aboard were Lt. Charles J. Ozuk, navigator; Sgt. Aden E. Jones, bombardier; Lt. Jacob

E. "Shorty" Manch, co-pilot; and Cpl. Leland D. Faktor, engineer–gunner. All had stuffed extra clothes, shaving equipment, and other belongings hurriedly into their B-4 bags but 6′4″ Manch took extra belongings he considered essential. "I stuffed in four boxes of Robert Burns cigars and two boxes of Baby Ruth candy bars," he recalled. "My phonograph and records would give us some American jazz in China so I decided to take it along. My records were in a cake tin and I asked Bob Clever to put them in his plane."[11]

Their takeoff was uneventful and they headed toward Japan. Although the cockpit was filled with fumes from the bladder tank on top of the bomb bay, Manch broke open a box of cigars and he and Gray smoked all the way to the coast. They tried to home in on a Japanese radio station and thought they would know when Doolittle's bombs hit because the radio stations would probably go off the air. They were concerned that because they were third in the line of B-25s, the fighters and ack-ack defending Tokyo would be alerted and pick them off.

Bombardier Aden Jones unloaded three explosive bombs on industrial targets and the incendiary on a dock area. Antiaircraft fire was light to moderate, Gray reported later. It had the correct altitude but not the correct aircraft speed. Gray had decided to make his run at an exceptionally slow speed to save fuel, a fact that may have saved the aircraft from ack-ack hits.

"Before reaching the target," Manch wrote later, "Bob Gray took a vote among the crew that if we were badly damaged by gunfire, what we wanted to do. All the members of the crew, with the exception of Gray, stated that if we had the chance, we would like to bail out. Bob said that if he had the chance, he would let us out, then he was going to pick out the biggest building in Tokyo and stick *Whiskey Pete* right in the middle of it."[12]

Just after Jones dropped the last bomb, Gray's B-25 was jumped by a half dozen fighters. Jones began firing with the .30 caliber gun in the nose while Faktor fired the top turret in the rear. They outran the fighters easily as Gray dropped down to a few feet off the ground and headed south.

"Several destroyers and cruisers in the harbor were firing at us," Manch said. "It looked like they were attempting to pick up our course heading so they could radio it on ahead. We flew a south heading, hoping they would think we were headed for the Philippines. We turned back after about 15 minutes to our heading to China."[13]

Just as with all the B-25s escaping to China, the headwind they experienced en route to Japan after leaving the carrier changed into a tailwind as they headed out over the China Sea, a rare situation since normally the winds would be on the nose flying from east to west. If they had not gotten this favorable wind for about seven hours, most would have had to ditch in the sea about two hundred miles from the China coast.

The navigator, Charles Ozuk, took a number of shots with the sextant while the sun was visible and felt confident that they would make landfall at the proper spot by dead reckoning as the visibility turned hazy.

When the weather worsened and night fell, Gray climbed to avoid the mountains and plowed ahead on instruments. He ordered everything thrown overboard they could spare to lighten the load. Ozuk gave Gray an estimated course to Chuhsien and when he figured they were over the destination, Gray turned south as the gas needles were on empty. He ordered the crew to bail out. Jones went out the nose hatch; Faktor pulled the hatch release and followed in the rear; then Ozuk, followed by Manch, who flashed his light in the rear to be sure that Faktor had gone.

Manch said:

> I grabbed a box of cigars and candy bars and stuffed them in my jacket. Then I bundled up my private arsenal, a 44-40 Winchester rifle, German Luger, two .45 automatics, and .22 automatic, and an ax and a bowie knife and got ready to go.
>
> As I went out, I watched the two exhaust stacks go over my head, then reached for the D-ring on my chute but couldn't find it. Scrambling frantically, I finally found it dangling at my side and pulled. Since I only had a twenty-four-foot chute which was too small for my weight, the opening shock was something I wasn't ready for. I saw red and the impact jerked my bowie knife, ax, canteen, and all my guns away, except the one in my holster. The box of cigars disappeared out of my jacket and the Baby Ruths were shucked, leaving nothing but the wrappers.

> Coming down, I thought I heard waves breaking on a beach and the horrible thought came to me that I had sent the rest of the crew out without their Mae West life vests on. They would surely drown if we were over the ocean and not over land as we figured. Just as I struggled to release my leg straps to get away from the chute in case I landed in the water, I hit the ground with a thud. What I thought was waves slapping on a beach was wind blowing through the pine trees.[14]

Each of the five crew members exited the plane without difficulty but Corporal Faktor's luck ran out that day. He either struck the plane after he left, his chute didn't open, or he hit the ground excessively hard. As near as can be ascertained, he died instantly. His body was found next morning by Chinese peasants and carried into a nearby village.

Meanwhile, the other four crew members began to strike out to seek help. Ozuk injured his left leg on landing and was barely able to walk, and Manch cut himself with his pocket knife trying to make a water bag out of his parachute's rubber cushion, but Gray and Jones were unhurt.

The tall Manch had his problems, though. As he started to walk, he came upon a Chinese man and woman who took one look at this giant and fled terrified into the woods. He came upon an old woman gathering firewood. "The site of me threw her into a panic," Manch said. "She threw her sticks down and hobbled off on her wrapped feet."[15]

Manch plodded on until, dead tired and hungry, he sat down in a creek with water up to his waist and wondered what to do next:

> About this time, the brush parted and a Chinese with a big smile on his face stuck out his hand to help me out of the creek. Several more Chinese then came out of the brush and tried to push and carry me up to a little trail on the mountainside. They were armed with old seventeenth-century flint lock muskets.
>
> I was so tired that I couldn't walk over one hundred yards without rest. One of the Chinese, about 5′4″ offered to carry me on his back. I laughed at him because I thought I would be too heavy for him. He insisted and when I did, he threw

it into high blower and went up and down those hills for two miles like a billy goat and like I wasn't even on his back. As we approached his village at dark, I became embarrassed because he was carrying me, a supposedly great aviator. I tapped him on the head several times, indicating that I could walk. I said to myself, "I'm going to walk into this damn village if it takes me all night. I won't come in with this little 5′4″ Chinaman carrying me."[16]

Manch spent the night in the village, and next morning his hosts indicated that an airplane had crashed nearby and that they would lead him to it. They passed some Chinese guerrillas carrying parts of Manch's plane, and at the village Manch was shown pieces of baggage, clothes, and navigation equipment. He was led to another village, where he found the body of Faktor, the engineer–gunner. Two soldiers gave him a note saying that Bob Gray and Aden Jones were a day ahead of him and had slept there the night before. He caught up with them and two days later the trio headed for Chuchow, where twenty or more men of different crews had gathered. Several days later, after rides on a boat, train, and bus, the group traveled to Hengyang and eventually to Chungking by C-47. Meanwhile, informed about the death of Faktor and told the location of his body, Doolittle made arrangements to have a proper funeral and burial. He asked Rev. John M. Birch, an American missionary, to hold a funeral service with several of his fellow crewmen there and gave Birch $2,000 (Chinese) to buy a burial plot near the Chuhsien Air Station. Maj. Y. C. Chen, the station commander, refused to accept any money for the burial; Faktor's coffin was donated by a local magistrate.

The fourth plane off the carrier was piloted by red-headed Lt. Everett W. "Brick" Holstrom, one of two of Doolittle's raiders who had already been decorated for a mission against the Japanese. (The other was Lt. Ross R. "Hoss" Wilder, co-pilot on crew no. 5 who had been Holstrom's co-pilot on the sub-hunting mission.) Both had received the Air Medal for attacking a Japanese submarine the previous December 24 off the Oregon coast.

After takeoff, Holstrom circled and came back over the carrier to check his magnetic compass, which he was certain had been pulled off during seventeen days on the carrier. As he flew west about seventy-five feet off the water, Bert Jordan, the gunner in the rear, kept trying to tell Holstrom something over the interphone, which had much static. When the crawlway gas tank was empty, Jordan came forward and told the others that the rear turret was out of commission and that the left wing tank was leaking gas, a common occurrence caused by siphoning. Holstrom solved the leaking gas tank by switching tanks.

Holstrom recalled:

> I told the navigator, Lt. Harry McCool, to make a landfall just south of Tokyo, under the assumption that the three planes ahead of us would make their landfall directly east of Tokyo and bring interceptor planes out in their direction and we could slip by them. We made our landfall south of Tokyo on a small group of islands at approximately 1230, still flying at seventy-five feet.
>
> Lucian Youngblood, my co-pilot, went back to transfer the last bit of gas from the bomb bay tank to the wing tanks. He was still back there when I saw two pursuits coming at us and I immediately turned under them. One fired and I saw tracer bullets going over the pilots' compartment. I yelled to Youngblood to come back to his seat. He pointed out two more fighters going across our bow at about fifteen hundred feet and they looked as if they were ready to peel off on us. I told the navigator [McCool] to tell Cpl. Bob Stephens in the nose to try and use his nose guns. I had given him previous instructions to have the bombardier salvo the bombs if we were intercepted, so the bombs were salvoed [into Tokyo Bay] from about seventy-five feet.[17]

Two more fighters flashed by the B-25 and crew members reported others above. Flying at a maximum speed of about 270 mph, Holstrom easily outran them. When no more were sighted after about ten minutes, Holstrom throttled back and headed south, then west toward China.[18]

Like the preceding three crews, Holstrom ran into steadily deteriorating weather. After climbing through the darkening overcast and unable to receive any radio homing signals, he ordered his crew to bail out at about 10:30 P.M. Each made the jump successfully, except that Harry McCool cracked his shoulder when he landed on a steep slope.

One by one, Holstrom's crew was rounded up by Chinese guerrillas. Bert Jordan described what happened to him:

> I came to a village and found a fire and dried myself off. Just outside of town I was jumped by a bunch of Chinese from both sides of my path. They took my .45 from me and marched me to a larger village. That night a guy with a Chinese-English dictionary came in and started questioning me. He got my name, rank, serial number, and nationality. They thought I was a German [but] I finally convinced them I was an American.
>
> The next day they marched me to another town and that night they brought Lieutenant McCool in. When they searched him and found his .45 they got really shook up and I thought we had had it. They threw me up against the wall and put a gun in my belly; they also roughed up Lieutenant McCool a little. Things finally cooled down and we slept on boards that night.
>
> Next day some big wheels came and apparently figured out what we had done and really treated us nice from that time on. As we were leaving next day, a bunch of firecrackers went off under my feet and I thought it was the end. I went about two feet in the air. They told me that was the way they treated their VIPs.[19]

Holstrom's crew, after much walking and by various means of transportation, made their way to Chungking. Although glad they had survived, they were unhappy that they had not bombed their target. Harry McCool was interrogated by Capt. John McGee, an intelligence officer in Washington, on August 23, 1942, who reported, "Lieutenant McCool appeared very much depressed about the whole affair. The fact that the electrical system failed to operate their guns, necessitating the discharge of their bombs, made the venture appear very futile."[20]

Years later, when the author asked Brick Holstrom if he had any regrets, he replied, "Had I had the experience that I gained in fighting the Japanese and being involved in several real scraps in the months following the Tokyo raid, I would not have jettisoned the bombs or at least my decision to do so would have been delayed. Although we were in serious trouble, I had obviously overestimated the capabilities of the Japanese and could have at least retained the bombs to use, if not on my primary target, on a target of opportunity."[21]

The engineer–gunners on each B-25 had fussed over their planes during all their waking hours aboard the *Hornet.* Sgt. Joseph W. Manske, mechanic on the fifth plane and one of the youngest men on the raid (he passed his twenty-first birthday on the carrier), had two pretakeoff experiences that "shook me up." Like other mechanics, he slept on deck when it wasn't raining to escape the heat below and be near his "baby." In the dark one night a sailor came running across the deck and accidentally kicked him in the face, breaking his glasses. The world looked fuzzy to him throughout the rest of the mission. He was not able to get them replaced until he returned to the States much later. One night during a raging storm with high seas, he went out on the slippery deck to check the tie-down ropes on his aircraft. As he did so, the storm increased suddenly and he was afraid to release his hold to go back inside the ship. "Fortunately, after about twenty minutes, I was able to get the attention of the navy men on watch during their rounds and they helped me back inside," he recalled. "Needless to say, I was much more careful in future trips to the deck."[22]

Capt. David M. Jones, pilot of the fifth plane, and his co-pilot, Lt. Ross R. "Hoss" Wilder, were concerned about the rubber bomb bay tank on their plane. The day before takeoff when the crews started fueling the planes, the bomb bay tank leaked badly. Manske took the tank out, patched it, and left it out all night to dry. Early on the eighteenth, the bombs were loaded, but when the signal to man the planes was given, the crawlway tank above the bomb bay had to be refueled and the wing tanks topped off.

During the confusion, Manske fueled the crawlway tank and then fueled the right wing tanks while a sailor fueled the left. When Jones checked the gas gauges, the left wing tank was thirty gallons short, so Jones ordered Manske to the left wing to finish the job. A fuel hose was passed up to him but, because the *Hornet* was in "battle condition," the gas was not turned on. "By this time the airplanes were taking off," Jones said, "and a dozen people were shouting instructions so I told Manske to get back in the airplane and started the engines."[23]

Jones had no trouble on the takeoff and proceeded on course after circling to compare his magnetic compass with the *Hornet*'s heading. Flying just under the clouds at fifteen hundred feet about an hour after takeoff, a Japanese twin-engine aircraft came out of the clouds and passed the B-25 on the right. Jones maintained course while the enemy plane turned to avoid a collision, the red ball markings plainly visible. It disappeared in the clouds behind the B-25 and was not seen again.

Visibility improved as Jones's plane neared the coastline but the navigator, Lt. Eugene F. McGurl, was unable to ascertain their exact position. After a few minutes, Jones believed they were too far north and turned south along the coast.

"After about 15 minutes we had not found Tokyo and I decided to drop our bombs on the first suitable target and get on our way," Jones said. "Just then we came to a bay and our navigator discovered it was the mouth of Tokyo Bay. I then turned north and approached Tokyo from the south."[24]

En route to the coast, Manske had worried about gas consumption. Like the other raiders, he had been so caught up in the excitement of the mission that "I gave little thought to just how dangerous a flight this would be," he said. "After we were into the flight for about thirty minutes we knew we wouldn't have enough gas to reach our destination. This was the first time that I fully realized what I'd gotten into. Being brought up in a good Christian home, I got down on my knees and prayed."[25]

On the flight deck, Jones was mentally figuring how far they might be able to go before having to ditch. "Since my gas was low and I had wasted time finding the area and there was a multitude of targets visible as I crossed the bay," he told the author,

> I decided to bomb along the bay in southwest Tokyo instead of turning east and flying around the city to get to my assigned target area, which was north of the business district.
>
> I informed my bombardier, Lt. Denver Truelove, of this and as I approached the docks, pulled up sharply to twelve hundred feet so the bomb fuses would function properly and the incendiary could spread to a good pattern. The first

> bomb made a direct hit on an oil storage tank. As [Truelove] let the second bomb go, I turned left because the area there looked more profitable. I looked down and could see a building, which I believe was a power plant, erupt in a great explosion. The next bomb was the incendiary and just ahead I saw a large building with saw-toothed roof construction which covered two or more blocks. It was easy to hit and every one of the bombs in the cluster hit on the roof of this plant.
>
> By this time my speed had increased considerably due to the urge given us by intense AA fire. The fourth bomb, which was aimed at another large building, hit a little over and probably damaged only one corner. At the instant of release I again descended to minimum altitude and took my course to the south for withdrawal.

As the preceding pilots had done, Jones flew south paralleling the Japanese coast, then turned westward. Lt. Gene McGurl, the navigator, made this report later to intelligence officers:

> Direct westerly course taken on 29th parallel. No landfall possible due to overcast. Computed ETA at coast and checked same on arrival. Checked ground speed and figured ETA at Chuchow (Chuhsien). Overcast and zero visibility made visual location impossible. Computation alone gave the position and the ruggedness of surrounding country made knowledge of exact position of paramount importance.[26]

Unable to see ahead in the lowering visibility and growing darkness, Jones climbed to fifty-five hundred feet. "By this time it was completely dark and raining hard," Jones explained. "It was becoming more and more evident that the chances of a safe landing were very slim. I informed the crew of our situation and decided to remain on course and jump out as close to Chuhsien as possible. I continued past our ETA there in hopes of finding a break. This proved futile so I turned 180 degrees and flew back until I found a small hole in the clouds. We put out a landing flare, which showed us that an attempted landing would be impossible. We then prepared to abandon ship."[27]

Truelove and Manske bailed out almost simultaneously, from the front and rear, followed by McGurl and the co-pilot, Hoss Wilder, who described what he did next:

> I put on my gun belt and grabbed a pint of whiskey, which I stuffed in my shirt and jumped. I landed on the side of a mountain in soft dirt. I was about halfway up a slope which was at least sixty degrees. I got out of my harness and climbed to the top of the mountain. I took a drink of whiskey to relieve the chill of the damp wind and went to sleep.[28]

When daylight came, Wilder heard a train and went down the mountain toward the sound. It was the village of Changsan where Jones had already arrived at the train station. Jones picked up the narrative:

> The stationmaster could write a little English and we conveyed our desire to go to Chuhsien. He called Yushan on the phone and a train consisting of two boxcars and three flatcars came out and picked us up. When we reached Yushan a large crowd had assembled. We were given a royal reception. How they knew about us and our mission I do not know, but certainly all the people knew about the "great deed of the brave American heroes." We were taken to the air station at Yushan where they washed our feet, cleaned our clothes, fed us, and put us to bed.[29]

Jones and Wilder arrived at Chuhsien next day and found Truelove, McGurl, and Manske there. Truelove had injured his left leg slightly but had been able to walk. McGurl had struck his head on landing and bled profusely for some time; he had also injured his side and suspected that he had broken a rib. Manske was uninjured.

Now all together, Jones and his crew remained at Chuhsien overnight. Next morning, six Japanese planes dropped bombs on Yushan and the crew remained in an air raid shelter. They were joined by three other crews and the group was moved to a large air raid shelter in the side of a sandstone mountain. Enemy planes flew over every day for a week. On April 25, the group traveled by train and truck to Hengyang. Truelove commented: "Reached Hengyang at midnight of our third day in a truck and too sore to walk." The group was flown by C-47 to Chungking on April 29.[30]

Lt. Dean E. Hallmark was a husky man by any standards. Nicknamed "Jungle Jim," he was six feet tall, weighed two hundred pounds, had a ruddy complexion, a loud laugh, and an aggressive personality. His crew consisted of Lt. Robert J. Meder, co-pilot; Lt. Chase J. Nielsen, navigator; Sgt. Donald E. Fitzmaurice, engineer–gunner; and Cpl. William J. Dieter, bombardier. Their mission: bomb steel mills in the northeastern section of Tokyo.

The sixth plane, named the *Green Hornet*, got off without difficulty and flew toward Japan at two hundred feet with two other planes in view all the way. They passed a Japanese patrol plane about a half-hour after takeoff and saw six fighters at about ten thousand feet when they neared the coast. Over Tokyo, Hallmark climbed to fifteen hundred feet in loose formation with the other two planes with intense antiaircraft fire all around them. Dieter triggered off three bombs amid the antiaircraft fire. Hallmark turned to get out of the flak area and made a second run on the target area to drop the last bomb. They received no hits from flak and were not intercepted. Fitzmaurice, the rear gunner, saw no reason to fire his guns at any time as Hallmark streaked for the coast. (This fact became an issue later as will become evident.)

Hallmark flew south over the same exit route taken by the other planes and approached China about sixty miles north of Wenchu at dusk. It was raining, clouds were low, and forward visibility was extremely limited, so he elected to continue under the clouds at about one hundred feet. With all gas gauges hovering on empty, Chase Nielsen estimated that the coast was still ten minutes ahead of them.

"We'll keep on your heading, Chase, until the engines quit," Hallmark said over the interphone. "Then I'll ditch it straight ahead. Count off the minutes for us so we'll know how far we'll have to row after we hit. Everybody strap yourselves in and wait until the plane comes to a complete stop before getting out. Make sure you've got your Mae Wests on."[31]

The crew acknowledged. When he estimated there was four minutes to go, the left engine and then the right coughed from fuel starvation. Hallmark held the plane straight ahead as it smashed into the waves and partially submerged. Nielsen, located at the navigator's station behind the pilots, had called Fitzmaurice in the rear compartment to make sure he was braced for the water landing. Bill Dieter elected to stay in his position in the nose. Nielsen described what happened next:

> It was a fast and very hard landing. As the aircraft hit the water, I heard Dieter scream. I saw the water pour up over the nose and then all went black momentarily. I had hit the side of my head against the back of the co-pilot's seat and was knocked out for a few seconds. When I came to, I was standing in water up to my waist and was bleeding from gashes on my head and arms. My nose hurt and I knew it was broken.
>
> The two pilots were gone and so was Dieter from the nose section. Not only was Dean Hallmark gone but so was his seat, which had catapulted right through the windshield.
>
> The water began to pour in so I climbed up through the hole, inflated my Mae West and joined Bob Meder, the co-pilot, on top of the slowly submerging plane. Dean came up right behind me. He had bad cuts on both knees but they didn't seem to bother him. Dieter was in the water and climbed up on the right engine nacelle, while Fitz came out the rear side window.
>
> Dean and Bob took the life raft from its compartment on top of the fuselage while I helped Fitz get up on top of the right wing. I noticed that the left wing and engine had been torn off and the severity of the situation suddenly came home to me. Waves twelve to fifteen feet high towered and slapped us viciously; it was dark now and our plane was sinking rapidly. All of us were bleeding and I could see that Dieter and Fitzmaurice were in very bad shape. Dieter was incoherent and evidently had been badly crushed on impact when the brittle Plexiglas nose slammed into the water. Fitzmaurice had a deep hole in his forehead where he must have struck something in the rear compartment.
>
> To add to our troubles, just as Bob pulled the lanyard on the CO_2 cylinder to inflate the raft, the cord broke off flush with the cartridge. The only way the raft could be inflated now was with the hand pump.
>
> While Dean, Bob, and I scrambled to locate the hand pump in the raft kit, Dieter slipped off the wing. Dean grabbed for him but missed. At the same moment, a huge wave washed the rest of us off the plane, which was now completely under water. Meder, seeing Fitz's condition, grabbed him as he was washed away. Each of us yelled to try

to locate each other in the dark but in a few minutes the voices of the others were out of range and I was alone.

I couldn't do a thing but ride with the waves. From the tide table studies I had made on the *Hornet*, I figured the tide had just started in so it was in our favor. I half swam and half floated for what seemed like hours. Thousands of thoughts flashed through my mind. I thought about my family, the fellows back at Columbia, S.C., who didn't go on the raid, the wonderful navy men who had brought us to the launch point and were probably now being chased by the whole Japanese navy. I wondered where the crews of the other fifteen planes were and whether Jimmy Doolittle's first combat mission might have been his last. I feared the worst might happen to Dieter and Fitzmaurice because they seemed to be badly hurt. Then I began to worry about whether my navigation had been accurate. Were we only a few miles off the coast of China or a couple hundred? I prayed that I was right but was overcome by doubt.

Just as I convinced myself that we must have gone down in the middle of the China Sea, I ran into some fishing nets suspended from floating bamboo poles but I was too weak to climb over them. But finding them was good for my morale because I knew if I couldn't make it to shore that sooner or later someone would come out to check the nets. I cut one of the large glass floats off as insurance in case my Mae West deflated.

Then a sickening thought struck me. Suppose they were Jap nets and not Chinese. After all, the Japs had occupied the coastal areas of China. Now I felt I had to get to shore before daylight and hide so I could get my bearings and then try to make contact with friendly Chinese.[32]

Nielsen swam with the waves and ran into more nets. His cuts and broken nose were burning fiercely from the salt water and his strength was dwindling fast. After about three hours in the water, he heard the sound of breakers smashing against the rocky shore. Soon, his feet touched bottom and he fought his way to the beach against an undertow that threatened to pull him under. Using his last ounce of strength, he managed to swim the last few feet and crawl up on the beach. Finally free of the sea, he rested a few minutes and then tried to tend to his wounds.

The fear of being discovered by the Japanese caused Nielsen to seek shelter. He left the beach for an area covered with trees and looked for signs of the other crew members but saw nothing. He flopped into some brush beside a cobblestone path leading into a village where he could observe but not be seen. At dawn, six soldiers armed with rifles, swords, and pistols passed by his hiding place and he assumed they were Japanese. Later, he saw a number of soldiers in different uniforms with Chinese insignia he recalled from pictures he had seen previously. Confused now, he didn't know whether to expose himself to the latter group, look for his crew, take off alone for the interior, or remain hidden.

While trying to figure his next move, Nielsen saw a group of villagers and two soldiers walk toward the beach and stand around what looked like two men lying on the sand. Thinking they might be two members of his crew, he decided to try to work his way around to a point on a dune where he could see the entire beach. "As I started to look," he recalled, "a voice in pidgin English said, "Stand up or me shoot!"

> I had no weapon and was sure I was a goner. I stood up to see what my chances were against whoever it was. As I did I saw the smiling face and hard set slant eyes of an Oriental. The insignia on his cap was the same as one of the groups I had seen I thought were Chinese. He had what looked like an ancient buffalo gun pointed at my stomach. The bore of the gun looked like a sixteen-inch cannon.
>
> I stood petrified for what seemed like hours and finally finding my voice asked, "You Japanese?" He replied with a heavy Oriental accent, "Me China. You American? You Japanee?"
>
> All the while that big gun aimed at my stomach never moved. I answered, "Me American."
>
> I could see the bodies on the beach now that I was standing up and knew right away it was Dieter and Fitzmaurice. The soldier saw me looking and said in his fractured English, "They dead. Bury them in hour. You go with me."[33]

Nielsen followed his captor to a garrison and met the commander of a guerrilla band, a young, well-built Chinese officer in a neat, clean-tailored uniform. He questioned Nielsen cordially through Chen, the soldier–interpreter who had captured him. The friendly interrogation was interrupted by an orderly who said another crew member had been located and would be hidden until the Japanese patrol that Nielsen had seen was safely out of sight. In the meantime, word had gone out through the mysterious Chinese grapevine system to look for the other crew members and protect them.

After a meal of boiled eggs and rice, seaweed soup, and semicooked fish "that smelled like it had been dead for a month," Nielsen was led out of the compound to the nearby village. They were met by an elderly Chinese wearing a small black skull cap, long black robe, and wooden clogs.

He spoke briefly to Chen and motioned for them to follow him into one of the shanties along the cobblestone street. Nielsen had an ominous feeling as he ducked inside a narrow doorway. He sensed someone was behind the door and threw up his arm to protect himself. As he jumped aside, there was Hallmark, ready to swing with a big club.

The two quickly compared notes. Hallmark was badly cut and bruised and barely able to walk. They returned to the compound with the interpreter and Meder joined them. He related how he had found the bodies of Dieter and Fitzmaurice, dragged them above the high-tide line, and gone into hiding. After a Japanese patrol left the area, the three survivors of the *Green Hornet* returned to the beach where the Chinese had hidden the bodies. The trio gently placed the bodies of their crewmates in two wooden boxes, selected a site high up on the beach, and buried them. The three officers prayed silently over the graves of the two faithful enlisted men who had made the supreme sacrifice.

Captain Ling, the guerrilla garrison commander, accompanied by Chen, the interpreter, took the three Americans aboard a sampan crowded with Chinese soldiers and civilians next morning. They were intercepted by a Japanese patrol boat, but a boarding party did not discover the three crew members hiding beneath some grass mats below the deck. They traveled for two days and reached the walled city of Wenchow where Ling went ashore. He returned with the news that many Japanese land and sea patrols were searching for the Americans who had bombed "the land of the dwarfs" as the Chinese referred to Japan. They would stay that night in Wenchow, however.

Ling left the Americans and Chen in the care of a Chinese named Wong who spoke perfect Oxford English learned while attending a college in England. He had once been a Buddhist monk but now described himself as "a poor fisherman." Wong told the three how the Japanese had sexually assaulted young Chinese girls until they died, beheaded men and boys with their heavy swords, and terrorized the villagers ceaselessly whenever their patrols passed through. Nielsen described what happened next:

> We didn't have long to talk because a young Chinese came running in and told Wong that the Japanese were at the gate to the city and starting to search on their side of the city. Wong said we had to move quickly. He rushed us out and down an alley, saying he would try to get us to a boat if possible. He shoved us in another building and ran to see where the Japs were. He returned and said they were coming toward us. We moved on to the northeast gate, and peering around the corner of a building, I could see that escape route was cut off as there were a dozen soldiers there with machine guns set up on tripods.
>
> I looked all around but couldn't see any place that would possibly conceal three Americans. The buildings were scantily furnished and one that Wong had suddenly pushed us into was barer than others we had seen. We made a fast decision. Dean dove into a corner where Bob and I covered him with sacks, grass mats, and a couple of old blankets and shoved an old bench in front of the pile. We both then climbed into the rafters as it was the only cover we could see. Mr. Wong sat down on the floor and busied himself by attempting to light a charcoal fire in a metal container.
>
> It seemed like an eternity and my body ached from trying to roost on that small rafter. At last, what I dreaded happened. The Japanese soldiers came down the alley. One stepped inside, looked at Mr. Wong who wore a real poker face. He looked in the corner where Dean was but then turned and left.
>
> I sighed with relief and prayed they would all leave the area. I could hear several soldiers stomping around outside and was surprised to see Captain Ling, who had protected us

so well, enter with a Japanese officer, followed by two heavily armed Japanese soldiers. Ling addressed Wong and slapped him hard across the face. One of the soldiers approached the corner where Dean was and kicked the pile of sacks. I could have jumped him but it would have cost me my life as the other soldier would have cut me in two with his automatic weapon. With two more kicks, Dean was uncovered. The Jap officer, speaking very good English, said, "You, stand up and walk out only two steps. If you don't, I'll have you shot immediately!" Dean obeyed reluctantly. As he did, the officer grunted several commands and guns appeared in the windows and soldiers filled the doorway.

The officer asked Dean, "Where are the other two men?"

Dean looked him straight in the eye and asked, "What other two men?"

The officer pulled out his pistol, and started yelling and beating on Wong. Wong fell to the floor right below me. I don't know if Wong told him where we were but a soldier in the doorway yelled and pointed a machine gun up at Bob. We were ordered to climb down and reluctantly complied.

I was so sick I couldn't even think. I could hardly hear him when he said, "You are now prisoner of Japanese. You have nothing to fear if you do as you're told. You will go with us now to our military camp."

The soldiers began to tie us up. Our hands were pulled behind our backs and secured with handcuffs. A rope about six feet long was attached to the handcuffs and the other end tied to the belt of a soldier.

While we were being tied up, the Japanese officer and Ling had quite an argument with much shouting and waving of pistols. After about three minutes, the Japanese officer cocked his pistol and pointed it at Ling's chest. Ling took a long look at us, holstered his pistol, and left without saying another word.

The Japanese officer said, "We now go to my superior officer. Do not try to escape or you will be shot and killed." As we left the building I heard someone yell, "Long live America and China. I hope they will kill all Japanese." I'm not sure but I think it was Mr. Wong.[34]

The three surviving members of the *Green Hornet* were now in Japanese hands. They did not know what anguish lay ahead for them and five members of the last plane to leave the carrier.

* * *

"We couldn't convince ourselves that we were halfway around the world from home on our own with a one-way fare and that we were doing a dangerous thing." So answered Lt. Ted W. Lawson, pilot of the seventh plane off the carrier, when asked what he was thinking about while aboard the *Hornet*. "I felt the mission was well-planned but certain that our losses would be necessarily high."[35] Although he guessed that they were going to bomb cities in Japan, he was surprised when told that their targets were in the major cities, including the capital, and that it was not to be a token raid on the smaller cities.

Lawson's crew consisted of Lt. Dean Davenport, co-pilot; Lt. Charles L. McClure, navigator; Lt. Robert S. Clever, bombardier; and Sgt. David J. Thatcher, engineer–gunner. Their takeoff in the *Ruptured Duck* was made without difficulty, although in the rush to follow the plane ahead, Lawson forgot to put any flaps down and the B-25 dipped below the deck level, which made onlookers gasp. He recovered, leveled off, and headed west a few feet above the water. Lawson recalled that both he and Davenport had terrible pounding headaches en route, which they attributed to "extreme apprehension and no food." Davenport recalled that they discussed the "unreality of being where we were and doing what we were about to do."[36]

Lawson made landfall northeast of Tokyo and turned south. As they approached their target area, which contained a number of factories near the Tokyo Bay waterfront, Jones's B-25 was ahead of them. When Clever toggled off their four bombs, they encountered antiaircraft fire that had the correct altitude. Dave Thatcher reported one burst just off the tip of their right wing and Lawson promptly made a steep dive to the left. Thatcher noted in a later report that "we left Tokyo going 300 mph."[37]

Lawson followed the southerly escape course along the Japanese coast and turned westward. About one hundred miles off the Chinese coast, the ceiling began to lower and rain began. In the growing darkness and poor visibility, Lawson and Davenport decided to ditch near the beach of a small island. Lawson told the crew to remove their parachutes and prepare for the water landing. As they lined up for the approach, Lawson called "gear down." Davenport pushed the gear handle down and the B-25 smashed into the water with a hard jolt that split the nose open and sent Lawson, Davenport, Clever, and McClure headlong into the sea still strapped to their seats. In the rear, Thatcher was knocked out. When he came to, water was gushing in through the top of the gun turret, which he thought was the rear escape hatch. He described what happened next:

> Still dazed, I pulled the strings to inflate my Mae West and tried to go through the opening but I couldn't make it. I finally figured that the plane was upside down so I found the rear hatch and got out there. I crawled up along thc belly of the plane toward the nose and found that it was badly smashed.
>
> Just at that time Lieutenant McClure called to me from the beach about a hundred yards away. The others were there, too. I swam to them and learned what happened. Lieutenant Lawson had changed his mind and tried to make a wheels-down landing on the beach but because of the rain hitting on the windshield and it being nearly dark, he had misjudged the distance and we hit just off the beach in about six feet of water doing about 140 mph.
>
> I was lucky. The other four crew members were all thrown out when we hit. The pilot, co-pilot, and navigator were thrown up against the top of the cockpit and not straight forward. Lieutenant Clever in the nose was thrown through the Plexiglas headfirst. The injuries he received were cuts around both eyes and the top of his head was so badly skinned that half his hair was gone. His hips and back were sprained so that he was unable to stand up and walk; all he could do was crawl on his hands and knees. His eyes were swollen shut so he couldn't see. His face was covered with blood but I thought it would be better to leave it that way because of what Doc White had told us about infections. I knew infection would set in soon enough if we couldn't reach help; besides I had my hands full with the other members of the crew.
>
> Lieutenant Lawson was, by far, the most seriously injured. His worst injury was a long deep gash just above his left knee. He had another deep cut on his left shin that left the bone exposed. His foot below the ankle was so badly bruised that it turned black within a few hours. He had other cuts on his left arm, head, and chin, and most of his teeth had been knocked out. He was in such intense pain and so

weak from loss of blood that I was afraid he would die if we didn't reach a hospital.

Lieutenant Davenport, the co-pilot, received severe cuts on his right leg between knee and ankle. He walked a little after the crash but not afterward. Lieutenant McClure, the navigator, only received a few scratches on his right foot but they got infected later. The serious injury was in his shoulders, which were swollen so badly clear down to his elbows that he could hardly move his hands. He was unable to lie down and had to try to sleep sitting up.

My injuries were minor. I had a slight gash on the top of my head. If I hadn't had my flying helmet on it would have been much worse. My back was badly bruised and I had a few small cuts, which later became infected, but I was in the best shape to take care of the others.[38]

In the hours following, Thatcher bandaged his crewmates' wounds as best he could. A group of Chinese fisherman came from a nearby village and helped the group to a hut. Next morning, Thatcher went back to the beach and tried to locate the first aid kit in the tail section of the mangled B-25 but couldn't find it. He spotted a Japanese patrol boat in the bay and rushed back to the village, where he met a Chinese guerrilla who spoke a little English. Thatcher pleaded with him to help get the four men to a hospital. That afternoon, they left with the four wrapped in blankets and carried on stretchers by peasants. By late afternoon they were headed for the mainland on a small river boat. Thatcher continued his narrative:

There was a covering over the middle of the boat, which kept us dry while it was raining. I was kept busy going from one to the other trying to make them as comfortable as possible. But they'd soon get tired lying in one position so I would help them move to another.

About midnight we stopped at one of the guerrilla hideouts to get something to eat. I went up to the house and got a bowl of something that looked like noodle soup. I was pretty darn hungry but whatever was in that bowl, I just couldn't swallow it. They gave me some for the rest of the fellows in the boat but it only added to their misery.

We didn't have any drinking water left by this time and I sure didn't want to drink any of the dirty water from the streams or the Chinese wells so I set my canteen up to catch rain water. Lawson was wanting water all the time because his throat was so dry from the blood in his mouth where his teeth had been knocked out. I didn't think that night would ever end. I had understood the guerrilla to say that it would only take two hours to get to the hospital but it took almost twenty-four.[39]

When they finally got to shore, the group was taken to Yai Hu, where two Chinese doctors and a nurse gave them their first medical aid. Thatcher sent a telegram to Col. Doolittle at Chungking telling of their condition. Next day, after helping as much as the Chinese could with the few medical supplies they had, "they gave us a royal send-off with a band and everything," Thatcher said. "We then traveled forty miles by sedan chair to Linhai, where there was a hospital. A Chinese doctor and his son, with the aid of missionaries from the China Inland Mission took care of the injured."[40]

The difficulties for this crew were not over. The injured were in desperate need of expert medical assistance. Lawson, the most seriously injured of the *Ruptured Duck*'s crew, would be near death. His life would be saved by Doc White, the physician who had insisted he be allowed to go on the mission as a gunner on the fifteenth plane off the carrier.

The left engine on B-25, serial number 2242, had given its crew chief, S. Sgt. Theodore H. Laban, trouble from the time he was assigned to it at Eglin Field. Although both carburetors had been changed at Sacramento and checked again on board the carrier, Laban was still apprehensive that the engines were not operating efficiently. It was imperative that they be operated with the leanest possible fuel mixtures in order to get maximum range out of the aircraft. His concern was well founded. Excessive fuel consumption was to lead this crew, the eighth in line for takeoff, on a strange saga of frustration and anger.

Capt. Edward J. "Ski" York, pilot; Lt. Robert G. Emmens, co-pilot; Lt. Nolan A. Herndon, navigator–bombardier; Sgt. David W. Pohl, gunner; and Laban, made up the crew. The takeoff was easy and the time en route to Japan seemed to pass quickly. York and Emmens watched the fuel consumption and figured time and distance to landfall. "I was fairly well convinced that none of us would come out of this thing alive," York recalled, the only West Point graduate on the mission. "I was surprised that with such a conviction my excitement and nervousness was replaced by a deep and unusual, for me, calm. My only real thought was that I had not been as good a husband as I could have been and I blamed myself for being such a bastard at times."[41]

As the plane bored westward, the low overcast burned away into blue sky. Herndon had York correct the heading to the right to compensate for wind drift. An hour before landfall, York turned the controls over to Emmens and began figuring furiously on a knee pad. He asked Emmens to look at his figures to see if the engines were burning fuel as excessively as his figures showed.

"His figures showed we were burning more gas than we should have been at those power and rpm settings," Emmens recalled. "York's figures were right. Maybe the gas gauge was inaccurate and would give the same reading after more time. Maybe we had developed a gas leak, letting pure gasoline spill into the ocean. We should have flown out our reserve tank and part of our bomb bay tank by the time we hit Japan. But we were more than an hour from Japan and had been on our bomb bay tank then for quite some time."[42]

It was very obvious to the four men in front that they were not going to get near the Chinese coast after bombing their targets. The only alternative, besides landing in Japan, which was unthinkable, was to set course across the Sea of Japan for Soviet territory. Herndon began drawing course lines to various points within the range that it looked like they could make on their dwindling gas supply.

Doolittle had warned the crews before the mission that it wouldn't be a good idea to go to the Soviet Union, even though the Soviets were American allies. Although requests had been made to Stalin by the American government to allow the B-25s to refuel at Soviet bases after the raid, Stalin had refused and wanted to remain neutral as far as Japan was concerned. He had enough on his hands fighting the Germans on his western front without having another powerful enemy to fight in the east.

The B-25 arrived over the Japanese coast and the crew looked for landmarks. "After flying for about thirty minutes after our landfall was made," York reported later, "we still hadn't spotted Tokyo itself so I started looking for any suitable target—something that was worthwhile bombing. About thirty-five or forty minutes after landfall we came across a factory with a main building about four stories high. There was a power plant with about three or four tall stacks and railroad yards and we decided to bomb it. I pulled up to fifteen hundred feet. We dropped our bombs there and Laban and Herndon said one had hit in the middle of the large building. They saw smoke and steam rising."[43]

York dived down to minimum altitude and turned northwest on a course of three hundred degrees, which Herndon said would get them to Vladivostok. Mount Fujiyama loomed skyward to their left and York began climbing slowly as the ground rose beneath them. They crossed the ridge of the mountain range, and ahead of them stretched some fifty miles of flatlands and the blue-green of the Sea of Japan.

The landfall was made about 5:00 P.M. York turned ninety degrees to the right to be sure it was Russian and not Korean coastline. Herndon identified some features along the coast on his map, which York and Emmens verified. They turned inland and suddenly saw an air base with a large number of orange-winged planes flying and on the ground. York lowered the nose and hugged the ground at high speed "just in case some Russian happened to notice a two-engine bomber roaring over an air base on that vulnerable east coast and decided to shoot it down first and ask questions later," he said.[44]

But time and gas were running out. They had to land soon. They spotted a large field and the two pilots made their decision. Emmens relates what happened next:

"We were about eight hundred feet above the ground. On my side I could see a couple of small buildings with a few men dressed in long black coats standing watching us. Just as I spotted a small plane under a camouflage net, Ski hit my arm and said, 'It's an airport!' "[45]

It was indeed. York landed the B-25 and taxied slowly toward the group of long-coated men. If they had slanted eyes, York and Emmens agreed they would take off immediately. The men did not have slanted eyes and were smiling. York put on the parking brake and cut the engines.

"For the moment no one spoke," Emmens said. "I saw about twelve men, all dressed the same, in long black coats with tight black leather belts, blue tabs on their collars, and wearing perfectly round, flat black caps with ribbons in the back and blue lettering on the bands. They were gathering around just off the right wing looking at our ship with curiosity—and they were grinning. We were in Russia!"[46]

The mission was not over for crew no. 8. They hoped that the Russians would allow them to gas up and take off for their destination in China. "When we went to bed that night we were fully confident we were going to leave the next morning," Emmens said.

> But the next morning a general showed up along with a division commissar—the equivalent ranking civilian town official. Evidently they had communications from higher headquarters and, after we finished eating, we were placed aboard a Russian DC-3 and flown to Khabarovsk, which is about four hundred miles north of Vladivostok. When we arrived there we were interviewed for a short time by the commander of the Far Eastern Red Army, who decided that we were to be interned.
>
> About three days later our personal belongings were sent to us. They had all been left at the station at Vladivostok. Anything that resembled airplane equipment had been removed. We were placed in a house about five miles out of town and very closely guarded. Five days later it was announced over the radio that we had landed in the country and had been interned. About five days after that we were taken aboard a train and sent to Penza in European Russia.[47]

The trip to Penza took twenty-one days. Here the men were shut up in a house with a surrounding fence beyond which they were forbidden to go. Three Soviet "companions" were assigned to them full time. The future looked grim since it appeared the five Americans were not to enjoy the relative freedom enjoyed by Americans interned in other countries like Switzerland and Sweden during World War II. They were prisoners except that they were not in a prison. Their plight was exacerbated by an overeager newspaperman in Moscow who had asked during a news conference five days after York and his men had landed what the Russians would do if any of Doolittle's raiders had landed in their country. He insisted so much on an answer that the Russians thought he must have had some information on York's crew being there. It was at this time that their presence was officially announced for fear of Japanese retaliation. To remain legally neutral, the Soviet Union was obliged to retain the five Americans for the duration. York, Emmens, Herndon, Laban, and Pohl faced a debilitating, boring, uncertain future.

Lt. Thomas C. Griffin, navigator on the ninth plane to take off, was eating an orange in the *Hornet*'s wardroom when the order came to man his aircraft. After hurriedly packing his equipment along with the other crew members—Lt. Harold F. "Doc" Watson, pilot; Lt. James M. Parker, co-pilot; Sgt. Wayne M. Bissell, bombardier; and T. Sgt. Eldred V. Scott, engineer–gunner—Griffin recalls lying prone on the deck, "hanging on for dear life," to keep from being blown overboard as the planes ahead took off.

At breakfast, before the call to man planes, Scott had asked Watson if it would be all right to change spark plugs on the left engine because they were fouled. "I figured we had plenty of time, so I told him okay," Watson recalled. "When the alarm sounded, I found all the cowling off the left engine and all the plugs out! The last piece of cowling was snapped in place as the ship ahead started its engines."[48]

Doc Watson did a good job lifting the plane off the deck, Griffin said, but the plans to fly formation to the target area were abandoned as they headed for Japan. No other B-25 was sighted after takeoff. They did see a few Japanese aircraft but were not attacked. Scott, in the rear, noticed that the bottom gas tank where the lower turret had been removed had sprung a leak and told Watson over the interphone that they were losing gas. Watson transferred gas out of that tank as soon as it could be burned out of the main tanks.

"Most of my thoughts on the way in," Watson recalled, "were concerned with what we were going to do after we left our target. I got the crew together and presented my plan, to which all agreed. After leaving Tokyo we would proceed on our planned course as long as our gas held. We would then strafe a small boat, ditch beside it, take it over and try to make our way to China. All agreed also, that if we were seriously hit over Tokyo we would crash into the Imperial Palace rather then attempt a bailout or crash landing in the Tokyo area."[49]

Griffin took a few sun lines as the weather improved en route. The weather was so beautiful as they neared the enemy coast, Griffin said, "I thought it was much too beautiful a day to be flying on a mission of destruction such as ours."[50]

Griffin gave Watson a course that would take them north of Tokyo as other pilots had done so that there would be no doubt that they should turn left after crossing the coast. Several small aircraft were sighted but did not attack. "As we came in over the city, we began to draw flak," he said. "We were quite surprised when it dawned on us that the black puffs of smoke we were seeing was flak, and that they were shooting at us!"

The target for this aircraft was the Tokyo Gas & Electric Co. on the shore of Tokyo Bay in the southern part of the city. The four bombs were dropped in quick succession and Bissell in the nose and Scott in the rear reported direct hits as Watson turned and dropped the nose to make the escape. An enemy Zero made a pass and Scott fired his turret guns. The fighter veered off and did not resume the attack.

To conserve fuel, Watson throttled back and the B-25 mushed along with the nose up and tail seeming to drag close to the water in an uncomfortable and unnatural flying position. "It was in this attitude and with fuel conservation on his mind that Doc flew us quite close to one of three Japanese cruisers which were heading towards Tokyo," Griffin said. "It was only after the Japs had shells hitting the water all around us that Doc finally and reluctantly pushed the throttles forward and got out of there. I think if we hadn't prodded him, he would have gambled on riding it through. He had fuel consumption on his mind!"[51]

Just as other aircraft ahead of them, Watson ran into deteriorating weather and climbed to get above it in the growing darkness. He leveled off at ten thousand feet on instruments. "All hope of reaching our airfield destination was now lost because of the storm, the rough terrain, and lack of radio contact," Griffin said.

Quite early in the evening our plans were formulated. We would head in a southwesterly direction, away from the Japanese-held area and fly as far inland towards Chungking as our fuel would permit. (As a result of this plan and because of Doc's outstanding zeal for fuel consumption, we flew farther inland than any of the other planes by a considerable distance.)

Early in the evening after we had crossed the Chinese coast when we were discussing our course of action, the other four crew members recognized that navigation was impossible. With no visibility downward or upward, we had to trust entirely on our watches and our compass to guess at our approximate position. As navigator, I felt like excess baggage.

It was true that if we somehow could know our exact position it would be of little value to us. We were in a storm over strange mountainous terrain at night with no radio aid whatsoever. If we knew our position and could somehow miraculously let down through the stuff into the clear, the possibilities of finding our Chuchow airport destination and making a landing would compound the miracle.

However, hope springs eternal. It was at this moment that a rift appeared in the clouds overhead and a lone star shone through! Four sets of eyes were turned on me. "Griffin! A star! Get a fix!" Their eyes told me that somehow this was to be our salvation—if I could produce.

I did not point out the dubious value of a fix. Nor did I attempt to point out that in celestial navigation at least two heavenly bodies must be used to obtain a fix and that they must be charted navigational bodies known to the navigator and that they must be separated so as to produce two lines, the nearer to perpendicular to each other the better. With those four sets of eyes on me it did not seem the moment to start a class in elementary navigation.

I stepped back and picked up my octant, wondering just what I was going to do. I started sighting our strange dim star. I could feel those eyes on me tensely. After several moments of sighting, the storm once more entirely engulfed the plane. The star appeared no more. I was off the hook and once more excess baggage.

> After fifteen and a half hours in the air our motors gave the sputtering sound we had long been waiting for. The bottom hatch was opened and one by one we eased down through the black hole into nothing.
>
> Jumping at night and in a storm is an experience one will never forget. There were times during that descent from ten thousand feet when I thought I had missed the earth. The wind currents at the time must have been violent because I remember just being able to see my chute. It would be level with me and sort of fold up. Then it would swing up over my head, fill up, and come down on the other side, once again spilling its air. However, it hung up on the tops of some bamboo trees and I was lowered to earth with the greatest of ease.[52]

Parker, the co-pilot, was fourth to bail out. "I sure hated to leave," he said, "but I finally pushed away, counted to ten, then couldn't find the rip cord. When I did find it, I pulled it so fast that I knocked myself out and put a big knot on the side of my head. When I came to I found that I had landed in a tree that had broken my fall. I decided to sleep in it and used the chute to tie myself in so I could sleep until daylight."[53]

Next morning, Griffin met Parker and tried to get directions from a farmer but the language barrier was too great. They followed a path they felt would lead to a village and met Scott; the trio stopped at a farmhouse where the farmer let them take off their wet clothes to dry. "Our guns were on the table and we were around the fire when suddenly a Chinese officer appeared in the doorway holding a scroll in one hand and a pistol in the other!" Parker said. "Turning around we saw that our pistols had disappeared from the table and that other Chinese were covering us with rifles from every window and door."[54]

Griffin, Parker, and Scott were held as prisoners overnight; next morning two Catholic missionaries identified them as Americans and they were given an unexpected welcome as heroes by the entire populace of the nearby town. Two days later, Doc Watson was brought in with a broken shoulder, which caused him great pain. He had caught his right arm in the chute shroud lines as it snapped open. Bissell came in two days later after being held captive by Chinese bandits. "He escaped by the simple expedient of running away," Griffin said.[55]

Watson and his crew stayed in the mountain village about a week. All but Watson visited their crashed aircraft where Griffin retrieved his suitcase intact. Chinese peasants were carrying off pieces of the B-25 for whatever use they could make of them.

The group, with Watson being carried by porters, traveled for two days and eventually was picked up at Hengyang for transportation to Chungking. Watson was quickly evacuated to the States for hospitalization; the rest of the crew followed. For them the adventure was not yet over. En route to India, Parker recalled: "While flying [in a C-47] at about sixteen thousand feet on instruments, we suddenly broke out in the open and there was a very high mountain in our way. The pilot made a very sharp turn which upset card players and sleepers alike. Just at dusk, the pilot admitted he was lost so we landed in a field and tried to find out the way to Calcutta from some natives. Finally, the crew got directions with a lot of gestures and we proceeded to our destination."[56]

The primary target for the tenth plane, piloted by Lt. Richard O. Joyce, was the Japan Special Steel Co. located in southern Tokyo; the secondary target was a nearby factory that was manufacturing precision instruments. Joyce's crew consisted of Lt. J. Royden Stork, co-pilot and mission photo officer; Lt. Horace E. "Sally" Crouch, navigator–bombardier; Sgt. George E. Larkin, gunner; and S. Sgt. Edwin W. Horton, engineer–gunner. They were delayed slightly before the takeoff because the right engine misfired, but Joyce was able to clear the difficulty and took off about five minutes after the aircraft ahead. En route to Japan, the crew sighted the same patrol plane others had seen but did not believe they were discovered.

Joyce elected to fly at altitudes of one to four thousand feet in order to stay in a thin overcast and possibly avoid detection. When he reached Tokyo Bay he dived out of the clouds, located the target area, and ordered bombs away. He reported to intelligence officers later, "I encountered heavy ack-ack fire over my target and since I took a long straight run on the target, by the time my bombs were out, I found myself in an AA bracket with puffs and bursts coming very close but generally behind me and catching up fast."[57] Sally Crouch, the navigator–bombardier, later reported that they had successfully bombed their alternate target, causing major damage to the precision instrument factory and the surrounding area.

"At that time a formation of nine Zero fighters came in above me and a little to my right in front," Joyce continued. "I increased power and went into a steep diving turn to the left to escape AA fire and pursuit. The fighters peeled off in attack and followed me but I dove underneath them."[58]

Joyce hugged the ground on the escape route with a speed reaching more than 300 mph at one time. Three Nakajima fighters attempted to intercept the B-25 but were too slow. The Zeroes were able to follow but did no damage. "They did not seem too eager to come in too close," Joyce reported, "as my rear gunner [Horton] was firing at them from time to time."[59]

Joyce followed the route taken by others across the China Sea and encountered the bad weather as it was getting dark. When his estimated time of arrival over Chuchow was up and there was only about ten minutes of gas left, he ordered his crew to bail out at about the eight-minute mark to assure that they would all drop into friendly territory. Crouch showed everyone their approximate position on the map and Joyce gave them instructions.

"Horton, you go first out the rear hatch," he said. "Then Larkin, then Sally [Crouch] and Stork out the front. Larkin, you wait until Horton is gone before you release the forward escape door—you might hit him." He asked Horton to let him know when he was ready.

"Okay, Lieutenant," Horton replied over the interphone. "Here I go and thanks for a swell ride."

"I couldn't help but laugh at that," Joyce told the author. "Here we had been flying for about fourteen hours, had been in combat, and now had to bail out, and he thanked me for the ride! Horton's spirit of discipline was typical of my whole crew and I was thankful."[60]

The bailouts of Joyce and his crew were successful with only a few bruises in evidence. Stork's report was typical of what happened to all of them:

> I landed on the side of a mountain and slid backwards down the slope of the hill. My chute caught on brush and

trees and I was on my back with my head pointing down the mountain. I cut my chute down, rolled it up, and tried to sleep in spite of the rain and cold wind.

At dawn I worked my way down the mountain and followed a small stream that led to a narrow path. I followed the path around many small rice fields and finally came to a small village. I was unsuccessful in making any of the natives understand me as I passed through some four different settlements. Finally, after about nine hours of hiking, I made the magistrate of one village understand that I wanted to go to Chuchow. He arranged things beautifully and I was on my way in less than an hour in a chair carriage.

One of the government men along the way had a card signed by Lieutenant Crouch and Sergeant Horton, which said they were in Suiyuan so I proceeded in hopes of overtaking them. I arrived there about 1:00 A.M. and they were asleep in the magistrate's house. Lieutenant Bowers's crew came in, followed by Sergeant Larkin, and we left two days later for Chuchow.[61]

Dick Joyce, the pilot, after his bailout, was able to locate the crashed B-25 and found a large number of Chinese picking through the wreckage. "I hailed them and made them understand that I was an American," he said. "They were friendly towards me. The plane had hit the side of the mountain and sprayed over a large area and burned. I was able to salvage nothing from it. It was a total loss. The Chinese farmers led me to a small village that day and the next day I met some Chinese soldiers who held me for a day, then led me over the mountains for two days until I reached Tunki Anhwei."[62]

Joyce got a ride on a truck and then went by train to Chuchow where he was joined by the rest of his crew. "My crew was safe and had no serious injuries," Joyce said. "We had a lot to be thankful for. Other crews were not so lucky."

The next plane off the *Hornet* was *Hari Karier*, piloted by Capt. Charles R. Greening; with Lt. Kenneth E. Reddy, copilot; Lt. Frank A. Kappeler, navigator; S. Sgt. William L. Birch, bombardier; and Sgt. Melvin J. Gardner, engineer–gunner.

Although Greening was in on the planning from the beginning, this crew was not originally assigned to him. Halfway through training at Eglin, the first pilot assigned lacked confidence and had the crew badly shaken up. Greening named himself as the replacement.

"From our first flight together, we knew that we were lucky to have him as our pilot," Kappeler said. "He was daring but knew his airplane and his own limitations, and was well coordinated and exceptionally strong. We had one of the best and we were fortunate in getting him."

Kappeler, as a navigator, worried about the proficiency of the pilots he flew with. "I'll have to admit that riding as a navigator and having to trust your life to the skill of another is not without its stomach-tightening moments."[63]

Sgt. Birch was below decks packing his B-4 bag when the alarm sounded; and he admitted that he was "scared and excited." He recalled that:

> the takeoff was surprisingly easy and, believe me, from my bombardier's station in the nose, I could see everything that was going on. Since the *Hornet* could swing directly into the wind, there was no drift as we started our roll. My biggest worry was that the pilot, Captain Greening, might catch the "island" with the right wing tip as he went by.
>
> Our targets were the docks, oil refineries, and warehouses between Tokyo and Yokohama. When we arrived over the coastline, it reminded me of southern California. People on the ground waved at us. We reached Tokyo northeast of the city when we were first attacked by enemy fighters. Four of them jumped us and we ran into flak. Sergeant Gardner put two of them out of action firing from the top turret. I released my bomb load of two incendiaries and two high explosives on a large oil refinery and tank farm from about twelve hundred feet. There was an immediate explosion and fire broke out.
>
> With the bombs gone, we headed out to sea at about fifty feet. We sighted several small fishing craft about five miles off shore so I machine-gunned them with the .30 caliber in the nose. The first one burst into flames and the crew jumped overboard.[64]

Greening pressed on south and then across the China Sea escape route. When the gas gauges were reaching empty at about 11:30 P.M. ship time, he ordered the crew to bail out. All of them stashed cigarettes and candy bars inside their jackets, grabbed hunting knives, canteens, and .45 caliber automatic pistols, and bailed out into the darkness from the front hatch. All left the aircraft successfully, but Sergeant Gardner sprained both ankles when he hit on the side of a mountain and had difficulty walking. Ken Reddy hit the ground head first and may have suffered a slight concussion. He still had a piece of rock lodged in his scalp when he arrived at Chuhsien.

When the group got together and talked about their respective experiences, they laughed about the name they had given the B-25 and how it had lived up to it by committing *hari-kari* on its first and only combat mission. Greening summed it up for the crew when he said, "I think they'll call the mission a success anyhow. But there's one thing we'll have to admit."[65]

"What's that?" the rest asked in unison.

"It was a mission that will have to go down in the official report listed under the heading "Not as Briefed."

Everyone nodded in agreement.

Lt. William R. Pound, Jr., navigator of the twelfth plane, was sound asleep when the klaxon sounded and, like many others, thought it was only a drill because they weren't scheduled to take off until much later in the day. He missed breakfast as he jammed maps and personal effects into his navigator's briefcase. Also like many others, he packed cigarettes and candy bars with his clothes in the B-4 bag and ran to his plane, not fully convinced that they were really going to leave. Lt. William M. Bower, the pilot, was already in the cockpit waiting for his crew to get aboard: Lt. Thadd H. Blanton, co-pilot; S. Sgt. Omer A. Duquette, engineer–gunner; and T. Sgt. Waldo J. Bither, bombardier.

"Bill is the most unruffled, unhurried man I know," Pound told the author. "It seemed like he was as unconcerned about this raid as he could possibly be. My impression was that it was just another cross-country trip to him. Only difference was that the takeoff strip was a little shorter than usual. Believe me, flying with a man like that is good for the nerves of a navigator and I wasn't a bit scared as we taxied onto the takeoff line."[66]

Bower lifted the B-25 off smoothly and settled on course at five hundred feet. Ahead was Greening's B-25, which was followed until Pound felt it was drifting too far north. Bower steered slightly left and made landfall northeast of Tokyo. The official interrogation report about this crew noted:

> Being unable to orient themselves quickly, an irregular course was flown in a southerly direction, paralleling the east coast of Japan, 5 to 20 miles inland to a point east of Yokusuka. On this course a large fire was observed at a point due east of Tokyo City, which appeared to be a burning tank farm believed to have been started by Capt. Greening. Several pursuit ships tailed this airplane for several miles but did not approach closer than 1,000 yards. The course was altered at this point just south of Yokusuka and the airplane was then flown west to a point just south of the Kisarazu Naval Air Station. The course crossed Tokyo Bay on a northerly curve and the target area was approached from the northeast . . .
>
> Because of barrage balloons over the targets originally selected (Yokohama Dock Yards), it was decided during the approach to attack other targets. The Ogura Refinery was selected and hit with one demolition bomb. The other two demolition bombs were dropped on factories and warehouses west of the Ogura refinery. The incendiary bomb was dropped on a warehouse . . .
>
> After the bombs were released, a power station was observed to the southwest and it was machine-gunned with the .30 caliber nose guns; sparks were seen to fly from the building and transformers.[67]

Bill Pound recalled: "We saw a few aircraft after leaving the target area but none of them came after us. We continued south and then west as most other planes had done, and as we passed away from Japan some naval craft turned broadside to us and started firing. Bill Bower took one look and calmly circled away from them out of the line of fire."[68]

Bower and his crew were delighted when Pound found that they were getting a tailwind across the China Sea. "We all felt a lot better then because we would never have made it with any kind of headwind," Pound said.

Darkness began about two hours before reaching the coast, along with heavy fog. Bower climbed and, when it was obvious that they had to bail out, leveled off at about 11,500 feet. He called the crew to the navigator's compartment. Waldo Bither recalled:

> I collected the things I thought most necessary. I weighed 117 pounds and figured I could take a good load with me. All this collecting was in the dark because my light in the nose would be detrimental for seeing any break in the clouds. The last thing I got was the parachute, a chest type, and in the darkness I either grabbed it by the ripcord or snagged the ripcord on the way through the tunnel. Whatever happened, it was open when I got in the navigator's compartment.
>
> I asked Bill Pound if he knew how to pack a parachute. He shook his head. I asked him to help me hold it and I would repack it. I did and it was a pretty neat job.[69]

Bower discussed the bailout procedure with everyone and indicated the order in which each man would go. Bither was first, followed by Duquette, Pound, and Blanton with Bower last. Bither continued:

> I went through the hatch and wanted to get on my back so that the shroud lines would not hit me in the face. It worked but on the opening shock I got stripped of most of my extras, including the canteen of water. I kept the flashlight lit all the way down and hollered trying to contact Duke. The clouds seemed to be getting darker below and I thought that just can't be the ground yet but it was because I saw stars in all directions as I contacted it.
>
> There was no wind so the chute dropped down on top of me. I stayed still listening for a call from someone but there wasn't a sound except the slow rainfall. I pulled the chute around me, made a pillow of the Mae West, and lay there thinking about the happenings of the day and imagining what would happen tomorrow. I smoked a cigarette and when I finished it, I flipped the butt away and it went sailing down and down and I suddenly realized I was on the edge of a cliff. I slept soundly and when I awakened at daylight, I could see I was on top of a mountain.
>
> I was cold now and didn't have a shirt. I had woolen pants and coveralls with an A-2 leather jacket, so I tore some strips from the chute and made a shirt by wrapping it around my body. I drank some rainwater that was flowing over some

rocks and started down the mountain. About five hundred yards down there was a faint trail that led into a small village. I saw a man watching me as I approached. I walked right up to him and grinned and bowed. He grinned and bowed lower and invited me to his house where by signs and motions I conveyed to him that I had parachuted from an aircraft. The villagers offered me food but I declined. I gave the kids most of my chocolate bars in small pieces so there would be enough to go around. I showed them some of the things I had such as my pocket compass but what interested them most was the leather jacket. One man came running up, pointing excitedly to my jacket and held up two fingers.

This meant two of my crew, so I started in the direction the man pointed and soon found footprints in the wet ground. I followed these prints until I was exhausted and sat down to rest. As I was resting, there came Bill Pound and Thadd Blanton. Bill had a map of China with names in English and Chinese and the people showed us where we were—about fifteen miles northwest of Chuchow. However, we walked a good thirty miles that day and just at dark we came to a village and there was Bill Bower. We spent the night and the Chinese people told us that one man with a broken leg was being brought to us. It was Duquette. Thirty-six hours after bailout, our crew was all together again.[70]

Duquette had broken his foot and the other crewmen were sore and stiff from their bailouts and hiking, so the Chinese made sedan chairs out of parachute harnesses and carried them the next day to where they joined Dick Joyce's crew. They eventually made it to Chuchow, where they stayed in a cave for six days during daylight hours because of Japanese air attacks.

Asked about his thoughts when he discovered his parachute had sprung open and he had to repack it before the bailout, Bither replied, "Well, I *was* concerned but if it didn't open, there's one thing about it. I didn't have anybody to blame but myself."[71]

The crew of the thirteenth B-25 in line for takeoff didn't realize they would have the dubious distinction of this numerical symbol of bad luck, but it wouldn't have made any difference. One crew had to be thirteenth and none on board this plane would have admitted to being superstitious. The crew was Lt. Edgar E. McElroy, pilot; Lt. Richard A. Knobloch, co-pilot; Lt. Clayton J. Campbell, navigator; Sgt. Robert C. Bourgeois, bombardier; and Sgt. Adam R. Williams, engineer–gunner.

McElroy had no difficulty getting off, although Williams said, "Like all the rest, I was very scared and prayed that we would make it."[72] Following Greening and Bower, McElroy flew about 250 feet above the water. As they neared the Japanese coast, Campbell estimated they were about one hundred miles too far north of Tokyo. McElroy immediately racked the B-25 into a left turn and paralleled the coast southward as Campbell suggested. Dick Knobloch noted, "The navigators in the other two planes must not have come to the same conclusion, although all three of us had the same target. Greening's ship turned right, while Bower continued straight ahead."[73]

Just as the target area was identified along Tokyo Bay, they were met with a heavy antiaircraft barrage; McElroy dived behind a hill. When the ships in dry dock were seen, McElroy climbed rapidly to fifteen hundred feet. He called for bomb bay doors open, and Bourgeois toggled off the first two bombs quickly, then the final two. Looking back, Knobloch saw a large ship-loading crane "fly into the sky and then break into a thousand pieces. A floating dry dock in which a merchant ship was being converted into an aircraft carrier suddenly toppled onto its side like a toy boat in a bath tub. Nearby workshops exploded."[74]

Williams, in the rear, reported that the first bomb hit an aircraft carrier in dry dock but he couldn't see where the last three hit. Bourgeois couldn't see the results of his work but "as we headed out to the ocean I could see smoke coming from the target area," he recalled.[75]

Campbell reported, "I was taking pictures with Dick Knobloch's candid camera and got one of the target on our approach to it and another just as the bombs were exploding, taken through the navigator's side window and as straight down as possible. I took two more photos later, one of them of a typical Japanese fishing boat about two hundred miles down the coast. These were the only combat photos to survive the raid."[76]

McElroy followed the escape route of the others, ran into the same foul weather, and prepared to bail out just before the engines quit. Campbell estimated that they were about twenty minutes past Chuchow. "About 10:00 P.M., all four gas gauges registered empty," Knobloch said.

> We went on for another ten minutes. Mac turned on the automatic pilot and called us amidships, over the escape hatch.
>
> "We're at 6,300 feet," Mac said. "If we jump quickly we may be able to land together."
>
> "Or drown together," I thought.
>
> Williams was to go first. We all said goodbye. I wish I had a picture of us. We had five long, long faces.
>
> Williams eased through the hatch. His head vanished. Then popped up again. "Well, goodbye," he said. Again his head vanished. Then up again. He grinned. "Well, goodbye," he said.
>
> "Goodbye for the last time," I said. I pretended I was going to step on his head. This time he went for good.
>
> Mac and I helped Bourgeois through the hatch, then Campbell. I squeezed into the hole. As I shoved downward I could see Mac's feet coming after me. I let go and fell out into the fog and rain.

McElroy and Knobloch, unhurt on the bailout, were able to get together quickly and seek help from the Chinese they encountered. They began walking near a river. Knobloch described what happened when they came to a small village:

> We had no idea where the Japs were so Mac stayed a short distance from the cluster of huts while I approached. Thirty or forty men, women, and children ganged around me, feeling my clothes and face. "Chiang Kai Shek," I said. It was the only thing I could think of. They all smiled and bowed. At least they were Chinese, I thought.
>
> Our instructions were to be calm, so I pulled out a cigarette lighter. As soon as I snapped it, the Chinese vanished. I waited and one by one they came out of their huts. One man, bolder than the rest, came up. I gave him the lighter. It was our key to China. The man took me to his house with the village following. He took out a map from a teakwood chest and studied it carefully. The room was packed with people.

"Do you speak English or American?" a voice said.

"Who said that?" I asked, startled. Everyone smiled and bowed. I went back to the map, thinking I was mistaken.

Again came the voice, "Do you speak English or American?"

I looked around quickly. More smiles and bows. I thought I was going out of my mind.

Then I saw one little old man open his mouth and say, "Do you speak English or American?"

I pushed through to him. "I'm American," I said. "Say, am I glad you speak English!"

He smiled and bowed. "Do you speak English or American?" he said again. Right then I realized that was all the English he knew.

The man with the map wasn't much help, either. I tried to ask him to locate his village on the map. Every time I pointed to a spot, he would nod, bow, and smile. It was my introduction to the land of the perpetual yes. I don't believe I ever heard a Chinese say no all the time I was in China.

I gave up hope of getting any information from my host when I saw that he was looking at the map upside down. I joined Mac and we headed down river. As we walked along, a young boy ran up and grabbed my arm. He shook his head violently and pointed downstream. He imitated guns with his hands, just as we did when we were kids playing cops and robbers. "Bang! Bang!" he said. He put his hands over his heart, made an awful face, and fell over backwards.

"Must mean Japs are that way," Mac said. Later we learned Jap soldiers were only two miles downstream. That boy probably saved our lives.

We followed when the boy started off across a field away from the river. After a mile or so we came upon a hut. A man in a ragged coat armed with a rifle jumped out and stood squarely in our path. On his lapel was a button which identified him as a soldier of China.

He pointed his rifle at us and snapped the bolt into place. The boy shouted at him. He let us advance. I didn't want to take any chances so when I got close enough I grabbed the rifle. It almost came apart in my hands. The barrel was tied to the stock with a piece of string. I pulled the bolt open. The breech was empty.[77]

The old man was a guard for a small military garrison. The commander, Captain Wong, spoke a little English and led them to a village where he saw to it that the villagers provided bedding and food. McElroy and Knobloch were joined by Bourgeois and Campbell. Williams arrived later, limping badly from a leg injury. The quintet proceeded atop small ponies, then sedan chairs carried by farmers who were pressed into service by Wong's soldiers when the bearers got tired.

The five crew members were taken to Poyang, a city of about 300,000, where they were greeted by hundreds of welcomers. Banners fluttered from windows, reading in Chinese and English:

> WELCOME BRAVE AMERICAN FLYERS. FIRST TO BOMB TOKIO. UNITED STATES AND CHINA RULE THE PACIFIC.

The "brave American flyers" were treated royally with warm baths and a meal of chicken, mashed potatoes, and pie. But, enjoyable as it was, they had to move on and were taken by boat around enemy-held territory. En route at Ying Tan, they met Father William J. Glynn, an American Catholic missionary, who helped them on their way by train to Chuchow, where Doolittle and eight other crews were waiting.

McElroy and his crew learned later that the village of Ying Tan had been torched and the inhabitants murdered by Japanese troops for helping them. The several hundred villagers were not the only ones to suffer the supreme penalty as the enemy troops took vengeance on the helpless Chinese and the missionaries who assisted any of the Americans en route to Chuchow.

Lt. James H. "Herb" Macia, navigator–bombardier on the fourteenth aircraft, no. 2297, kept a precise log of his flight. He noted the takeoff time as 0905 and the pass over the *Hornet* to check the plane's compass as 0913. His report follows:

> Ship position approx. 35°10′N 153°10′E. Wind at takeoff 300° 26K [knots]. Course into coast 282° compass or 286° true. At 10:20 patrol ship sighted at approx. 35°N 149°E. Plane apparently did not sight our ship. Sun observation taken between 11:50 and 13:00 showing D.R. [dead reckoning] position 25 miles north of desired course. Drift increased from 5°L to 1°L and course altered to 277° compass or 263°

> true. Japan mainland sighted at 13:50 on approx. 34°30′N. At 09:45 we attempted to set up A.F.C.E. [automatic pilot] but it did not function properly. A.F.C.E. had not been flight tested following repairs at Sacramento. Altered course at 13:50 to follow along coast. At 14:00 we altered course toward Nagoya. Sgt. Eierman had tested .30 cal. machine gun in bombardier compartment and in charging gun had lodged cartridge case in barrel and gun was put out of commission. At 15:15 anti-aircraft fire opened from ground as we passed east of city on a northerly heading. First incendiary bomb dropped at 15:20 and three others followed at intervals of approx. 1 to 2 minutes. All bombing equipment functioned properly and all bombs fell on or very close to targets. Upon passing last target smoke from first three bombs was visible. At 15:30 we could see great columns of dark smoke over the city from a distance of about 30 miles.[78]

The targets for this plane, piloted by Maj. John A. Hilger, were the military barracks surrounding Nagoya, an oil and gas storage area, an arsenal, and the Mitsubishi Aircraft Works. All of them were hit with precision, especially the latter. Hilger remarked in his diary that "Macia hit it dead center and if there is anything in that building that is inflammable, it is probably still burning."[79]

The postaction reports of Lt. Jack A. Sims, co-pilot; Sgt. Jacob Eierman, engineer; and S. Sgt. Edwin V. Bain, gunner, confirmed Macia's success as the B-25 fled southward and then across the China Sea. Macia's log noted that they encountered bad visibility and low clouds at 2010 and Hilger went on instruments. He gave Hilger a course five degrees left of their desired course "to insure being south of occupied China."

Hilger climbed into the overcast, and as he noted in his war diary later:

> I had a premonition then as to what was waiting for us and I was right. As we crossed the coast and continued inland the weather got worse with heavy driving rain and zero visibility. I passed the word for everyone to prepare to bail out and got ready myself. At 1920 (Chungking time) Macia estimated that we were over our objective in unoccupied China, Chuchow (Chuhsien), and I gave the order to bail out. Everyone went out with no excitement. I've never been

as lonesome in my life as I was when I looked back and found that I was all alone in the plane. I trimmed the plane for level flight and slid my seat back to get out. I had a little trouble getting between the armor plate but finally managed it and picked up my musette bag which the other fellows had laid out for me. I sat down on the edge of the escape hatch, leaned over and let go.[80]

All five crew members had similar experiences on their respective bailouts. Most of the cigarettes, candy bars, and emergency supplies they had stuffed inside their jackets were lost when their chutes opened. All suffered bruises and assorted minor injuries. Hilger had been knocked cold, sprained his left wrist and hand, and wrenched his back. Bain was also knocked out when he struck the ground. One of his teeth was broken off and another cracked.

Jack Sims, third man out of the plane, reported, "I hooked my musette bag on my gun belt. The bag contained four cans of rations, pair of gloves, compass, and flashlight. To this I wish I had had the foresight to include socks, underwear, handkerchiefs, and important papers such as orders, etc. On my belt I carried canteen, pistol, clips, first aid kit, and knife. All this weight made quite a jolt when the chute opened, and also when I hit the side of the mountain."[81]

All five flyers slept where they landed, not daring to venture far in the darkness. Hilger's diary noted:

> I spent a horrible night last night. I awakened when the wind died down and could hear what sounded like surf on three sides of me. That meant the other four fellows were out in the ocean. The last thing I had seen on leaving the plane was two life jackets near the hatch. This thought kept me awake all night and it was not until more than an hour after daylight when the fog cleared that I discovered a beautiful flat valley below me and a tumbling mountain stream on either side, that had given me the illusion of surf. Columbus was never happier with a discovery than I was at that moment.[82]

Each man met Chinese farmers who tried to assist them but the language barrier was formidable. However, by signs and gestures, they managed to communicate their need to get to Chuchow. The mysterious Chinese grapevine communicated their presence. The villagers treated each with great respect and care as they were led to a reunion at Kuang Feng, where an impromptu parade was staged in celebration of their heroism. Hilger's diary notes: "Their honesty, willingness to help and hospitality were unequaled by anything we have ever seen."[83]

Hilger and his crew arrived at Chuchow at daybreak on April 20 and "were immediately whisked out to the quarters near the airport where our gang was to stay," Hilger noted. "I was never so glad to see anyone in my life as I was to see Jones, Greening, Bower and all their crew members. It was like a homecoming and we were all as happy as kids. There's nothing like a familiar face in a foreign country."

The assigned target city for the fifteenth plane was Kobe, part of an industrial complex 270 miles southwest of Tokyo on the western shore of Osaka Bay. The plan was to follow Major Hilger's plane to Nagoya and then proceed to Kobe, about twenty miles farther. The crew consisted of Lt. Donald G. Smith, pilot; Lt. Griffith P. Williams, co-pilot; Lt. Howard A. Sessler, navigator–bombardier; Sgt. Edward J. Saylor, engineer–gunner; and Dr. (Lt.) Thomas R. White, gunner and physician.

Smith followed Hilger easily as they paralleled the coastline toward Nagoya. When Hilger turned toward his target area, Smith continued at twelve hundred feet altitude and 240 mph to the northeastern part of Kobe and aligned himself with the steel works assigned in his target folder. "We had no trouble finding our targets," Smith reported later. "No antiaircraft fire was encountered, and nothing happened to prevent us from completing our mission. The bomb release light was not working and didn't light until the fourth bomb was dropped, so we couldn't tell from the pilots' compartment when the bombs were released. After Lieutenant Sessler called and said 'bomb doors closed,' a gun on the south edge of town opened fire at us, and we dove for the water, pulling out just above it, indicating 325 mph. We did not have an opportunity to see how much damage was accomplished."[84]

Smith continued south and then west and approached the Chinese coast about twenty-five minutes earlier than expected and ten miles north of their planned point. Smith's report noted:

> The visibility was almost zero, the ceiling about 300 feet and it was almost dark, when we caught the outline of a mountain sticking out of the sea directly ahead. I immediately started a bank to the right, began to climb and turned due east to head back out to sea. The right engine was giving very little power, and the left one was back-firing. It was evident we could not remain in the air so we prepared for a water landing alongside the island.[85]

Doc White recalled that Smith "did a beautiful job of ditching the plane. None of us was hurt in the least. The plane floated for eight minutes. I was able to get my medical kit out and we got the life raft launched but, unfortunately, the raft was punctured on one side and it turned over on the way to shore. We lost almost everything we had managed to save."[86]

In his diary, White described what happened next:

> Sessler swam ashore. We paddled. Bucked current and wind for awhile, then turned with it. Nearly an hour in the cold yellow water. Dark. Rocks all around with big waves breaking over them. Turned over three times. The last time I was too tired to climb in so popped my life vest and swam, towing the raft. Current nearly swept us past the point but finally made it. Climbed up nearly vertical rocks through surf and looked for signs of life. Nearly fell over several cliffs and finally huddled to get warm for we were thoroughly chilled and exhausted. Too cold and no shelter from wind and rain so we went exploring again. Saw a dim light and headed toward it. Found a haystack and finally a goat shed. We curled up in the straw. The owner came out with a candle and dragged us into the house. Built a fire of straw on the floor and we took off our wet clothes. Four of us went to bed family style—two each way!
>
> At first the people said they were Japanese but finally found a book with some English words in it and the Chinese equivalents. Then we established ourselves as Americans ("Negua") and found out they were Chinese ("Chunqua"). We were fed and given dry, if inhabited, clothing. They were much pleased that we had bombed Japan.[87]

Sessler, when he swam to shore, had not found the group and had spent the night in a sheltered cleft of rocks. "For the first time I could really see what a predicament we were in," he said. "I really did some sincere praying that night." Next morning, he found the others and they began their trip to safety by Chinese junk, often evading Japanese search parties with the help of Chinese guerrillas, headed by Gen. Jai Foo Ching. White's diary for April 20 states:

> In late afternoon we got word that Japs were coming so we split up, all going different ways. The General and I and another guerrilla went over some hills. Finally reached a canal where we got into a boat and went for a long ride, collecting eggs along the way. Much shouting back and forth—the grapevine telegraph. Occasional stops for heated discussions.
>
> We reached the end of the canal about dusk and then walked a mile to a kind of barracks where we had supper of eggs, rice, shrimp, tea and wine. Got into another small boat and finally wound up in an old Taoist temple. The old priest had fine features, wild hair and beard and wore a black gown. He had a long pipe he used for a staff. Our guerrilla and the priest offered prayers for us and then tested the omens with the "jumping sticks" three times—once for them, once for us, and once for Chiang Kai Shek.[88]

The crew got together again and spent the next several days traveling by boat, sedan chair, and hiking along the guerrilla network of friendly villages, where they were treated to baths, good food, and restful sleep. They were presented with scrolls honoring their presence; the crew gave their hosts American coins.

As they progressed toward Chuchow they were given news of other crews. They learned that Lawson and his crew were injured and had preceded them by about three hours, going toward a missionary hospital at Linhai. Smith decided they should follow their route to see what help was needed. When they arrived at Linhai, White found that Lawson, Davenport, Clever, and McClure were in no shape to travel. He elected to stay with them while the other members of Smith's crew plus Dave Thatcher of Lawson's crew would proceed to Chuchow.

"This providential linkup of the two crews probably saved the lives of the injured," Doolittle told the author. "If Doc White had been on any other aircraft, he may not have been able to get to Linhai to tend to them before the Japanese got there. We were all glad that Doc insisted he be allowed to go along as a crew member."[89]

The book entitled *Thirty Seconds over Tokyo*, written by Lawson with Bob Considine in 1943 before the full story of the raid was known, documents the plight of the four injured crewmen of the *Ruptured Duck*. Doc White's diary tells the story this way:[90]

April 24

Lawson in very poor shape with compound fracture of left knee and badly infected leg, right front teeth knocked out and cuts about the chin and face. Davenport not too good—badly infected cuts on right leg. McClure suffering sprained or possible fractured right shoulder and nerve injury to left arm, small infected cuts. Clever has infected cuts above left eye, scalp and right leg, sprained right ankle and cuts on right hand. Thatcher, one small cut on head. The Drs. Ching, a father and son, are looking after them. This hospital once belonged to a Britisher, a Dr. Bevington, who built up such a reputation for cures that even though he left 20 years ago the place still shines in his reflected glory. It later belonged to the Church Mission Society and now to the Drs. Ching.

Went to work on the boys. Wired Chungking to fly some supplies down. Found some sulfanilamide and put Lawson and Davenport on it. Dressed wounds, wearing gloves.

The Chinese newspaper came out with news of our raid, causing much excitement. Deputations from the town, schools and all sorts of organizations came and brought eggs, cookies and oranges.

Wire from Major Hilger to pick up two bodies at San Men. None were there but two or three in hands of the Japs. Worse luck, Lishui and Chuhsien bombed.

April 25

Lawson had a bad night. Gave him two transfusions of 150 and 200 cc by two-syringe method. The co-pilot, Lt. Williams, was donor. Syringes clogged! He was better afterward.

All of us given Chinese names. I'm "Way Esong" meaning "great and powerful doctor." It rained. We had several air raid alarms. Planes apparently on way to bomb Lishui, a nearby town.

April 26

Made a splint for Lawson's leg at Mr. England's and installed it. Very painful. Had a table made for McClure to get his arms up. Put a splint on his left hand to prevent contraction.

April 27

Gave Lawson an intravenous and he had a very sharp reaction. Running out of sulfanilamide. Smith, Williams, Sessler, Saylor and Thatcher left via [sedan] chair for next town. Sent letters with them.

April 28

Cold and rainy. Lawson no better so gave him chloroform and operated to improve drainage. He nearly went out under the anesthetic.

May 1

Our gang reached Chuhsien last night. Heard one of our ships went to Russia.

Lawson's wounds don't look so good. Put in sulfa powder. Dr. Ching got us some more, thank goodness.

May 2

Rainy. Met Dr. Ding from Plague Prevention Unit. He brought a little morphine and sulfa and a blood transfusion set. Dressed the boys' wounds. I'm feeling better today but still very rheumatic. Lawson no better. Gave him another blood transfusion—Clever and McClure, donors.

May 3

A Chinese professor, Dr. Seng, arrived from Provincial Medical School. Checked on river for possible seaplane landing. Lawson no better. Afraid he'll lose the leg. Rainy. Wired for seaplane to pick up Lawson.[91]

Lawson much worse. Decided to amputate. Did a high mid-thigh under spinal. Gave him 1500 cc. blood for transfusion. Changed dressings. Lawson not reacting very well.[92]

May 5

Lawson much better. Very little drainage so far.

May 6

Lawson definitely more lucid. Changed dressings.

May 7

Lawson better but still running some temperature. Gave him a second pint of my blood. Felt this one a bit. Other boys doing well.

May 8

Lawson looking somewhat better in the a.m. but bloody stump is infected. Changed dressings. Feeling somewhat shaky from transfusions. Lawson much worse in evening. Not eating. Gave him an intravenous and some morphine.

May 9

Lawson some better but stump plenty infected. Did some dentistry and put in two fillings for Mr. Sharmon, a Welshman visiting the Englands. There have been several patients who wanted me to look at them but I've explained that I'm a military doctor. I can't take them except on consultation with Dr. Ching. They seem to understand and honor me for it. There is no other hospital nearby.

Had three more dentistry patients and three eye patients. Ophthalmoscopy and retinoscopy by candlelight!

Doc White cared for the four crewmen over the next three weeks; all had their respective problems recuperating. News about Japanese troops advancing toward Linhai, destroying and murdering, came in almost hourly, and it was obvious the Americans had to be moved. On May 17, Chinese villagers carried the five men to Sien Ku where White sent a message to Chungking:

ENROUTE CHUHSIEN WITH FOUR INJURED OFFICERS. EXPECTED TIME OF ARRIVAL MAY 22. REQUEST PLANE MEET US.

News that Japanese troops were dogging their movements prompted the Chinese to detour the Americans through a number of small villages for the next thirteen days. Although they were feted at each village and were well cared for, the group was continually exhausted by each nightfall. They arrived at Kweilin on May 29, where they were to meet the evacuation plane but they had to wait until June 3. Meanwhile, on June 1, they learned that the village of Linhai had fallen to the Japanese onslaught. Hundreds of Chinese and the missionaries who had befriended the Americans were paying with their lives in one of the cruelest retaliatory expeditions ever recorded.

For their heroism and devotion to their fellow airmen at the risk of their own lives, Doolittle recommended Dave Thatcher and Doc White for the Distinguished Service Cross. However, both received the Silver Star for their gallantry, an award slightly lower in precedence.

Tall, red-headed Lt. George Barr was the navigator on the last plane to leave the carrier. He was eating breakfast when the alarm sounded and recalled that he was "as unprepared as anyone else. The running around, the bag packing, and the rushing to board our planes was real enough but, somehow, I couldn't make myself believe we were really going."[93]

When Barr arrived at his plane, Lt. William G. Farrow was already strapping himself in the pilot's seat. Co-pilot Lt. Robert L. Hite climbed in beside him. Cpl. Jacob D. DeShazer, the bombardier, loaded his equipment in the nose. However, since this last plane's tail was hanging out over the end of the deck, Sgt. Harold A. Spatz, the engineer–gunner, couldn't enter the rear hatch until the plane was moved forward.

"Out in front of the plane," Barr said:

> the navy deck hands were swarming around pushing and pulling, and it seemed to me that it wouldn't take much for someone to get hurt in all the confusion. Sure enough, before we could do anything about it, a sailor slipped in front of our left prop and the blast from Lieutenant Smith's plane blew him right into it.
>
> It was an unfortunate accident and there was nothing we could do about it. The seaman's arm was practically cut off and he was carried away by his buddies. This accident unnerved me and it was all I could think about as we lined up for our takeoff.[94]

The route to Nagoya, the target city assigned to this aircraft, was covered without incident. However, being last off the carrier, the crew was apprehensive about the reception they would receive by the time they got there. When they reached the coast, Farrow hedgehopped toward the city and, spotting three enemy fighters above them, pulled up quickly into the twenty-five-hundred-foot overcast.

"A short time later," Barr said:

> we let down to the deck again. We had four incendiaries in our bomb bay because of the nature of our targets. Up ahead we saw antiaircraft fire. We spotted our first target, a battery of oil storage tanks, and let go our first bomb. We had three more to go. To the north (on our right side) I could see smoke and fire coming from two different places. This meant that Jack Hilger and Don Smith had found their targets. The air around their targets was speckled with ack-ack bursts. I saw Hilger's plane flying in a southerly direction and at a lower altitude than ours. (We were at fifteen hundred feet.) Then we realized the Japs were firing at him and coming close to us, since we were crossing his line of flight.
>
> But our job wasn't finished yet. Up ahead I saw a nice long aircraft factory loom up to our left. Bill saw it, too, and without any direction from me, changed course, lined the building up, and we made a run for it end to end, dropping our incendiaries.[95]

Farrow kept the other two planes in sight as they flew the escape route but lost them as the weather deteriorated. He elected to continue inland as far as possible rather than attempt a water landing. As the fuel warning light came on, Farrow spotted a break in the overcast and Barr was able to verify that the lights below were those of Nanchang. Although they had been warned that the area around Nanchang was presumed held by the Japanese, they had no choice. Farrow ordered everyone out and followed when all were clear.

Barr landed easily in a rice paddy up to his waist in water. Except for a slight sprain, he was unhurt. He picked up the narrative:

> I wandered around in the maze of rice paddies in the dark trying to find a path. I finally found one and followed it until I reached a position that was guarded by wild jackals that the Japs used as sentries. To avoid them I headed out into the flooded rice paddies again but I couldn't bypass the area where they were kept.
>
> Unable to make any headway I decided to go back to the path and head in the opposite direction which would take me toward the town. I followed this path for about half a mile to a river. The bridge that spanned the river had been completely bombed out but I managed to get to the opposite bank by jumping from one piling to the next. In the dark, this was no easy task. Directly in front of me was a dirt barricade with an entrance. I walked through it. Just as I did, a soldier shouted something at me and shoved a rifle in my back. My heart stood still. Was he Japanese or Chinese? Was he going to shoot me in the back or what?
>
> He didn't shoot me but prodded me to a dugout where he woke up some other soldiers sleeping on the ground. They searched me and then tied my hands in front and my elbows behind me and marched me into a nearby town. I was still hoping they were Chinese just doing their duty but when we got to the town I was brought into a room where there were about ten to fifteen Japanese officers in full military dress sitting around a table overloaded with wines, whiskies, cigarettes, and delicacies.
>
> Needless to say, they were delighted with their captive. I was a rare prize. They immediately interrogated me through an interpreter. After refusing the food and drink and giving them only my name, rank, and serial number, I was directed to a room where I could sleep. During the night, Bob Hite was brought in, and the following day we learned that Farrow, Spatz, and DeShazer were also captured.[96]

There were forty months of torture, solitary confinement, and starvation ahead for this luckless crew. Two of them, along with a member of the sixth crew, would be executed. Three from this crew and one from another would barely survive the next forty months under a life sentence receiving "special treatment" as prisoners of the enemy. In a strange turnabout, one of the survivors would return to Japan as a missionary and convert a famous Japanese pilot to Christianity. The last of Doolittle's raiders to return to the States would be "lost" in an incredible medical record mixup and would seem destined to spend the rest of his life in a mental ward.

9

A Psychological Blow to the Japanese

Vice Admiral Matome Ugaki, chief of staff of the Combined Fleet headquarters in Tokyo, was at lunch when the call came over his classified telephone announcing an enemy attack. He tried to confirm the bad news. "At 1300 (1:00 P.M.) I heard various reports from headquarters that Japan had been attacked," he wrote in his diary that night, "but I doubted their validity, and had difficulty in making any plans or decisions."[1] He recorded his actions:

> I repeatedly ordered the Third Submarine Fleet, which was located two hundred miles west of the enemy aircraft carriers to attack but no units came in contact with the enemy, and in spite of the fact that our primary purpose was to catch the enemy, the enemy's position was unknown. I did not know what was happening, and all I could do was order a pursuit to the east. Today I was very irritated when the sun went down at 1700; at 1600 I received a message from the Kirarazu unit that had departed to attack. It stated that the unit had gone seven hundred nautical miles without finding a trace of the enemy. According to later reports the attack planes were twin-engine long-distance bombers, which took off from aircraft carriers, bombed nine places in Tokyo, and dropped incendiary bombs. Casualties were twelve dead and more than one hundred wounded. Fifty houses were burned down, fifty were half destroyed. Kobe, Wakayama, and Nagoya were bombed and it is reported that one plane bombed the Nitsu oil wells in Niigata. The bow of a large whaling vessel that was at anchor at Yokosuka sustained some damage. Apparently, there were more than a few planes, and it is not clear whether they returned to their mother ship, headed toward Siberia or China, or contacted a Soviet vessel that was sailing twenty nautical miles south

of Ashizurizaki. However, the enemy aircraft carrier seems to have pulled back to the east, and it is regrettable that I missed my chance three or four times. It had always been my motto not to allow Tokyo or the homeland to be attacked from the air, but today my pride has been deeply hurt and my spirits are low as today I gave the enemy his glory.

The next day, April 19, Ugaki had more information and wrote:

> One enemy plane was captured in Nanchang. It is reported that it took off from Baiel Island south of Midway. There is no such island on the map. The intelligence reports come from low-ranking army officers who do not know English, have no knowledge of the sea, and are unreliable, so I have dispatched an intelligence officer from the navy. Anyway, it is clear that thirteen B-25s landed in Chung-shui. Those planes might return from China and attack our homeland again. Since sufficient measures had to be taken, after lunch I ordered my staff to solve the riddle of the American planes.[2]

Ugaki ordered the Second and Fifth Fleets and all the planes he could muster to chase the American task force, but no trace of its presence was found. Exhausted after two days of nervous pacing and waiting for news that the Americans had been located, he was moved to note that "I am at the end of my resources. The enemy casts an eye of contempt at the clamoring Japanese. Thus we were invaded, but missed our chance to fight back; this is most regrettable."[3]

The reaction of the Japanese public to the raid seemed relatively mild in the first few hours after the raid. Father Bruno Bitter, a Catholic priest, reported to Army Air Force intelligence officers after he was allowed to leave Japan that the sudden intrusion seemed to have little effect on the population where he was in Tokyo. "It was just twelve o'clock noon when the alarm was given," he recalled. "Most of the people did not believe it, thinking it was just another drill. But when they learned it was a real raid, nobody could hold them back to go outside, to climb the roofs or the chimneys to get a better view. In other words, it was a thrill rather than a frightening event."[4]

Joseph C. Grew, U.S. ambassador to Japan, and still in Tokyo, kept a personal diary of his ten years in Japan. His entry for April 18, 1942, reads:

> The Swiss Minister came again, and just as he was leaving before lunch we heard a lot of planes overhead and saw five or six large fires burning in different directions with great volumes of smoke. At first we thought it was only maneuvers but soon became aware that it was the first big raid on Japan by American bombers which are reported to have attacked first in Hokkaido and then, in turn, Tokyo, Yokosuka, Nagoya and Kobe. We saw one of them, apparently losing altitude and flying very low, just over the tops of the buildings to the west, and at first we feared that it had crashed but then realized that it was intentionally following these tactics in order to avoid the dives of pursuit planes and the anti-aircraft fire. To the east we saw a plane with a whole line of black puffs of smoke, indicating anti-aircraft explosions, just on its tail; it didn't look like a bomber and we are inclined to believe that the Japanese batteries lost their heads and fired on their own pursuit planes.
>
> All this was very exciting, but at the time it was hard to believe that it was more than a realistic practice by Japanese planes. The Japanese press claimed that nine enemy planes had crashed, but we doubt if any were lost since, if even one had crashed on land, the papers would have been full of triumphant pictures of the wreck. They appeared too large to have come from an aircraft carrier, and they may have been flying from the Aleutian Islands to the new air bases in China. We were all very happy and proud in the Embassy, and the British told us later that they drank toasts all day to the American flyers.[5]

While Ambassador Grew was under loose restrictions in the American embassy, Otto D. Tolischus, a *New York Times* reporter, viewed the attack from a different vantage point: solitary confinement in a Tokyo jail. Jailed when the war began, he was interrogated continually for six months before being released on June 25, 1942, to return home on the *Gripsholm* with other Americans. In his book *Tokyo Record*, he recalled the events of April 18:

> This afternoon, the air raid sirens began to scream, and the guards came rushing through the corridors to double-lock the cell doors. During the day, the cell door could be opened from the outside by just turning a handle. But during the night, during earthquakes, and during air raid drills, it was locked with a key and could be opened only with a key. My friendly floor guard opened my door long enough to indicate to me this was no drill, but the real thing. He made a long face and shook his head. An air raid—a real honest-to-goodness air raid—was apparently something the Japanese had not counted upon. I felt like cheering. I had heard sirens during the first few nights in prison and had rushed to the windows to listen, filled with the hope that this was an American air armada come to smash the whole town into smithereens, and the whole blasted prison with it. But every time I had realized that what I heard was merely the siren of fire engines going by. Now there was no mistake. Soon I heard gunfire, some close by. It was an air raid! I listened for the bomb explosions, but could hear none. After about half an hour, the doors were unlocked. It was all over. But I felt much, much better.[6]

It took a while for the full impact of the raid to sink into the minds of the average Japanese. There was a creeping realization that, despite propaganda to the contrary, the confidence of the people was severely shaken. Toshiko Matsumura, thirteen years old at the time, lived in the suburbs of Tokyo toward Yokohama. She told the author she did not realize there had been a raid until she overheard her elders discussing it in hushed tones a few days later.

"My people had always placed emphasis on spiritual strength and the medieval belief that Japan would never be attacked," she said. "As children we had been taught to believe what the emperor and his advisors told us. It was a severe psychological shock to even the most ardent believer when it was officially announced that we had been attacked. We finally began to realize that all we were told was not true—that the government had lied when it said we were invulnerable. We then began to doubt that we were also invincible."[7]

A martyr to the "inhuman" bombing was needed to prove the bestiality of the Americans and was quickly invented. The

Asahi Shimbun published a story on April 19 about a group of school children on their way home from school "when an enemy plane flew over at terrific speed." Hinosuke Ishibe, fourteen, was about to enter his classroom when "the enemy plane which had descended to an altitude of fifty meters fired about ten rounds of ammunition at the schoolyard. One of them went through the corridor window glass and struck Ishibe in the right thigh. At 2:00 P.M. the same day he breathed his last in the arms of his teachers."[8]

The feeble attempts to cover up the effects of the raid continued in the press and government propagandists worked overtime on statements to convince the public there was nothing to fear. The air raid alert warning was officially lifted on the morning of the twentieth, but the announcement was not made in the press until the next day. There was a caution: "We must imagine that, as the enemy did not achieve his objectives in the first air attack, he will make several more vain attempts."[9]

The government publicists were directed to counter the visible effects of the bomb damage that had been seen by thousands of citizens. Proof that the bombers had been destroyed was badly needed. Since no planes had been shot down over Japan, orders went out to the occupation troops in China to obtain some wreckaage of the American planes at any cost.

On April 25, the Saturday following the raid, an extra attraction was announced for the Yasukuni Shrine Provisional Festival. It was an exhibit consisting of a twisted wing and landing gear tubing from a B-25, and a parachute. The authenticity of the display could not be doubted. The words "North American" were stamped on the torn metal of the wing and "U.S. Army Air Corps" was stencilled on the parachute harness. The parachute was marked as having been manufactured in June, 1941, by the Switlick Company.

Over two million people passed by this display as they paid homage to their war dead during the festival. The government had said that nine planes had been shot down and here were the remains of one of them.

A final attempt to minimize the effects of the raid was made in *Shashin Shuho*, an illustrated weekly, on April 29, 1942. In a long discourse about the bravery of the people and the futility of the raid, the article disclaimed the potential effects of any future air raid against Japan:

> There is no country which has been defeated only by air raids, regardless of how many it has sustained. Moreover, our country will not be reduced to ashes by incendiary bombs, as the enemy has schemed. Judging from the modus operandi of this first enemy air raid, the enemy did not live up to his threats and war cries and, acting as if he acknowledges this fact, he used only a few planes and gained little success even though he conducted a broad-scale attack. Also, the fact that the bombing targets were streets and towns rather than military installations means that he was not aiming to destroy completely all facilities, but had schemed to rally the public opinion of his own country since his people have suffered defeat after defeat. His attack was intended as effective propaganda to be broadcast to other countries and to produce the psychological warfare effect of disturbing the spirit of the Japanese people on the home front. This plan of the enemy met with failure in his first attack. The enemy will probably repeat persistent guerrilla-type raids. However, we must be firmly resolved not to become disturbed, regardless of how many times we are attacked from the air. To become disturbed is to fall victims to the enemy's intended scheme of psychological warfare. We must respond to the brilliant battle achievements of our officers and men on the front lines and in order to win the Great Asian War, we must rouse our warrior spirit and vow to defend our homeland to the death.[10]

Ever since the day that the raid had been conceived in Washington, its objective had been to affect adversely the morale of the Japanese people as well as to inflict some damage on their war effort. When measured in terms of the later raids on Japan by B-29 Superfortresses, which ended with the single-plane attacks on Nagasaki and Hiroshima in August, 1945, the two-thousand-pound bomb loads of the B-25s did not cause much damage. But the impact on Japanese national morale, the primary objective of the raid, was considerable. Public confidence was shaken and for the first time, the people began to take a cynical view of government propaganda.

Interned Americans who were allowed to return from Japan on the *Gripsholm* in June, 1942, were unanimous in their belief that the B-25s had scored direct hits on the Japanese psyche and that from that standpoint alone, the operation was magnificently justified. "I did not know one American in Japan who would even question that fact," said Otto Tolischus, the interned *New York Times* correspondent.[11]

Ramon M. Lavelle, a commercial attaché at the Argentine embassy in Tokyo, agreed with Tolischus. He had witnessed the raid from the roof of the embassy and reported his impressions upon visiting the States later in the war. "That raid by Doolittle was one of the greatest psychological tricks ever used," he said.

> It caught the Japs by surprise. Their unbounded confidence began to crack.
>
> The day after the raid, the Tokyo newspapers said nine American planes had been shot down. . . . The people knew such a statement was a lie. The officer in charge of the Japanese antiaircraft defenses was compelled to commit suicide.
>
> The results of the Doolittle raid are still evident in Japan. They are stamped into the daily habits of the Japanese people. Where before they imagined themselves safe from aerial aggression, they now search the skies each morning and each night. . . . Fearlessness has turned to fear.[12]

While Japanese morale was shaken, the feat lifted the morale of Americans as nothing else had during five months of bitter defeats. It seemed a promise that America was now going on the attack and had avenged the raid on Pearl Harbor. The good news countered the bad news that Bataan had fallen a week before the Doolittle raid. Newspapers in the United States gave large headlines in "war extras" to the news of the raid and that it had been led by the famous Jimmy Doolittle. The *Los Angeles Times* titled its lead story "Doolittle Did It"; the *Nome Nugget*, the Alaska newspaper that Jimmy had delivered while a young lad in the frontier Alaskan town, claimed "Nome Town Boy Makes Good!" in the largest typeface the editor could find in his back shop.

President Roosevelt, ecstatic that his request to retaliate had been carried out, told the press with gusto on April 21 that the bombers had taken off from Shangri-La, the mythical, timeless place featured by James Hilton in his novel, *Lost Horizon*. This created an air of mystery that confounded the Japanese and delighted the Allies. The Shangri-La remark added the exact psychological note that the nation had been wanting to hear. It proved that the United States *could* strike back. The boast that Premier Hideki Tojo had made that "Japan has never lost a war in all the 2,600 years of her glorious history" was going to be destroyed.

Meanwhile, in China, eight of Doolittle's raiders were being tortured and starved in an effort to get them to reveal the details of their mission. They were being flown to Tokyo where experts at extracting "confessions" from innocent captives were waiting. Four of them were destined to make the supreme sacrifice.

10

The Chinese Pay with Their Lives

In the days immediately preceding the raid, Chiang Kai Shek had received reports in Chungking that the Japanese were concentrating their forces at Hangchow in preparation for a march against Chuchow, the intended landing spot for Doolittle's planes. This impending threat to his supply lines, especially the Chekiang–Kiangsi Railroad, was serious. He objected strenuously to the use of the Chuchow airfield by the Americans because he felt certain the Japanese would react violently to an attack against their homeland.

Chiang's prediction was correct. When the news of the bombing reached the Japanese military leaders operating in China, a three-month campaign of fury and fanaticism began against the Chinese people, which was preceded by more than six hundred air raids to cover the advancing army. As Chiang feared, fifty-three Japanese battalions slashed their way through Chekiang Province where most of the raiders had landed. On April 28, the China Expeditionary Forces were given orders to "thwart the enemy's plans to carry out air raids on the homeland of Japan from the Chekiang Province area."[1] To carry out the orders, the commander-in-chief ordered his troops to annihilate enemy forces in the area and destroy the principal airfields. Murder, rape, and plunder became the order of the day.

When the reports began coming in to Chiang, he sent a bitter cable to Washington. "After they had been caught unawares by the falling of American bombs on Tokyo," he said, "Japanese troops attacked the coastal areas of China where many of the American flyers had landed. These Japanese troops slaughtered every man, woman and child in those areas—let me repeat—these Japanese troops slaughtered every man, woman and child in those areas, reproducing on a wholesale scale the horrors which the world had seen at Lidice, but about which the people have been uninformed in these instances."[2]

Chiang did not exaggerate. In describing the campaign of retaliation in his memoirs, Gen. Claire Chennault recalled that Japanese forces drove two hundred miles into East China to wreak revenge. Twenty-thousand square miles of Chinese territory were searched; landing fields were plowed up; hundreds of villagers were murdered if there was the remotest suspicion that they had seen or aided the Americans. Chennault reported that entire villages the raiders had passed through were burned to the ground and every inhabitant murdered on the spot. "One sizable city was razed for no other reason than the sentiment displayed by its citizens in filling up Jap bomb craters on the nearby airfields," he wrote. "A quarter million Chinese soldiers and civilians were killed in the three-month campaign."[3]

A report written by a member of the magistrate's office in Hsiangshan was typical of reports of Japanese retaliatory measures that were forwarded to Gen. Joseph Stilwell, commander of U.S. ground troops operating in the China–Burma–India theater. The account documented the revenge committed against the innocent Chinese who attempted to help Lt. Dean Hallmark and his crew:

> At about 6 p.m. on April 18, 1942, a plane force-landed on the sea off Numeachiae (2 li from the coast of Chiachsi, Hsiangshan). Yang Shib-diao, the village alderman, heard it and went out to see when he saw three foreigners trudging on the road wet with water and in great distress. He knew at once that they had swam in the sea and tried to find out their trouble. But owing to the language barrier Yang could not get anything that would help. Thereupon, both tried to draw pictures of flags in the sand with their fingers from which Alderman Yang understood that the survivors were American Pilots who after bombing Tokyo had dropped on the sea. He found out also that two other members of the crew who could not swim were drowned in the sea. Seeing the importance of the matter Alderman Yang led the American members to his home where he gave them such comforts as were available.
>
> On the following morning Yang led by a secret path the American Pilots to the Magistrate's Office under an escort

of some ten inhabitants hoping to save them out of danger. But unfortunately the puppet troops heard it and told the enemy about it. On arriving at Paishawan some forty to fifty enemy troops suddenly came and took them up.

The American Pilots were sent to Macyang but the Chinese inhabitants were ordered to stand in a row when all of them were machine-gunned by the enemy. After killing the local inhabitants the enemy then went into Chiachsi in search for more. Whilst in Chiachsi Village they committed many atrocities killing and robbing the inhabitants. Alderman Yang though escaped death at first died of shock afterwards when his home and those of many other local inhabitants were robbed and destroyed by the enemy.

On the morning of May 1, however, an enemy vessel arrived covered by an airplane which hovered over Numenchiao. The enemy then picked up the wrecked plane from the sea and carried it away. The bodies of the two American Pilots who had been drowned floated for sometime on the sea but were afterwards picked up by Alderman Yang and buried at Shatow, Chiachsi. Stone tablets were set up at the tombs.

We are sorry that what we had done toward saving the American Pilots was very little and at the same time our hearts burn with rage for the cruel deeds of the enemy who killed our inhabitants.[4]

Reverend Charles L. Meeus, a Belgian-born missionary who had become a Chinese citizen, gave further testimony of the vicious retaliation against the Chinese. Traveling through Kiangsi and Chekiang provinces, he had followed the trail of revenge and estimated the number of murdered Chinese at twenty-five thousand in the towns he passed through. The Japanese had warned the villagers that no one was to assist the American fliers or "the very stones of your towns and villages will be crushed into dust."[5]

"Little did the Doolittle men realize," Father Meeus said, "that those same little gifts, which they gave their rescuers in grateful acknowledgment of their hospitality—the parachutes, gloves, nickels, and dimes—would a few weeks later, become the telltale evidence of their presence and lead to the torture and death of their friends."[6]

The tragedy of the vengeance-seeking was that hundreds of

the Chinese peasants massacred never even heard of the Tokyo bombing. Meeus had found the wreckage of the *Whirling Dervish*, Lt. Doc Watson's plane, near Ihwang in Kiangsi Province and learned what had happened there.

"They found the man who had given shelter to Lt. Watson," he wrote to Bishop Paul Yu Pin, Vicar Apostolic of Nanking, in the fall of 1942. "They wrapped him up in some blankets, poured the oil of the lamp on him and obliged his wife to set fire to the human torch. They threw hundreds of people to the bottom of their wells to drown there. They destroyed all the American missions in the vicinity (29 out of 31); they desecrated the graves of all these missionaries; they destroyed the ancestor tablets in the various villages they went through. Cannibalism is the only terror they spared the Chinese people of Kiangsi."[7]

Chuchow, the city toward which most of Doolittle's raiders headed, was taken and the airfield was destroyed. When the campaign was deemed completed, the Japanese withdrew and allowed the Chinese army to reoccupy the area. An estimated fifty thousand Chinese troops had been killed trying to stop the enemy. The helpless civilian population lost an untold greater number as the Japanese tried to teach the Chinese a permanent lesson about the consequences of helping the Americans. To their eternal credit, they spurned the lesson and its teachers. Hundreds of American airmen owe their lives to the aid given them by humble Chinese peasants during the next three years of war.

In the closing days of April, 1942, while the Japanese were hacking their way through the countryside looking for Doolittle's crews, Reverend John M. Birch, twenty-seven, a tall, gaunt, dark-eyed American missionary, was wending his way unobtrusively through the villages of Chekiang Province. He was trying to organize a new chain of Baptist missions to replace those lost when the Japanese interned Americans in Hangchow. Cut off from his church through the severing of communications with the outside world, this dedicated man of God was determined to carry out his missionary work, war or no war. Although he would never know it, his name was to become synonymous with ultraconservatism in America. The John Birch

Society, a highly vocal postwar anticommunist organization, was to bear his name and he would be called "the first casualty of World War III" because he was killed by Chinese communists on August 25, 1945—ten days after World War II was officially over.

Birch, the son of Baptist lay missionaries, had been born in Landaur, India, graduated from Mercer University in 1939 and the Bible Baptist Seminary in 1940, and was sent to Shanghai to begin his missionary work. After six months of intensive study of the Chinese language, Birch went to Hangchow, which he used as a base of operations.

Soon after December 7, when Japanese troops began to round up all the Americans they could find, Birch fled to Changjao, 250 miles to the southwest. Three or four days after the Tokyo raid, Birch was returning to Changjao from a trip down river. En route, tired and hungry, he stopped at a crowded Chinese inn in a small village and seated himself to begin a meal of boiled rice, bamboo shoots, and meat scraps. A Chinese came over from a corner of the room and sat down silently across from him. When he felt he wouldn't be overheard, the Chinese whispered, "You American?"[8]

Birch, startled to hear someone speak English, looked up and nodded.

The Chinese went back to his meal. A few minutes later, the Chinese said, quietly, "You finish. You follow me."

Again, Birch nodded. The Chinese left and made his way to the nearby river. Birch followed at a distance and saw the man climb aboard a riverboat at the dock. Hesitating at first, Birch quickly swung aboard.

"Americans," the Chinese said, pointing toward a closed cabin door.

Birch knocked on the door and said in his southern accent, "Are there any Americans in there?"

Behind the door five Americans tensed. It was Jimmy Doolittle and his crew, Dick Cole, Hank Potter, Fred Braemer, and Paul Leonard. They looked at each other and finally Leonard said, "Hell, no Japanese can talk American like that" and opened the door.[9]

Birch was as delighted to see his fellow Americans as they were to see him. Doolittle quickly briefed him on their situation and Birch agreed to help them get to Lanchi on the Chientang River, about halfway between Hangchow and Changjao.

"John Birch was a fine young man who was living 'off the cuff' in China and having a rough go of it," Doolittle told the author. "He wanted to join the American military forces in some capacity, preferably as a chaplain, and do his part to drive the Japanese invaders out. I promised to put in a word for him and get in touch if we needed him to help round up our men."[10]

When Birch left the Doolittle crew he did not know if he would ever get a response to his offer to serve in uniform. But on April 27, Birch received a telegram from the Chinese air force base at Chuchow asking him to proceed there and await instructions from the American Military Mission in China. When he arrived next day, he met Capt. Dave Jones and other raiders and acted as their interpreter. Doolittle and others had already left for Changjao and Chungking.

Birch was told that Doolittle had left $2,000 (Chinese) and instructions to buy a burial plot near Chuchow, bury Corporal Faktor, obtain as much information as possible about other dead or missing raiders, and accompany the last group to Chungking. Birch filed this report later in Chungking:[11]

> The Chinese officials at Chuhsien told me that outright purchase of a burial plot was prohibited by existing international law, but that Major Y. C. Chen, representing the Chinese Air Force, would like to present to the U.S. Army Air Corps the free use of a plot for one hundred years or so long as the Air Corps wanted it. I thanked them for their kind expressions, and asked them to wait until May 5; meanwhile (May 2) I sent the following telegram to the Military Mission:
>
> COLONEL DOOLITTLE'S INSTRUCTIONS TO BUY PLOT RECEIVED. MAJOR CHEN CHUHSIEN AIR STATION OFFERING PLOT NOT FOR SALE BUT FOR FREE AMERICAN USE. SHALL ACCEPT IF NOT OTHERWISE INSTRUCTED BEFORE MAY 5. BIRCH.
>
> . . . No contrary instructions came, so I accepted Major Chen's offer on May 5. He offered to supply the labor con-

nected with the burial, and asked me to instruct the workmen. Hindered by constant air raid alarms and air raids, the workmen failed to have the grave and stone ready until May 19, on which date Faktor's body was buried. The burial plot is located about one thousand meters southeast of the main group of buildings at the Wan Tsuen headquarters, approximately eight hundred meters south-southeast of the center of the village of Wan Tsuen, and is just south of the motor road from Chuhsien.

As to information gathered: For what I could learn regarding Faktor, see Report on Death and Burial enclosed. Concerning those who came down outside of free China—unofficial and uncertain reports locate them as follows: In Siberia, five men, condition and identity unknown here; near Nanchang, five men, probably those in Captain York's plane, two reported dead, two captured, and one rumored to be safe in free China; in Hsiang San Bay, five men, two reported dead and three captured, identity unknown to me.

On May 18, a telegram came to Chuhsien from Dr. White at Linhai, just as his party was leaving there for Chuchow (Chuhsien). He expected to reach us at Chuhsien by May 22. On May 20 I wired the Military Mission, asking whether or not I should accompany him to Chungking; at that time I could not anticipate the subsequent change of his route which kept him from coming by way of Chuhsien. The reply calling me to Chungking reached me on May 23. Also on that date the Chinese Air Force officers at Wan Tsuen turned over to me a number of personal articles salvaged from the B-25 which crashed near Shuei Chang, Chekiang, these articles to be carried to the Military Mission at Chungking.

The funds I received . . . are untouched; as regards board and lodging, I was the guest of the Chinese Air Force from April 28 to May 26, 1942.

Jimmy Doolittle never saw John Birch again, but he had relayed Birch's request to serve in uniform to the American Military Mission in Chungking. On July 4, 1942, the official birthday of General Chennault's Fourteenth Air Force, the young missionary was sworn in as a first lieutenant. Chennault already had a chaplain assigned but he needed someone to run his intelligence net—someone who could be trusted, knew the Chinese people, could speak the language, was aware of their intricate social customs, and could live in the field on Chinese food. Birch filled the specifications perfectly and never became a chaplain. However, he was ever mindful of his religious calling while serving in uniform. Wherever he found himself on a Sunday, he conducted religious services, often at the risk of his life when behind Japanese lines. He was promoted to captain and served honorably with total dedication. Chennault, fearful that Birch would crack under the strain of continual clandestine ventures into occupied territory, tried to persuade him to take a leave of absence or temporary duty in the States. Birch refused. "Thank you, General," he said, "but I'll leave China only when the last Jap is gone."[12]

11

"Guests" of the Kremlin

Before the takeoff from the *Hornet*, Capt. Edward J. "Ski" York had felt sure that he and his crew would not survive the mission. He was one of the few who had known from the beginning where they were headed and how they would be launched to get to the target areas. The only West Point graduate among the crews, he had changed his Polish name from Cichowski to York and had been given the nickname "Ski" by his classmates. His wife, Mary Elizabeth, was pregnant when he left Florida and he thought he would never see her again or know whether they had a boy or girl.

Justine, the wife of Lt. Robert G. "Bob" Emmens, York's co-pilot, was also pregnant when they left Eglin Field. Their child was due in mid-May. The other members of the crew—Lt. Nolan A. Herndon, navigator; S. Sgt. Theodore H. Laban, engineer; and David W. Pohl, gunner—were single. Pohl, at age twenty, was the youngest crewman on the raid.

York's decision to land in Vladivostok was not a difficult one, although Doolittle had warned all crews not to head for Soviet territory. The fuel consumption on the B-25's engines was so great from an overrich mixture that it would have to have been ditched in the middle of the China Sea. The problem could be traced back to the maintenance personnel at McClellan Field near Sacramento. Both carburetors on York's plane had been removed without his knowledge and in disregard of Doolittle's orders that no work was to be done without permission. No record of the change had been made on the plane's maintenance forms.

Sergeant Laban, the crew chief, discovered on board the carrier that the serial numbers on his records did not agree with those on the carburetors. When this was reported, Doolittle asked York how he felt about it: York had replied, "All right," hoping that the new carburetors would at least have normal fuel consumption and allow the aircraft to get to the Chinese coast. But when they had to be launched farther away from Japan than planned, York knew he would have to make a difficult decision.[1]

After landing safely near Vladivostok, York and his crew hoped they would be detained only briefly and allowed to fly to China after refueling. York later described to intelligence officers what happened after he and his crew were met by a Russian officer and a half-dozen Russian soldiers, all with automatic weapons at the ready position:

> They took us into an office and we sat there for about two hours and a half, at which time an interpreter came in and told us that they were fixing something for us to eat. They didn't question us about where we had come from—except that pilots would come in now and then and, out of curiosity, point to the map with an inquiring look. We pointed generally in the direction of Alaska. There was no interpreter present. None of the Russians could speak English, and no one in our party could speak Russian. A very poor interpreter was finally brought in as we were being fed black bread, soup, and tea. We got the idea of our being on a goodwill flight through to this interpreter, which seemed to satisfy this group of Russians. Nothing in our attempt at conversation suggested anything about Japan or Tokyo's having been bombed earlier that day. Communications within the USSR in early 1942 left much to be desired. The interpreter seemed to understand through the familiar sounds of certain words our request for gasoline, and the friendly smiles and nods from our hosts seemed reassuring.
>
> When we went to bed that night we were fully confident we were going to leave the next morning. But the next morning a general showed up along with the divisional commissar—the equivalent ranking civilian town official. Evidently they had communications from higher headquarters. It was during a five-hour breakfast next morning with the general and the commissar that when questioned specifically about Tokyo's having been bombed, we admitted that we had been part of that mission. After we finished eating, we were placed aboard a Russian DC-3 and flown to Khabarovsk,

which is about four hundred miles north of Vladivostok. When we arrived there we were interviewed for a short time by the commander of the Far Eastern Red Army, General Stern.[2]

Bob Emmens described the meeting, which was interpreted by a woman:

[The general asked] what our target had been, the route we had taken across Japan, the route we had taken across the Sea of Japan, with special cmphasis on whether or not we had been followed by Japanese planes. He returned to that question at least three times during the session. Only once did he ask from what point we had departed, but we declined to give the location of "Shangri-La."

At the end of the questioning the general made a long statement, slowly and deliberately, with his eyes going from one to the other of us. When he finished, the woman stood up and said, "The general has asked me to tell you that according to a decision reached between our two governments and by direction of orders from Moscow, you will be interned in the Soviet Union until such time as further decisions are made in your case. You will commence your internment immediately in quarters which have been prepared for you outside the city of Khabarovsk. You will be given proper protection and attempts will be made to make you comfortable. I must ask you to obey all orders from the officer who will be in charge.' "[3]

York continued:

About three days later our personal belongings were sent to us. They had all been left at Vladivostok. Anything that resembled airplane equipment had been removed, including our pistols. Some items were misplaced, indicating everything had been thoroughly searched. We were placed in a house about five miles out of town and very closely guarded.

Five days later it was announced over the radio that we had landed in the country and had been interned. About five days after that we were taken aboard a train and sent to Penza in European Russia.[4]

The trip to Penza, about three hundred miles south of Moscow, took twenty-one days on the Trans-Siberian Railway. Mihaiel Constantinovitch Schmaring, whom the crew promptly named "Mike," was assigned to them as a "companion" who would remain with them for most of their stay in Russia. When the group arrived in Penza, accompanied by a group of military "companions," they were taken to a house in Okhuna, a small village about ten miles from Penza.

There was a fence around the house and they were allowed outside only with escorts. Three Soviet military officers, all captains, were assigned to them full time. Peasant women were assigned to cook and clean. Most meals consisted of black bread, thin cabbage soup, red caviar, "kroopa," and tea. The future looked grim as the five men faced an indefinite period of doing nothing in a land ravaged by war whose people were living on the ragged edge of poverty.

Internment for any American in the neutral Soviet Union was in stark contrast to Americans interned in Sweden, Switzerland, or Turkey. Doolittle's men were prisoners except that they were not in a prison. Their plight was attributed to an overeager American newspaper reporter in Moscow who, during a news conference about five days after the raid, asked what the Russians would do if one of the planes involved in the raid landed in the Soviet Union. He insisted so much on an answer that the Russians thought he must have had some information on York's crew being there. Their presence was then announced for fear of Japanese retaliation. To remain neutral under international law, the Soviet government was obliged to retain the five Americans for the duration.

On April 22, four days after the raid, Ambassador William H. Standley radioed Washington that a twin-engine North American B-25 bomber had made a forced landing in Primorskkai and reported, "The Soviet military authorities would like to have this information kept secret and especially do not wish that the press should know that a United States Army plane had landed in the Soviet Union."[5]

It was over a month before any American representatives were allowed to visit the five internees. On May 24, Col. Joseph A. Michela, American military attaché to the Soviet Union, and a man named Page from the embassy staff, flew to

Penza to talk with the five men and to report on their condition and morale. The next day Michela radioed the ambassador from Kuibyshev:

> At this time crew members are lodged in a large, clean bungalow in a village approximately ten miles outside of Penza. The bungalow is surrounded by lawns and gardens and adjoining a second house which contains the dining and recreation rooms and also houses three Soviet companions, one of whom is an interpreter. For recreation the Americans have been provided with books, billiards, athletic facilities, and other distractions. All in all, the Soviet authorities have been extremely considerate in providing for the crew. The food which the men receive is superior to that obtainable by the diplomatic corps in Kuibyshev and the men are allowed the same freedom of movement permitted to chiefs of mission at Kuibyshev. All men seem to be in excellent mental and physical condition. It is stated that their only complaint is that they are urged to eat and drink too much. . . .[6]

York and his crew stayed at Penza until August, 1942, and then were moved to Okhansk, a small village eighty miles south of Molotov, where they remained for the next eight months. About four months after their arrival in Okhansk, the "companions" were withdrawn and the five men lived by themselves with Mike acting as occasional interpreter and go-between with the local Russian authorities.

Ambassador Standley with an entourage that included Michela, now a brigadier general, and the same Mr. Page, visited the crew at Okhansk, bringing them mail and news of the outside world. On September 13, he wired the State Department that the men were "found to be comfortably housed, adequately fed, in good health and generally well cared-for" and that their principal concern was the welfare of their families. Emmens learned that Justine had had a boy one month after the raid; York was told that he had been promoted to major but had no news about Mary Elizabeth and whether or not he was a father yet.

Although the men were generally in good health, the boredom began to grow on them. They pleaded for something useful to do. On November 6, a formal request was sent by

Crew No. 9 (Plane No. 40-2303): *from left to right*, Lt. Thomas C. Griffin (Navigator); Lt. Harold F. Watson (Pilot); T. Sgt. Eldred V. Scott (Engineer–Gunner); Lt. James M. Parker (Co-Pilot); Sgt. Wayne M. Bissell (Bombardier). (Air Force Photo)

中國時事照片
悪虐無道空襲帝國本土之美機
依据軍法断然加以嚴罰

Photographs of the crew of Lt. William G. Farrow taken after their capture were used for Japanese propaganda purposes. The circular shown above was spread throughout occupied China. The text, in Chinese, reads: "The cruel, inhuman, and beastlike American pilots who, in a bold intrusion of the holy territory of the Empire on April 18, 1942, dropped incendiaries and bombs on nonmilitary hospitals, schools, and private houses, and even dive-strafed playing schoolchildren, were captured, court-martialed, and severely punished according to military law." *Front row:* Cpl. Jacob D. DeShazer and Sgt. Harold A. Spatz. *Rear row:* Lts. William G. Farrow, George Barr, and Robert L. Hite. Farrow and Spatz were executed by firing squad after a mock trial. The other three, given life sentences, survived forty months of torture and imprisonment. DeShazer returned to Japan after the war as a missionary. (Air Force Photo)

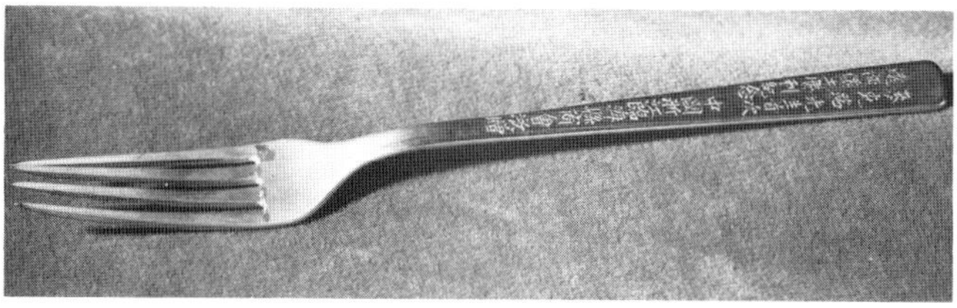

This inscribed fork, given to Lt. Charles L. McClure, is typical of the many gifts presented to Doolittle's raiders by grateful Chinese. The inscription reads: "In remembrance of Mr. Mai K'e Lu's [McClure's] first long-range attack and victory over Japan [Dwarf Land]. Respectfully presented by the Business Association of Linhai, Chekiang Province, China." (Photo by Guy R. Dyke)

Crew No. 10 (Plane No. 40-2250): *from left to right*, Lt. Horace E. Crouch (Navigator–Bombardier); Lt. Richard O. Joyce (Pilot); unidentified; Lt. J. Royden Stork (Co-Pilot); Sgt. George E. Larkin, Jr. (Engineer). The fifth member of this crew was the gunner, S. Sgt. Edwin W. Horton (*inset*), who was substituted at the last moment because of his expertise with gun turrets, a constant source of trouble. Surviving raiders are unable to identify the man in the center who did not go on the mission. (Air Force Photo)

Madame Chiang Kai Shek presented Chinese medals to all of Doolittle's raiders who arrived at Chungking. Shown here before the ceremony are Lt. Col. James H. Doolittle, Maj. John A. Hilger, and Lt. Richard E. Cole. (Air Force Photo)

As the raiders were making their way to Chungking, the Japanese searched for them continually. During the many air raids on the nearby airfield, Doolittle and his men stayed in this air-raid shelter carved out of the mountainside.

Crew No. 11 (Plane No. 40-2249): *from left to right*, Lt. Frank A. Kappeler (Navigator); Capt. C. Ross Greening (Pilot); Sgt. Melvin J. Gardner (Engineer–Gunner); Lt. Kenneth E. Reddy (Co-Pilot); S. Sgt. William L. Birch (Bombardier). (Air Force Photo)

Crew No. 12 (Plane No. 40-2278): *from left to right*, Lt. William R. Pound, Jr. (Navigator); Lt. William M. Bower (Pilot); S. Sgt. Omer A. Duquette (Engineer–Gunner); Lt. Thadd H. Blanton (Co-Pilot); T. Sgt. Waldo J. Bither (Bombardier). (Air Force Photo)

After the raid, Doolittle was promoted to brigadier general, skipping the rank of colonel. He was later decorated with the Medal of Honor by Franklin D. Roosevelt in a surprise White House ceremony. Looking on is Lt. Gen. Henry H. Arnold, Chief of the Army Air Forces, Mrs. Doolittle, and Gen. George C. Marshall, Army Chief of Staff. (Air Force Photo)

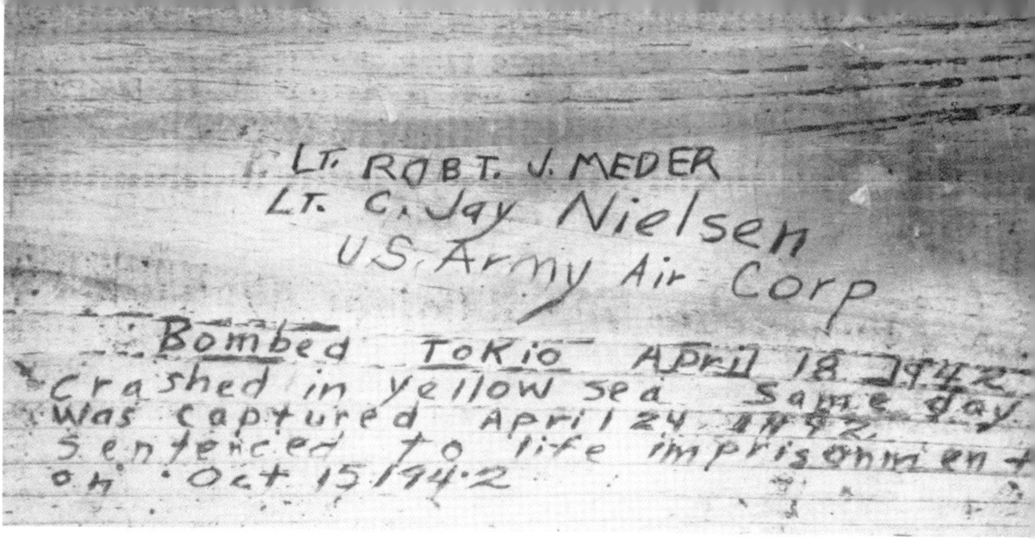
LT. ROBT. J. MEDER
LT. C. Jay Nielsen
U.S. Army Air Corp
Bombed ToKio April 18 1942
Crashed in yellow sea same day
Was captured April 24 1942
Sentenced to life imprisonment
on Oct 15 1942

This photo shows a section of flooring removed from the cell of Lt. Chase J. Nielsen for use as evidence at the 1946 war crimes trials. Nielsen made the inscription with a nail "so that if we died or were later executed, some record would be left behind as to where we had been and what happened." Nielsen returned to China to testify against the Japanese. (Air Force Photo)

Crew No. 13 (Plane No. 40-2247): *from left to right*, Lt. Clayton J. Campbell (Navigator); Lt. Edgar E. McElroy (Pilot); Sgt. Adam R. Williams (Engineer–Gunner); Lt. Richard A. Knobloch (Co-Pilot); Sgt. Robert C. Bourgeois (Bombardier). (Air Force Pilot)

Crew No. 14 (Plane No. 40-2297): *from left to right*, Lt. James H. Macia (Navigator–Bombardier); Maj. John A. Hilger (Pilot); S. Sgt. Jacob Eierman (Engineer); Lt. Jack A. Sims (Co-Pilot); S. Sgt. Edwin V. Bain (Gunner). (Air Force Photo)

Each year, Doolittle's raiders hold a reunion. These silver goblets are taken to the reunion site and used for toasts to the crew members who are no longer living. These men are represented by the cups that have been turned down. The last two surviving members will open the bottle of brandy and drink a final toast. Between reunions the goblets, presented by the City of Tucson, are on display at the Air Force Academy Museum, Colorado Springs, Colorado. (Air Force Photo)

Jimmy Doolittle and some of his raiders held an informal reunion in a farmhouse in North Africa on the first anniversary of their historic mission. Four raiders became prisoners of the Germans. (Air Force Photo)

Crew No. 15 (Plane No. 40-2267): *from left to right*, Lt. Howard A. Sessler (Navigator–Bombardier); Lt. Donald G. Smith (Pilot); Lt. (Dr.) Thomas R. White (Gunner); Lt. Griffith P. Williams (Co-Pilot); Sgt. Edward J. Saylor (Engineer). (Air Force Photo)

Crew No. 16 (Plane No. 40-2268): *from left to right*, Lt. George Barr (Navigator); Lt. William G. Farrow (Pilot); Sgt. Harold A. Spatz (Engineer–Gunner); Lt. Robert L. Hite (Co-Pilot); Cpl. Jacob D. DeShazer (Bombardier). (Air Force Photo)

Three of the four survivors are shown as they arrived at Chungking after release from forty months of imprisonment. *From left to right*, Lt. Robert L. Hite, Cpl. Jacob D. DeShazer, and Lt. Chase J. Nielsen. Lt. George Barr, the fourth survivor of the eight captured, was too ill to be moved and was returned to the States several weeks later. All had been sentenced to life imprisonment and were not to be released even if Japan lost the war. (Air Force Photo)

Three people pose by small crosses in the same manner as the three Doolittle raiders who were executed by firing squad. This photo, taken at Kiangwan Cemetery, Shanghai, was used as evidence at the 1946 war crimes trials. (Air Force Photo)

Maj. Gen. Follet Bradley, on special assignment in Moscow, to the Pentagon recommending that the secretary of war "direct Amembassy Moscow arrange with Soviet authorities permit Maj. York and crew . . . to participate in useful professional work. They have not been asked nor have they given their paroles which would be necessary if they are permitted to fly. They are most anxious to work and I believe would give necessary paroles. If official request is made to Soviets I believe they would comply."[7]

While waiting for word from Washington, the five airmen were allowed free run of the village of Okhansk, which wasn't much of a privilege. The people were wretchedly poor, food was scarce, and the luxuries of life were nonexistent. They had no soap, tobacco, matches, or even the barest of extras. Schools had been closed for the duration and there was only one newspaper for the entire population, which was posted in the center of town. There was only one radio, which had loudspeakers attached so that everyone could hear the news from Radio Moscow. The only fringe benefit was a motion picture theater, housed in an old barn, which showed propaganda films and, much to the delight of York's crew, old American films.

Time seemed to stand still for the internees. There was no reply from Washington to General Bradley's request. For the five, the days and nights ran together monotonously. They talked, slept, read and reread the magazines and letters they had received from the embassy visitors, and studied the Russian language using a Russian–English dictionary Mike had obtained for them from one of the local grade schools.

It required a major effort to study or take an interest in anything. They found themselves numbed as the days went by endlessly without any real contact with the outside world. After the New Year, they began to talk of escape as soon as the intense minus 50°F. weather subsided. On the off chance that they could make a plea for relief from their enforced idleness, Ski York suggested a bold initiative: write a letter to Premier Joseph Stalin. Emmens recalled drafting the letter:

> First we congratulated the Red Army on its great feats in its struggle with the Germans. Then we told of our "wonderful" treatment, but wished to point out that we were a

> liability to them, doing ourselves no good, and would like very much to be allowed to join American forces and continue the struggle against our common enemy. We likened our case to a hypothetical case of a German pilot bombing Russia and landing in Japan. We indicated that his probable treatment would be a dinner party given him by the Japs, and that he would probably be returned to Germany within forty-eight hours. We pointed out that we were familiar with international law, which technically bound us to internment, since the Soviet Union was not at war with Japan. But we stated that we felt that because of the length of time since the incident which landed us in the Soviet Union, our departure could be managed with a fair assurance of secrecy. Then we told him that in the event a clear way for our departure could not be seen, we would like to be moved to a warmer climate; that none of us had ever experienced such weather as the fifty below we had seen in Okhansk, and that we desired to be put to work.[8]

Mike, aghast at the idea of writing to Stalin, reluctantly translated the letter into Russian and promised to mail it. Emmens thought he would be afraid not to since it was addressed to the nation's leader. None of the five really expected to have a response to the letter, but it was a way to pass the time and nothing ventured, nothing gained. The Soviet bureaucracy moved in strange ways. Maybe someone up the hierarchy ladder would get the hint and do something for them.

On March 25, the unexpected *did* happen. Two Russian officers arrived and told them that their letter had been received at the headquarters of the Red Army in Moscow and that they were to be granted the second and third parts of their request; it would be impossible to grant the first part. Within an hour, they departed by automobile for Molotov, by plane to Chkolov, and then by train for eight days to Ashkhabad, not far from the Persian border. En route, they met an importer named Kolya, who made frequent trips to India, Afghanistan, Iraq, and Persia (now Iran) from his headquarters in Ashkhabad. Kolya spoke reasonably good English and was generous with food and drink, which, surprisingly, included Maxwell House coffee and Spam. He promised to try to do something for them during their stay. The meeting was to be fortuitous.

Upon arrival in Ashkhabad, the quintet noticed the distinctly different way people dressed. The majority wore the old-fashioned Turkish clothes, and most of the women were veiled. Emmens described what they saw as they were taken by auto to their new quarters:

> We drove up a long street toward the outskirts of the town. Back of us and to the right and left, there was not a hill to be seen. Land formed a straight line with the sky. But directly ahead of us, as we drove up the street—we were heading south—we could see the high mountains which form the natural boundary between the Soviet Union and Persia, now called Iran. In the section where we were driving there were rows and rows of low mud hovels. Mud fences about six feet high kept one from getting a view of the inside. But the roof of a tiny house was visible in each plot of ground bounded by fences. Each plot was about fifteen feet across the front, and appeared to be about one hundred feet in depth. They seemed all the same. In the corner nearest the street, just inside the fence, was the house. The roof was higher than the fence by about a foot.[9]

The mud house assigned to the five had only two rooms. The larger of the two had two beds, a table, and five wooden chairs. The smaller room, about six feet square, had three beds. The beds were iron cots, with iron springs. Each bed had one blanket; there were no sheets, pillows, or mattresses. In the back yard was a water faucet sticking up out of the ground, the group's water supply. At the back of the lot was a three-sided board screening with a two-by-eight board over a pit. There was no roof. This was their toilet.

Their morale sank as they inspected their new home away from home. An old man who spoke a little English was assigned to cook for them. A Russian officer was also assigned to check on them daily. The future seemed grim. However, true to the promise of the two officers who had escorted them to Ashkhabad, on April 10, 1943, nearly a year after the raid, they were given work permits, outfitted with baggy coveralls, and assigned to an aircraft overhaul shop for biwinged training planes. York and Emmens were put to work dismantling fuselages and tearing away old fabric from the frames. Herndon and Pohl cleaned instruments, while Laban, an experienced mechanic, worked on small engines. While doing useful work helped their morale, the urge to escape, which they had discussed many times, quickly returned.

On the evening of the second day, after the Russian officer had counted noses and the old man said he was going out for a couple of hours, Kolya, their new-found friend, knocked on the gate. Over the next weeks, Kolya met a number of times with the five, who continually expressed their desire to escape. After much coaxing by York and Emmens, Kolya finally said he would try to help them but pleaded with them not to try to cross the border on their own. "It is absolutely impossible," he told them. "The mountains are very high and very rough. They are for the most part inhabited by unfriendly tribes. The border is manned by Russian troops, dogs, mines, and barbed wire. You cannot do it alone. Do not try!"[10]

Kolya arranged for a border smuggler named Abdul Arram to have a clandestine meeting with Ski York. After intensive bargaining, Arram agreed to smuggle the five airmen across the border for $250 in U.S. currency, payable when they were assured of leaving. Fortunately, among themselves the five men had about $380, which gave them a cushion if they needed more for other arrangements.

After midnight on May 27, taking only a few essential articles and a little food, Arram and a driver took the quintet to the foothills near the border in an ancient truck, with the frightened airmen hiding under a tarpaulin in the back. After several hours, the truck left the road and stopped. A third individual, a Persian border runner, met them and, in the darkness, set off up the mountain on foot, over shale, loose rock, and gravel at a brisk pace with the five Americans gasping behind him. After about two hours of stumbling, running, and falling behind their guide, they were stopped suddenly at the crest of the mountain by their guide, who turned southward and said very softly, in Russian, "My Iran!"[11]

It was about 3:30 A.M. now and quite dark. The unknown guide led them to a truck and disappeared. Once more they hid under a tarpaulin while the driver inched his way down the mountain, still in Soviet territory, to a well-lighted wooden archway with a large picture of Stalin and a red star in the center—a Soviet road block. Emmens described what happened next:

> There was animated conversation between the driver, Abdul, and at least two other persons outside the truck. They were yelling at each other in typical Russian fashion. It was difficult to tell whether they were mad at each other or not. Then I heard footsteps coming around toward the back of the truck. I wished that I had covered my head entirely with the tarpaulin. But it was too late then. We didn't stir, scarcely breathed. Certainly the edge of the tarpaulin meeting a perfectly obvious cap with a bill on it would be a dead giveaway if anybody looked back there.
>
> All of a sudden I heard someone grab the edge of the truck close to my head. Almost immediately I was staring directly into a face a bare twelve inches above mine. There was a growth of stubble on the face, and a fur cap with a red star on it above the face. I closed my eyes and stopped breathing. Another movement outside—I opened my eyes again, and the head was gone. I exhaled and drew in another breath and held it. There was more wild talking from the front of the cab, then a squeaking noise as I saw a wooden guardrail rise above the front of the cab of the truck at an angle from the ground. The truck started to move again. Slowly the guardrail, the arch, Stalin, and the red star passed over our heads and behind us. I began to breathe again.[12]

There were more roadblocks ahead, mostly guarded by uniformed women, but the truck was allowed to pass each time. It was just dawn when Abdul stopped the truck with the men hiding in back bruised and battered. He motioned for them to get out, threw their bags down, and demanded his money. He pointed to Meshhed, their destination, still about a mile away. Ski York protested that the deal was to take them all the way to Meshhed.

"No! Impossible. Guards—Russians," he answered. "Now give—money!"[13]

Since he was probably armed, York didn't argue and handed over the wad of bills. Abdul, without counting, stuffed the wad in his pocket and turned the truck back north. There was now only a single Russian sentry stationed on a bridge between them and freedom. York and Emmens decided to go by themselves and try to get by the sentry. If successful, they would then locate the British consulate, using the map Kolya had drawn for them. The other three would wait and if no help was forthcoming within two hours, they would be on their own. Looking like tramps in their Russian clothes, York and Emmens joined a group of natives who were not stopped walking through the checkpoint and made their way to the British consulate.

The vice consul, incredulous that the Americans had escaped, sent a lorry to the spot where Herndon, Laban, and Pohl were hiding. They were taken through the checkpoint without being stopped by the Russian guard. The relief and happiness at being back on the other side of the Soviet border was almost mind-boggling to the five airmen.

The five relieved Americans were not yet in safe hands, however. The American ambassador to Teheran requested the British consul to assist in getting the group close to the Afghanistan border and into northern India, now Pakistan. The trip from Meshhed to Qetta took five days. Emmens recalled:

> We rode in a lorry with Persian soldiers for guards, were delayed one day because Kurdish tribes had raided a Persian village, took the women and girls, and murdered the males. Our driver ran the border and crashed through the guard rail into India. The Indian soldiers departed, and British soldiers then took us in a station wagon to Qetta on the eastern border of what is now Pakistan. An American C-47 airlifted us to Karachi. A four-engine military troop transport plane carried us to the States via Khartoum, Accra, and Belem.[14]

Because of their special status as escapees from a neutral country, the five men were told not to reveal to anyone where they had been and they were instructed that they were not to be separated en route. They were whisked to Washington, where they underwent interrogations for about two weeks by representatives of the army, navy, army air forces, marines, OSS, Coast and Geodetic Survey, and State Department, and then were flown to Dayton, Ohio, for questioning by military map-makers.

"I can recall our stating in our interrogations that the Russians were anything but our Allies," Emmens said.

> There were officers up to the rank of general who said, in effect, "These young punks don't know what they're talking about—the Russians are the greatest allies we've ever had!"[15]

While their treatment, bad as it was, could not be compared with that received by the eight men imprisoned by the Japanese, it had a lasting effect on York and his crewmates. They were among the first Americans to realize that the citizens of the Soviet Union were as Bob Emmens expressed it, "controlled by terror and violence, nurtured on fear and suspicion." He was one of the first Americans in uniform to warn his countrymen about the Soviet brand of communism through publication in 1949 of a book entitled *Guests of the Kremlin*. He warned that "communism, like a malignant scab on the skin of the world, is spreading north, south, east, and west. FIGHT IT!"[16]

12

Forty Months of Hell

The three survivors of the crew of the sixth plane off the carrier—Dean Hallmark, Bob Meder, and Chase Nielsen—were handed over to the Japanese by the Chinese guerrillas, tied up, and marched out of town. As they moved away, a Japanese officer pushed and shoved the three reluctant prisoners. It was more than Nielsen could take.

"I was a little agitated to find we were in Japanese hands," he said, "and, quite naturally, did not think we had much longer to live." He lashed out in fury at the officer but missed. His reward was a vicious kick on his left shin, which opened a nasty wound. Shin-kicking, the prisoners were to discover, was the favorite counterblow administered to all prisoners.

The three men were taken to a jail near the airport in Shanghai and placed in solitary confinement. "The Japanese took me out of my cell about three o'clock in the afternoon of April 24," Nielsen recalled, "and started questioning me about our mission through an interpreter. I gave them my name, rank, and serial number, and told them that was all the information I was going to give.

"The first thing they did was to put pencils between my fingers, squeezing my hands and forcing the pencils up and down causing the skin to break."[1] When he wouldn't talk, Nielsen was stretched out on the floor and given the infamous "water cure." Four soldiers sat on his arms and legs while a fifth placed a wet towel over his face and poured water on it. Every time he gasped for breath, more water was poured on the towel, which had the effect of drowning him.

The more they tortured, the more Nielsen was determined he was not going to talk. His resolution caused him to be subjected to another favorite Oriental torture. A bamboo stick about three feet long and two inches in diameter was placed behind his knees and he was forced to kneel and sit back as far as he could. One of the soldiers held him in this position while another jumped up and down on his thighs. Excruciating as it was, Nielsen still didn't give in to their questions.

The Japanese officers seemed to tire and the interpreter told Nielsen, "If you insist on not telling us anything we might as well finish the job right away. You will face a firing squad for execution immediately." The blindfold was replaced and Nielsen was led from the room.

"Outside the sun was warm and pleasant on my face," Nielsen recalled.

> We seemed to be walking on a gravel path. The soldiers kept a tight grip on my arms but said nothing. My mind was in a whirl and I couldn't think straight. When we were in the Chinese garrison before the Japs captured us, Hallmark, Meder, and I had talked about the possibility of execution. We had told each other that they would surely kill us, but we really didn't believe it. Now it began to dawn on me that the Japs were perfectly capable of doing it and that they could easily get away with it. It's awful hard to understand that you are about to die, especially when you are not conscious of having done anything wrong. I didn't feel any fear then, just a numbness in my body and an empty feeling in my stomach.
>
> As we marched along I became aware that several men were marching behind me. I could hear the cadence of their steps and I knew they were soldiers. This is the firing squad, I thought, and my heart seemed to turn over and stop. My throat felt dry. I wanted to say something—ask a question, but I knew the soldiers wouldn't understand me and probably wouldn't answer if they did. We had marched about a thousand feet when I heard a gutteral command and the men behind me halted. I heard their rifle butts hit the gravel path. I was marched along a few feet farther and then brought to a halt.
>
> They turned me so that my back was squarely to the squad behind me. The blindfold was still on and I couldn't see what was in front of me. The sweat was pouring down my face and neck now. I wanted desperately to wipe my face but my hands were handcuffed and tied behind me. I heard another gutteral command and I thought I could hear the noise of the rifles being raised to firing position.

> I began to feel weak and nauseated. I thought my heart was actually going to stop. Then I heard another command followed by the sound of marching feet. The interpreter then laughed.
>
> "Well, well, well," he said. "We are the Knights of Bushido. We do not execute men at sunset—only at sunrise. It's now sunset so your execution will take place in the morning. We will shoot you then unless you decide to talk in the meantime."[2]

Nielsen was marched back to his cell but the torture was not over. About an hour later, three husky guards entered his cell. "They examined the handcuffs and the chain between them," Nielsen said.

> "Then they pushed me over to a wall and raised my arms above my head. There was a stout wooden peg in the wall that I hadn't noticed before. They boosted me up and hung me on the peg by the chain of the handcuffs. When they let go my toes just barely touched the floor but not enough to ease the strain on my arms.
>
> In a few minutes, the pain in my wrists was so intense that I was almost sick to my stomach. Then stabs of pain began to shoot in my chest and shoulders and my left arm that had been injured in the airplane crash was swollen and looked like it was getting blood poison in it. I don't know how long I hung there before I passed out.[3]

Nielsen was taken down about 6:00 the next morning and had difficulty standing. He had no use of his arms: "I thought they would drop off when I lowered them. They merely hung down and I couldn't move them."

Nielsen was led to a room where Meder and Hallmark were waiting, disheveled, bruised, and grim. They had received the same treatment but they had also resisted the interrogations. The three officers were then moved to another jail on April 24 and again tortured throughout the night. On the twenty-fifth, handcuffed, blindfolded, and tied to individual seats, they were flown to Tokyo in a transport plane.

Meanwhile, Lt. Bill Farrow, the tall, lanky pilot of the last plane, and his crew consisting of Lts. Bob Hite and George Barr, Sgt. Harold Spatz and Col. Jacob DeShazer, had been captured near Nanchang, given the same crippling tortures as the others—water cure, finger-squeezing, and knee beating—and flown to Tokyo on the twentieth.

The eight airmen were held in Tokyo for about forty-six days—all but the last four days in solitary confinement. The Japanese gendarmerie, experts in torture methods, questioned them day and night for hours at a time, trying to force information about the mission out of them. They were beaten, slapped, kicked, starved, and not permitted to wash, shave, or remove their clothing, and were kept in leg irons all this time. For the first eighteen days all eight successfully resisted answering vital questions and only made replies concerning their personal lives. This was not enough for the Japanese, who finally showed them maps and charts that had been recovered from one of the crashed planes in China. It was then they knew the tortures had been needless. The Japanese had pieced together all the important details such as the targets, the training they had received, and the departure from an aircraft carrier.

On May 22, the eight prisoners were forced to sign papers written in Japanese, which they were told contained only statements about their personal lives. What they signed were actually false confessions about their "crimes" and admissions that they had strafed and bombed only schools and hospitals instead of military targets. Following are excerpts from the translated 7330 Noboro Unit Military Police Report No. 352 which alleged to be the official transcript of each prisoner's interrogation:

> *Q.* Did you do any strafing while getting away from Nagoya?
>
> *Hite:* Heretofore, I haven't revealed any information on this point, but the truth is that about five to six minutes after leaving the city we saw in the distance what looked like an elementary school with many children at play. The pilot steadily dropped altitude and ordered the gunmen to their stations. When the plane was at an oblique angle, the skipper gave firing orders, and bursts of machine gun fire sprayed the ground.

> *Q.* While heading out to sea from Nagoya, didn't you strafe children of an elementary school?
>
> *Farrow:* There is truly no excuse for this. I have made no

mention of this before, but after leaving Nagoya, I do not quite remember the place—there was a place which looked like a school, with many people there. As parting shot, with a feeling of "damn these Japs," I made a power dive and carried out some strafing. There was absolutely no defensive fire from below.

Q. What are you thinking of after killing and wounding so many innocent people?

Hallmark: Since it was our intention to bomb Tokyo and escape to China quickly, we also dropped bombs over objectives other than those targets specified, and made a hasty escape. Therefore, we also bombed residential homes, killing and wounding many people.

Q. After the bombing of Nagoya, did you not actually carry out strafing?

Spatz: It was an extremely inexcusable deed. Shortly after leaving Nagoya, while flying southward along the coast, the pilot immediately upon perceiving a school, steadily reduced altitude and ordered us to our stations. I aimed at the children in the school yard and fired only one burst before we headed out to sea. My feelings at that time were "damn these Japs" and I wanted to give them a burst of fire. Now I clearly see that this was truly unpardonable and in all decency should not have been committed.

Q. Even if you were instructed by the pilot to drop the bomb properly, didn't you, as the bombardier, think that in the name of humanity you shouldn't have bombed innocent civilians?

DeShazer: With our technique and methods used in that air attack such things, even if we thought about them, would have been impossible.

Q. State the conditions at the time of the bombing.

Nielsen: At that time I was mainly observing the situation outside from the windows. At an altitude of 1,500 meters, as soon as we crossed the Noka River in the northeast part of Tokyo, the pilot frantically ordered the bombing. In general the main objective was the factories but with such a bombing method, I believed we missed completely.

> *Q.* You not only bombed the factories but you also bombed homes of innocent civilians and killed many people. What are your reactions in that respect?
>
> *Meder:* It is natural that dropping bombs on a crowded place like Tokyo will cause damage in the vicinity of the target. All the more so with our technique of dropping bombs while making a hit-and-run attack, so I believe it was strictly unavoidable. Moreover, Colonel Doolittle never did order us to avoid such bombings and neither were we particularly worried about the possible damages.
>
> *Q.* Did you not strafe an elementary school while headed out to sea after the Nagoya raid?
>
> *Barr:* I am quite sure that was done. Only when the pilot steadily dropped altitude and the strafing was executed was I aware of it.[4]

On June 18, the eight fliers were handcuffed in pairs and sent by train to Nagasaki; from there they returned by ship to Shanghai and put in a cell with fourteen Chinese prisoners at Bridge House, a small apartment building converted into a jail by the Japanese.

"We remained in the Bridge House for 70 days," Bob Hite said in a deposition after his release in 1945.

> The Chinese in our cell were removed a few days after we arrived, and for the rest of the time the eight of us were in the cell together. Here we were particularly troubled by the conditions of our imprisonment. We were bothered by bugs, rats, and lice which bit us continually until finally our faces and hands swelled out of proportion from the bites. We slept on the floor with one blanket to each man. Our only sanitary facility was a small bucket in the corner of the cell called a "benjo" which was emptied periodically, usually only after we complained because it was overflowing.
>
> For the first 120 days after we were captured none of us was given the opportunity to shave or bathe. We received three meals daily. For breakfast we received about one-half pint of wormy, watery rice. For lunch and dinner we were generally given some bread which usually amounted to about five ounces. We were given one-half cup of water per man per day.
>
> While we were in Bridge House we were not permitted to

> leave the cell for exercise. Usually we were forced to sit cross-legged and motionless on the floor facing the door of the cell. We were not permitted to talk or move during the whole day. There was a light in the ceiling which was left burning 24 hours a day and made it difficult for us to sleep.[5]

On August 28, the eight weakened men were transferred to Kiangwan Military Prison, several miles outside Shanghai, a top security facility under the jurisdiction of the Japanese Expeditionary Army in China. By this time all eight had dysentery and were in the first stages of beriberi. Hallmark was by far the sickest of all. He was so weak that he could not stand by himself and had to be transported to Kiangwan on a stretcher.

When they arrived at Kiangwan, the eight bedraggled Americans were brought before an assembly of about ten Japanese officers. Hallmark, still on a stretcher, was placed on the floor while the others stood. Five Japanese officers sat on a raised platform. There was the solemn atmosphere of a courtroom as the five stared down stonily at the eight captives.

After a few seconds of silence, the Japanese in the center of the five nodded to a short man standing at the side of the room. He was Caesar Luis dos Remedios, a half-Portuguese, half-Japanese who had been sentenced to seven years imprisonment for spying. Since he could speak Chinese and English as well as Portuguese and Japanese, he was used as an interpreter by his captors.

Remedios stepped toward the men and began questioning them about their life histories. "This was translated to the Court after which some conversation ensued in Japanese," Hite said. "When we realized that this was a trial of some sort, we asked for a translation but this was refused. We were not told what the charges against us were or what our sentences were. No interpretation was made to us of any part of the proceedings."[6]

When the mock trial was over, one of the Japanese stood up and read from a manuscript in Japanese, which Remedios did not translate. The seven standing prisoners were then led off to solitary confinement in five-by-nine-foot cells. Hallmark, delirious and too weak to take any interest in what was going on, was carried out and taken back to Bridge House, where he was put in a cell with about twenty Chinese, one Japanese, and a

Russian named Alexander Hindrava. Hindrava could speak a little English and had been sentenced to prison for three years, presumably for spying, but he wasn't sure since he spoke no Japanese and had not been allowed a translation of his trial proceedings. At the war crimes trials after the war, he testified that Hallmark and the others received only an ounce of rice, four ounces of some kind of punch, and three ounces of water for breakfast, and four ounces of bread or rice and a little fish at noon. Three times a week they received a soup made from water in which vegetables had been washed.

Hallmark could not improve under these conditions and was near death. Meanwhile, back at Kiangwan, the seven others were kept in solitary confinement for twenty days and then permitted to exercise outside for a few minutes each day. They were now fed a bowl of rice and some soup three times a day. Chase Nielsen described their days as "Get up at 6:00 A.M. Breakfast at 8:00. Exercise with a guard between 10:30 and 11:00. Lunch at 12:00. Supper at 5:00 P.M. Bed at 9:30. The rest of the time we had nothing to do and nothing is the hardest thing in the world to do."[7]

Prior to their mock trial on August 28, a curious rationalization had taken place to determine the fate of the eight Americans. A draft of a law concerning the punishment of captured enemy airmen had been sent in July from the Japanese War Ministry in Tokyo to the headquarters of the China Expeditionary Forces in Nanking with instructions for the latter to "establish" the law. At the same time, the Thirteenth Japanese Army was ordered to defer its trial of the eight Americans until the new military law had been enacted. Gen. Shunroku Hata, supreme commander at Nanking, "established" the Enemy Airmen's Act officially on August 13, 1942, and issued it to the Thirteenth Army.

This law, to take effect immediately, was to be applicable to all enemy airmen raiding Japanese territories. It explained that anyone who participated in the bombing or strafing of nonmilitary targets or in any other violation of international law would be sentenced to death. "Should the circumstances warrant," the Act stated, "this sentence may be commuted to life imprisonment, or a term of imprisonment for not less than ten years."

As soon as the act was published, a staff officer was sent to China to give instructions regarding the trial of the eight Doolittle raiders and to demand that General Hata have the prosecutor require the death sentence. Thus, the mock trial for the eight was held on August 28, but their guilt and the death penalty had already been prescribed.

A record of the trial, found after the war, showed that the defendants "have been found guilty as charged, and are hereby sentenced to death." Under the "reasons for the sentence" the defendants were said to have arrived over their respective targets and "suddenly exhibited cowardice when confronted with opposition in the air and on the ground, and with the intent of cowing, killing, and wounding innocent civilians, and wreaking havoc on residences and other living quarters of no military significance whatsoever . . . did carry on indiscriminate bombing and strafing. . . ."[8] This record, dated August 28, was signed by Lt. Col. Toyama Kakajo, chief judge, Lt. Yusei Wako, and Lt. Ryuhei Okada of the 7330 Nōboro Unit Military Tribunal, and forwarded to Tokyo.

The fate of the eight was sealed in Tokyo by October 10, when General Sugiyama, chief of the staff of the Grand Imperial Headquarters, approved a message to China that approved death sentences for Hallmark, Farrow, and Spatz. The death sentences for the other five were reduced to life imprisonment. "As war criminals," the message stated, "their treatment shall not be that accorded ordinary prisoners of war (and) even in the event of an exchange of war prisoners they may not be repatriated to the United States forces."[9]

The date of execution of the three was set for October 15, 1942. In passing on the decision to spare the other five to Gen. Sadamu Shimomura, commander of the Thirteenth Army, General Hata instructed that, "in making this announcement to the convicted men, special mention must be made of the Emperor's leniency."[10] No reasons were ever given why the death sentences were imposed on the two pilots and one engineer–gunner and not any of the others. The only rationale could be the false "confessions" made in Tokyo while they were being tortured.

On the afternoon of October 14, Dean Hallmark, unable to walk alone, was brought to Kiangwan and placed in a cell by himself. That evening Hallmark, Farrow, and Spatz were told that they had been sentenced to death and would be executed next day. They were given paper and pencils and told through interpreter Remedios that they could write letters to their friends and relatives. In testimony at the war crimes trials after the war, Remedios described what happened:

> On October 14, 1942, I was instructed by Sergeant Sotojiro Tatsuta [later Captain] to have Lieutenant Farrow, Lieutenant Hallmark, and Sergeant Spatz sign their names on two blank sheets of white paper. One page was signed by each of them in the middle of the sheet, and the other page was signed at the bottom. They asked me why they were made to sign these papers. Tatsuta told me they were signing these as a receipt for their belongings and that he would fill in the rest in Japanese later on.
>
> Later Tatsuta gave each two sheets of paper, one on which to write a letter to their family, which he said he would send through the Red Cross; and the other sheet was to be used to describe the treatment they received by the Japanese while they were confined. At that time I didn't know what the Japanese were going to do to these airmen. The fliers asked me what they should write. My opinion was to give a little "top hat" for the Japanese, so that they would be given good treatment later on. I didn't read the letters, but gave them to Sergeant Tatsuta early the next morning.[11]

The letters, later introduced as evidence during the 1946 war crimes trials, were poignant farewell messages to their loved ones.

Dean Hallmark wrote to his mother and sister in Dallas, Texas:[12] "I hardly know what to say. They have just told me that I am liable to execution. I can hardly believe it . . . I am a prisoner of war and I thought I would be taken care of until the end of the war . . . I did everything that the Japanese have asked me to do and tried to cooperate with them because I knew that my part in the war was over." He asked his mother to "try to stand up under this and pray."

Harold Spatz wrote to his widower father in Lebo, Kansas, saying that he had nothing to leave him but his clothes. "If I have inherited anything since I became of age," he wrote, "I will give it you, and Dad, I want you to know that I love you and may God bless you." Then he added, "I want you to know that I died fighting for my country like a soldier."

Lt. Bill Farrow, the twenty-three-year-old pilot from Darlington, South Carolina, wrote to his widowed mother: "Don't let this get you down. Just remember that God will make everything right, and that I will see you again in the hereafter."

In a separate letter to his fiancé, Farrow wrote that "you are, to me, the only girl that would have meant the completion of my life" and thanked her "for bringing to my life a deep, rich love for a fine girl." He added, "Please write and comfort Mom, because she will need you—she loves you, and thinks you are a fine girl. . . ."

The orders to execute Hallmark, Farrow, and Spatz specified they were to be shot by firing squad on the afternoon of October 15 with proper military ceremony. That morning, at Public Cemetery No. 1 outside Shanghai, Tomoichi Yoneya headed a detail to erect three small wooden crosses made at the regimental carpenter shop the night before. Shigeji Mayama, one of the detail, cut the grass in the vicinity of the execution ground and helped erect the crosses. A small table was placed nearby to serve as a ceremonial altar.

At half past four, the three Americans were brought to the cemetery under heavy guard in three separate trucks. They were led to the crosses, turned around, and placed on their knees; their arms were tied in two places to each cross. White blindfolds were placed over their eyes and a black ink mark was put on the cloth directly over the center of their foreheads.

While these preparations were being made, a firing squad of six men marched into position in a double rank about twenty feet away. Two riflemen were assigned to each prisoner—one primary who would fire first, and a secondary in case the first missed or had a dud cartridge.

Other Japanese arrived. According to military custom, they were the prosecutor of the district in which the trial was held, Col. Akinobu Ito; prosecutor for the case against the accused, Maj. Itsuro Hata; warden of the military prison, Sgt. Sotojiro Tatsuta; and clerk of the court that tried the raiders, Chosei Jujita. Three medical officers, three members of the Shanghai Military Police Headquarters, and an interpreter were also present.

Lt. Goro Tashida, commander of the firing squad, posted four men as security guards around the cemetery. An incense burner was lighted on the altar table. The fifty-five-year-old Tatsuta, in his postwar trial testimony, described what happened when he arrived at the cemetery:

> Major Hata was looking after the execution preparations and I read the statement which was prepared by the prosecutor. . . .
>
> Then I told the fliers, "I do not know what relation I had with you in the previous life but we have been living together under the same roof and on this day you are going to be executed, but I feel sorry for you. My sympathies are with you. Men must die sooner or later. Your lives were very short but your names will remain everlastingly. I do not remember if this was Lt. Farrow but one of them said, "Thank you very much for all the trouble you have taken while we were in your confinement, but please tell the folks at home that we died very bravely." And I told them that "your ashes will be sent through the International Red Cross to your homes."
>
> I told them that Christ was born and died on the cross and you on your part must die on the cross but when you are executed—when you die on the cross you will be honored as Gods, and I told them to pray and they made a sign which resembled the sign of the cross and they prayed. I told them "you will soon be bound to the crosses and when this is done it is a fact that it is a form that man's faith and cross shall be united. Therefore, have faith." Then they smiled and said they understood very well. Then I asked them if they had any more to say and they said they had nothing more to say. That was all that was said.[13]

Hata, the prosecutor, and a medical officer spoke briefly with the trio through the interpreter. When Tatsuta was asked during the postwar trial if he thought Hata was sorry, he replied, "I believe so because he gave them the deepest bow at the end of his speech."

Tatsuta, the official in charge of the execution, nodded to Lieutenant Tashida, who turned to his firing squad.

"Attention! Face the target!" he commanded. The six riflemen turned toward the helpless men tied to the crosses.

"Prepare!"

The three soldiers in the front rank raised their rifles and aimed at the black marks on the blindfolds twenty feet away. Tashida raised his arm.

"Fire!" he shouted as he snapped his arm down. Three shots broke the afternoon stillness. Each of three bullets found their marks. Death was mercifully instantaneous; no second shots were necessary.

Tashida about-faced his squad and marched them away. The medical officers checked the pulse of each man and, finding none, bandaged the wounds. Three coffins, freshly made the night before, were brought up; the bodies were untied and placed inside. The coffins were carried to the altar and laid side by side. The assemblage stood on one side of the table and after a few moments of silent meditation, saluted the three coffins and departed.

The coffins were taken to the Japanese Residents Association Crematorium, where the bodies were cremated. The ashes were placed in small boxes and put on an altar at Kiangwan Prison. About a month later the boxes were removed and taken to the International Funeral Home in Shanghai where they remained until the end of the war. However, the names on the boxes were deliberately changed by unknown persons in an attempt to conceal the real identities. Fortunately, the record of the real and fictional names was found after the war and the ashes were returned to the States for interment in Arlington Cemetery.

In Kiangwan Prison, the remaining five prisoners were unaware that their buddies had been executed. Still in solitary confinement, each was trying to maintain his sanity against the loneliness and uncertainty. While Hallmark, Farrow, and Spatz were being executed, the other five were roused out of their cells and marched to the same room where they had been "tried" in August. Standing solemnly in a row, they were told in English that although they had been sentenced to death, Emperor Hirohito had mercifully commuted their sentences to life imprisonment "with special treatment." They were not told what "special treatment" meant nor what happened to the other three.

The days of deadly boredom in their cells continued for the survivors. Each man's health was now deteriorating rapidly. All were suffering from dysentery and malnutrition and were developing dropsy and beriberi from the lack of fruits and vegetables. On April 18, 1943, the first anniversary of their mission, the quintet was transferred to the military prison in Nanking.

While their strength slowly ebbed, their spirits were uplifted considerably when they were allowed to exercise together thirty minutes a day. Although the exercise in the sunlight helped, each was growing steadily weaker, and Bob Meder was the weakest of the five. Normally weighing about 175 pounds, he was now down to about 110. Although he always came out with the others each day, it was obvious he needed medical attention. As the spring passed into summer and late autumn, Meder looked like a walking skeleton. On December 1, 1943, the once sturdily built, athletic Meder died quietly in his cell.

The following deposition about Meder's death was taken from George Barr after the war:[14]

Q. Do you have any knowledge as to how much medical treatment was given to him?
A. Very little was given to him. A medical orderly came around with pills, approximately every three days.

Q. What is the source of your information as to the medical care that he received?
A. You could hear the cell doors open, and the medical orderly would stop at our cells when he came by.

Q. Did the men talk back and forth?
A. No, sir.

Q. Did you have tapping signals?
A. Yes, sir.

Q. Were you able to talk [by Morse code signals] to Lieutenant Meder?
A. No, sir. Lt. Chase J. Nielsen could talk to Lt. Robert J. Meder and I could talk to Lt. Chase J. Nielsen, and Lt. Robert J. Meder told Lt. Chase J. Nielsen that he wasn't being given medical care.

Q. Did Lieutenant Meder continue to exercise with the rest of you?
A. Yes, Sir. He even exercised the last day—the day of his death.

Q. Describe Lieutenant Meder's physical condition as you remember when he went out and took exercise on the day that he died.
A. I would say he was extremely thin. He was very weak but would not admit it.

Q. What exercises did Lieutenant Meder take that day?
A. Just light exercise. Arm exercises and body bending exercises.

Q. Did Lieutenant Meder take all the exercises that the rest of you took that day?
A. No, Sir. We used to run around for about five or ten minutes, but Lieutenant Meder would stand over in the corner of the yard and do arm exercises.

Q. When did you learn of his death?
A. At approximately 4:30 the day he died.

Q. Do you know the approximate time of his death?
A. Between two and four o'clock P.M.

Q. Who informed you of the death of Lieutenant Meder.
A. I happened to be out serving meals and when he didn't answer when I passed his meal in, the guard opened the door and there was no response from Lieutenant Meder and that was when we found out he was dead.

Meder's body lay in the cell for two days before being removed for cremation. His ashes were placed in a jar, which in turn was put in a cardboard box tied with string. The box was then placed in a cell across from Barr's and remained there until the men were later transferred to Peking. The medical report filled out by 1st Lt. Soshi Yasuharu certified that Meder's death was due to "heart failure resulting from beriberi and inflammation of the intestines."[15]

Meder's death caused a slight improvement in the diet of the four survivors. Their daily ration increased to two and one-half cups of rice and soup for breakfast, with occasional hot tea. Lunch consisted of more rice with occasional greens and half a fish. Supper included tea with rice curry spiced with occasional pieces of unidentifiable chopped meat.

The day's routine, however, was the same hour after hour of complete boredom, punctuated only with the short exercise periods and a once-a-week bath. There was no heat in the cells and their clothing was inadequate. They slept on straw mats on the floor with only one blanket each. However, after Meder died, a second blanket was issued. Strangely, none of them had any respiratory difficulties even though their resistance was low and it was cold enough to freeze water in the wash bowls outside. They believed this was due to the inoculations, including one against pneumonia, that Doc White had insisted each raider have before the raid.

Weeks became months and the seasons came and went monotonously. No reading material had been allowed, although they asked for something to read whenever a sympathetic guard who could speak a little English was on duty. Finally, because of Meder's death, a few books in English were provided. One of these was a Bible and its message provided the link to sanity each needed so desperately. As Nielsen said later, they suffered desperately from a "gnawing hunger in our heads and stomachs."[16]

Up to this time, each man resorted to various methods to pass away the hundreds of lonely hours. Nielsen tried building a house in his mind. Barr worked mentally on an elaborate neon sign while Hite planned a model farm down to the last fence post. DeShazer, son of an Oregon minister–farmer, recalled his childhood and composed poetry. While these mental exercises helped, it was the Bible, they admitted unanimously later, that had a profound impact on their respective outlooks. Each one of them read it every hour of daylight that he had it before passing it on to the next man.

None of the four men would have called himself religious and none had ever read the Bible through before. Between turns, they thought about the passages they had read and memorized them. The words took on a deep meaning and conveyed a new hope for their future.

The summer of 1944 turned out to be the hottest in Nanking's history. The cells were almost unbearable because there was no circulation of air. The cells' doors were of solid wood and there was only one small window in each cell. Bob Hite developed a high fever and was dangerously close to death. When the guards recognized that he might be dying, a medical assistant was sent to live in the prison and nurse him back to health. Under this kind of attention and with cooler weather, Hite recovered.

While the summer of 1944 was the hottest in Nanking's history, the winter of 1944–45 shared the opposite dubious honor. Snow fell on December 1 and stayed until March 1. Heavier clothes were issued to the prisoners and, as the winter became more severe, their own American uniforms were returned, which they put on over their prison garb—a small but important morale factor.

A high point in the long months of imprisonment was reached on Christmas day, 1944. Some strange fighter planes the prisoners could not identify roared over the prison headed for oil refineries and storage tanks nearby. Explosions followed, interspersed with machine gun fire. Black smoke billowed slowly up into the sky. Nanking had just been bombed by American planes!

The prisoners were beside themselves with joy. It shouldn't be long now before they would be released but weeks went by and no more planes came. On June 15, 1945, for some reason unknown to them, the four men were transferred hurriedly to Peking by train. En route they had their hands and legs tied with belts. Each man had a guard who hung on to a rope tied to his waist. A large green raincoat was thrown around each man and a hat placed on his head, with a mask attached that fell down over his face.

After three days of traveling by train, they arrived in Peking and were placed in solitary cells in an inner section of the Japanese military prison. Their treatment changed drastically from what it had come to be in Nanking. They were made to sit all day in their cells on small wooden stools made out of a two-by-four about eight inches long and were required to face the wall three feet away. Their spirits sagged as they stared at nothing for hours on end all day long and lay on their straw mats staring at nothing all night.

DeShazer now became the weakest of the four. Huge boils—he counted seventy-five at one time—broke out all over his body. He became delirious and couldn't sit on the stool. Since he was apparently near death from malnutrition, a Japanese medical officer finally gave him vitamin shots and his condition slowly improved. On August 9, 1945, DeShazer awakened in the morning to a voice that said, quietly, "Start praying." He describes what happened next:

> I asked, "What should I pray about?" Pray for peace and pray without ceasing, I was told. . . . I started to pray for peace although I had a very poor idea of what was taking place in the world at that time.
>
> About seven o'clock in the morning I began to pray. It seemed very easy to pray on the subject of peace. I prayed that God would put a great desire in the hearts of the Japanese leaders for peace. I thought about the days of peace that would follow, Japanese people would no doubt be discouraged, and I felt sympathetic toward them. I prayed that God would not allow them to fall into persecution by the victorious armies.
>
> At two o'clock in the afternoon, the Holy Spirit told me, "You don't need to pray any more. The victory is won." I was amazed. I thought this was quicker and better than the regular method of receiving world news. Probably this news broadcast had not come over the radio to America as yet. I thought I would just wait and see what was to happen.[17]

It was several days before DeShazer would know that August 9, 1945, was the day that the second atomic bomb had been dropped on Nagasaki and that the Japanese were considering complete surrender. The guards said nothing, but a few days later they appeared on duty wearing fresh uniforms and began breaking into their supply rooms. DeShazer knew that it would not be long before they were free men again. He was certain now that Japan had been defeated.

"I could not help wondering what would happen to Japan now," he said. "Their hopes had been set on victory. It would be an awful blow to suffer defeat. But, if the Japanese found out about Jesus, the military defeat to them would in reality be a great victory."

It was then that DeShazer heard the same voice tell him, "You are called to go and teach the Japanese people wherever I send you."

Ten days after DeShazer heard the voice tell him peace was at hand, a Japanese guard opened the cell doors of the four Americans and said, simply, "The war is over. You can go home now."[18]

The four dazed and weakened men were taken from their cells to the Peking Hotel where they were offered haircuts and shaves. While Hite, Nielsen, and DeShazer were able to walk, Barr had to be helped by the guards, now solicitous and friendly. It was then the four men learned that the war had actually ended on August 15.

From evidence revealed much later, it is certain that the Japanese did not intend that the Doolittle raiders were ever to be released. Their life sentences "with special treatment" meant that they were to be kept hidden in captivity for their daring mission against the Japanese homeland. When American parachute teams dropped into Peking to accept the surrender of all troops and release all POWs, the Japanese told the Americans that they had all been executed but American and Chinese intelligence had reported otherwise.

Within a few hours, Hite, Nielsen, and DeShazer, badly emaciated from their experience, were being interviewed by newsmen in Chungking and were soon en route back to the States. Their forty months of hell were over. It wasn't over for George Barr.

13

"Four Doolittle Raiders Located"

Light rain pelted T. Sgt. Nestor Jacot in the face as he tapped out a coded message on the portable high-frequency radio transmitter in Peking in August, 1945. Beside him S. Sgt. Dick Hamada vigorously turned the hand crank on the power generator. Around these two American soldiers stood a ring of Japanese soldiers watching the operation stoically.

"We're getting through to Hsian now," Jacot said, patting his head set. "Now I'll send the good news."[1]

The good news that Jacot sent to headquarters of the OSS (Office of Strategic Services) made world headlines next day:

> FOUR DOOLITTLE RAIDERS LOCATED IN MILITARY PRISON PEKING. NAMES ARE LT. GEORGE BARR, LT. ROBERT HITE, LT. CHASE NIELSEN AND CORPORAL JACOB DE SHAZER. BARR IN POOR CONDITION. OTHERS WEAK. WILL EVACUATE THESE MEN FIRST. ADVISE ETA OF AIRCRAFT.

The word traveled fast from Hsian to Kunming to Chungking. American war correspondents immediately flashed the story to the world that four missing members of Doolittle's Tokyo Raiders had been found alive. It was August 20, 1945.

The discovery of the four survivors of the April 1942, mission had been preceded by weeks of undercover forays by OSS teams of five and six men each, who had been traveling behind Japanese lines searching for prisoner-of-war camps. When the Japanese began to put out peace feelers toward the end of the war, it was not known what retaliation they might take against POWs. If the prisons were accurately located in time, the

Japanese might be prevented from killing the prisoners in a last gesture of defiance.

Col. William R. Peers, the OSS commander given responsibility for sending the teams behind enemy lines, organized them from among the highly trained veterans who had operated there previously. Some had parachuted into Japanese strongholds in the dead of night. Others, disguised as Chinese, walked right through the Japanese lines. Still others, some of Oriental descent, successfully bluffed their way into the enemy-held coastal cities. One Hawaiian-born Nisei had even arranged to have himself "commissioned" a Japanese captain, armed himself with fictitious orders, and made "routine" inspections of every Japanese POW camp in his area of penetration.

A three-man team was sent into the Peking area in the early spring of 1945 and located a large POW camp at Fengtai, about five miles outside Peking. They learned that more Americans were being held in a military jail inside the city. They made their way into Peking but couldn't get out. Each time they tried to leave the city their escape route was blocked by sentries who had been alerted to be on the lookout for American spies. They were incommunicado for nearly three months and virtual prisoners as they hid among friendly Chinese contacts.

The identity of these three men, how they obtained information, and how they eventually escaped from a city teeming with thousands of armed Japanese must remain a secret even now. Suffice it to say that three brave men were able to report on August 6, 1945, that American prisoners were confined in Prison #1407. Their report, code-named "Magpie Mission," gave the size of the cells, the furnishings in each cell, and the daily routine of the prisoners.

Three days later, after the second atomic bomb was dropped on Nagasaki, Maj. Ray A. Nichol, a tall, impressive Alabaman; Lt. Mahlon Perkins; Sgt. Richard Hamada, interpreter; Sgt. Nestor Jacot, radioman; Pvt. Melvin Richter; and Dr. (Lt.) Fontaine G. Jarman were assigned to liberate the Americans at Fengtai and inside Peking. Dr. Jarman recounted the adventure that followed:

> We were briefed that Colonel Devereux, the senior Marine officer and Commander W.S. Cunningham, commander of

Wake Island, were still alive and probably located in a heavily guarded prison inside the city.

We flew from Kunming to Chungking and then Hsian on August thirteenth. At noon on the seventeenth, the six of us were loaded aboard a B-24 which had the belly turret removed. Our destination was a small Japanese fighter strip outside Peking.

The weather was perfect—hot, sunny, and beautiful. We arrived over Peking fully expecting to be met by swarms of Kamikaze fighters foresworn to knock us down and make the supreme sacrifice doing so. There were no other planes in the air. We circled slowly while the B-24 crew members threw thousands of leaflets out which told the Japanese that the war was over and that they were not to harm the American troops that were coming to accept their surrender.

When the last leaflet was gone, the pilot circled the airfield where we were supposed to make our jump. The idea of the jump didn't scare me because I had qualified as a paratrooper in the States. But I was surprised to learn that Major Nichol was the only other member of our party who had ever jumped before and he had only one jump to his credit.

We made one pass over the field. Down below I could see hundreds of Jap soldiers scurrying to take up positions around the field. We were low enough so that I could see they were all armed with rifles and pistols. I was praying that they had all gotten the word to quit but I had no way of knowing and it worried me to see them all running with no indication that they intended to give up their weapons and surrender. When I started to go, there wasn't a soldier in sight.[2]

One by one, the six-man OSS team jumped and landed in a line across the open field. They unhooked their chute harnesses and gathered in the yards of silk. Dr. Jarman described the events that followed:

I started walking slowly across the field toward what looked like an administration building about six hundred yards away. I looked back and saw that the others in my party had all landed safely so I thought that if we walked foward singly that we would present smaller targets than if we all gathered in a group. The plane circled once more, dropped our equipment and supplies, and then departed. An almost overwhelming feeling of desolation swept over me as the B-24 faded away.

The equipment I carried seemed like a strange assortment for such a mission but it all had a purpose. I had three pistols, a carton of cigarettes, a pair of swimming trunks, and $10,000 in American cash. Each of us had the same amount except for Major Nichol, who carried $50,000.

Each of us carried a letter from Gen. A.C. Wedemeyer, commanding general of the U.S. Forces, Far East, addressed to the Japanese, saying in firm words that no harm was to come to us and that we were representing him until American troops arrived to take over the city. One thing bothered me. The letter was in English.

I had walked about one hundred yards when a burst of small arms fire split the air. I froze as bullets flew over my head sounding like a swarm of angry bees.

There wasn't anything I could do. If they were aiming at me, they had missed. There was no place to hide and no place to run. The firing finally stopped so I kept on walking as if I wasn't scared. I fully expected to be mowed down in the next few seconds. If that was what they intended to do, there wasn't anything I could do about it.

In the distance I heard a motor and saw a truck coming onto the field bearing a white flag. It steered straight for me at high speed and I thought they intended to run me down. It would be a strange way to die, I thought.

The truck roared up and stopped in front of me. A Japanese lieutenant and three soldiers armed with rifles and bayonets surrounded me. The officer spoke a few words of English so I explained that I was not in charge but that Major Nichol, several hundred yards to my right, would discuss our mission with him.

I don't know what was going through the officer's mind but after a moment's hesitation, he ordered the soldiers to pick up my equipment and put it in the truck. Then they picked up the other members of the party and took us to their headquarters building.[3]

Maj. Ray Nichol was the ideal man for the strange task ahead of him. Towering over the Japanese, he took charge of the situation from the beginning as he confronted the commanding officer of the field. "I am Major Nichol, United States Army," he announced authoritatively. "I wish to speak to your commanding general as soon as possible."[4]

There were two Japanese intelligence officers present who

had been educated in the States, spoke English with a British accent, and had actually been in the States on Pearl Harbor Day. They had been repatriated along with other Japanese in an exchange during the spring of 1942.

The commander of the field placed several telephone calls and, after an hour of uneasy tension, General Takahashi and the Swiss consul in Peking arrived. Nichol saluted courteously and then got right to the point.

"General, I have been sent here to arrange for the release of Allied prisoners of war," he declared. "We know you have a number of them, including the men taken at Wake Island. I want them released immediately!"

Takahashi was nervous and perturbed at the effrontery of the American towering over him. "Major, I think your commanding general is premature in sending you here," he said through an interpreter. "The war is not officially over. Only a few high-ranking officers know that peace negotiations are underway. You are in extreme danger coming here like this!"[5]

The Swiss consul, seeing that he should assume the role of mediator, quickly interjected that the general was right but that the Americans were not asking him to surrender. Their mission was a humanitarian one.

"Tell the general," Nichol said, "that I have a letter from General Wedemeyer which tells him exactly why we are here. Tell him also that *he* will be in extreme danger if harm comes to any of us."[6]

Takahashi was visibly agitated and insisted that he could not control all the elements of his forces. It would help the situation if Nichol and his men would surrender their weapons since he could not guarantee their safety.

"Tell the general that we will not surrender our weapons and we are not asking him to surrender his—yet." he told the interpreter. "We want suitable quarters for ourselves and we want him to start releasing the prisoners at Fengtai. I will not accept any delays or stalling around!"

After about an hour of discussion among the Japanese, the Americans were taken to the Grand Hotel de Pekin, one of the two best hotels in Peking. Takahashi strongly suggested that they remain there because if they wandered around the city fully armed, some of his dedicated troops might think they would be honored by the emperor himself if they killed the conquering Americans.

Nichol agreed to remain at the hotel but, after many hours of discussion and no action on Takahashi's part, he announced on the afternoon of August 19 that he and his men were going to leave the hotel regardless of the danger and visit the prisoners. Takahashi, seeing he could stall no longer, finally agreed to release the prisoners that day. The first truckloads were taken to the two major hotels. It included about three hundred British, French, and Australian prisoners, a few Americans and several hundred Allied civilians. All were suffering from malnutrition, dysentery, and assorted illnesses, including malaria.

By the morning of the twentieth, all POWs at the Fengtai prison had been released. Nichol invited the ranking ex-prisoners of the camp to sit in with him while he talked with Takahashi. By this time, he had been well briefed by the ex-prisoners on the cruelty and tortures they had suffered during their imprisonment. He knew the names of those who had died from tortures. When Takahashi arrived, the air was tense with excitement.

Hilaire du Berrier, an American civilian who had flown for the Spanish Loyalists and later for Chiang, had joined a French Resistance Group spy network in Shanghai after Pearl Harbor. He had been captured and had survived almost three years at Fengtai. He describes the confrontation between Nichol and Takahashi:

> There were about fifteen Japanese officers present, including Colonel Odera and Lieutenant Hondo, a lieutenant in the Kempetei, who ran the prison camp. The meeting began pleasantly enough with Major Nichol obviously in charge of the affair. He was magnificently self-controlled as he exchanged pleasantries in the cultured Oriental manner. He talked about the weather, the excellent facilities in the hotel, and how pleased he was that the Fengtai prisoners had been released.
>
> The general and the other officers, their huge samurai swords clanking against their chairs, were ill at ease but began to relax as Nichol smiled and continued to converse amiably.
>
> Then, without warning, Nichol's mood changed and he

asked a direct question. "General, I know exactly how many prisoners were moved from Nanking to Fengtai. Two of them did not arrive. What happened to them?"

When the question was translated, the Japanese stiffened and Lieutenant Hondo quickly answered that they had died. "But," he added quickly, "we have kept their ashes for you."

Hondo was visibly shaken by the question and his personal answer had confirmed a suspicion that Nichol had about him. Nichol glared at the lieutenant, who shifted nervously and then sat down in a chair.

Nichol shouted at him in a voice so commanding that everyone jumped. "You will *not* sit down!" he exclaimed. "I know now that you are not an officer in the Japanese Army. You are an interrogator for the Kempetai. Therefore, you will interpret but you will not have the privilege of volunteering information at this meeting."

Hondo jumped up as if he had been kicked, his hands shaking. After this exchange, Nichol lapsed back into talking about trivial things until the Japanese relaxed again. As soon as they leaned back in their chairs, Nichol suddenly changed his mood and shot another question that shattered the atmosphere like a thunderbolt.

"What happened to the man named Hutton?" Nichol asked. Hutton had died of tortures on August 15, 1944. Colonel Odera, sensing now that Nichol knew more than they realized, answered truthfully that he had died. Nichol asked about other men and then lapsed back into his pleasant mood again.

The room was hot and Nichol was fanning himself with a Chinese fan. His manner was the coolest of anyone I have ever seen. The Japanese were weakening as the room got hotter and Nichol calmly fanned himself.

Commander Cunningham, the naval commander of Wake Island when it fell, was observing the proceedings and thought it was an opportune time for Nichol to mention that he knew that four of Doolittle's raiders were in the military prison in the city. He whispered the information to Nichol who then demanded that Takahashi release the Doolittle fliers being held in special confinement immediately.

The Japanese were obviously stunned. Apparently, they had believed that no one but themselves knew they were in Peking. Without blinking, Nichol stared at the Japanese general and waited for an answer. No one moved. The general

> nervously unbuttoned his collar and squirmed in his chair. Nichol waited patiently and then made a striking gesture that spoke more than words. He carefully folded the fan he had been using and handed it to the general. Takahashi reached for it and began to fan himself. The gesture was, for that moment, the superb *touché*. Takahashi knew that this American was truly the master of the situation. He promptly ordered an aide to arrange the release of the men.[7]

Within an hour the four emaciated Doolittle fliers were taken from their cells to the hotel. A few hours later the world learned for the first time of the fate of two of Doolittle's B-25 crews that had gone down in enemy territory. The world also learned how deeply the raid had affected the Japanese psychologically and how their wrath and frustration had been directed toward the eight airmen they had captured and the friendly Chinese who had tried to help them and the other Doolittle raiders. Four of the eight had paid the supreme penalty. The remaining four, sustained by their faith and fortitude, had barely survived to tell the story of their suffering.

14

Last to Return

George Barr was, by far, the sickest and weakest of the four survivors on their liberation day. He could not have survived another week of imprisonment and he knew it. Hovering between life and death, he fell unconscious for periods of time. Like Meder, who had died quietly in his cell twenty-one months before, Barr thought his life would end the same way.

On the evening of August 20, Barr's cell door creaked open and a gush of light startled him awake. He felt an overwhelming relief that death had finally come. Through the haze of blinding light, he saw the face of a Japanese guard and felt himself being picked up like a child and carried to a small room at the end of the cell block and laid on a table. A voice seeped through his fading consciousness. It was Chase Nielsen's.

"Hi, George. How do you feel?"

Barr couldn't answer. Death seemed pleasant, if that was what it was. Another voice sounded. It was Bob Hite. Or was it? He hadn't heard his voice for a long time.

"Come on, George, wake up! It's all over now. The war's over, George. We're free!"

The word "free" was like a hypodermic. Barr opened his eyes and focused guardedly on the scrawny, unshaven, smiling faces looming over him.

"I couldn't believe it was true," Barr recalled. "I *knew* I was dead now but I didn't care. If death meant that I could be with my three buddies, I was as happy as they were."

Since Hite, Nielsen, and DeShazer were able to travel, they were returned to the States a few days after their release after getting physical exams, some good food, and uniforms. Barr, however, was kept behind in the hotel, which was being used as a hospital. Unable to stand, he didn't have enough strength to eat at first. He was semiconscious for several days and his mind wandered between reality and a dream world in which he kept asking himself questions. Was he dead yet? Was he still in jail? If he had been released, why was he still in bed? Where were the guards and where were his three buddies?

Barr's doubts and fears grew as his mental disorientation became more pronounced. He was flown to Kunming as a "mentally disturbed patient" on September 12 and placed in an open ward where he was given shots to ease abdominal and leg pains. He dozed fitfully that night and fell out of the high hospital bed. He screamed. The medics tried to quiet him with an injection. When he awoke he was in a barren room in the psychiatric ward. He recalled his reactions:

> All my past suspicions and doubts were now confirmed. The barren room, the bars on the window, the occasional face at a slot in the locked door, and the solitary confinement spelled prison as far as I was concerned. I lay there a long time thinking things over and decided that I would pretend to go along with anything my captors were trying to make me do—but I would try to escape when the opportunity arose. If they wanted stories for me, I would give them stories. If they wanted to experiment with my body, I didn't have the strength to stop them. If they were going to punish me for something I would try to learn why and prevent any recurrence. But I would prepare myself for an escape at the first opportunity. No one, I told myself, would ever brainwash me as they had apparently done to all the white people I had seen since getting out of the Peking prison.[1]

The medical reports for the next two weeks reflected Barr's gain in physical strength but also his continual struggling with reality. Words like "apprehensive," "restless," "agitated," and "disturbed" were frequently used in his medical records. His irrational behavior kept him in a padded cell.[2]

When it seemed that he was able to travel, he was taken to an airport and while waiting to board, had a sudden panic attack and began running away from an accompanying orderly. The wide open space of the airport, the clear air, the blue sky, and the lack of any physical restraint was too much.

Barr's promise to himself to escape had become overwhelming. Out of nowhere came a blow that knocked him to the ground unconscious. When he awoke, he was on a C-47 lying on a stretcher under a restraining sheet with his arms encased in a straitjacket.[3]

Barr was offloaded at Calcutta.[4] He asked the medics about his status, why he was in Calcutta, and what was going to happen next. The medics checked his restraints periodically and said nothing. Several days later, without explanation, he was placed aboard a C-47 again and flown back to Kunming, accompanied by three officers, two of them doctors who had earned enough "points" to be discharged when they returned to the States. Under their continuing watch, Barr was released from restraint but the questions continued in his mind. How was it that so many Americans seemed to have been fooled by the enemy? Had the Japanese discovered some drug that had enabled them completely to brainwash their captives? The skin of the three men was yellow and when he asked them why, they told him it was atabrine they had taken for malaria prevention, something he had never heard of. If they were not under Japanese mind control, why did all three of them have samurai swords sticking out of their barracks bags?

After several days in a Kunming military hospital, Barr seemed much better and was next flown across the Pacific and arrived at Letterman General Hospital, near San Francisco, California, on October 17. The three physician escorts said goodbye and left for the nearby separation center. Barr was put aboard a bus alone and taken to the base hospital. He had no baggage, no identification, no records, and no personal belongings. He had only the rumpled, ill-fitting uniform he had been given in Kunming and a small shaving kit.

The sergeant at the admissions desk asked questions, which Barr answered hesitantly. Name? Age? Last station and unit of assignment? What was he being treated for? Where was his baggage? What happened to his records?

Disgusted at Barr's feeble attempts to explain his plight, the sergeant gave up and told an orderly to show Barr to a room, take his clothes and give him pajamas. Barr was led to a small room containing two beds, a chair, and a night stand. He disrobed, handed the uniform to the orderly, and put on his pajamas. The orderly left without further explanation and Barr was alone. It was a weekend and there were few patients or medical personnel around. There was no one on his floor.

That old feeling of being alone in a cell returned to Barr and so did the questions. Why hadn't he seen a doctor when he checked in? Why wasn't anyone else around? What was the significance of some coins and a pocket knife lying on the night stand?

After several hours of being alone and afraid to venture out of the room, Barr suddenly had an overwhelming urge to kill himself. But how?

The pocket knife! That was it! The Japanese were going to let him commit *hari-kari!*

Barr seized the knife, opened it and jammed the blade into his chest. Strangely, he felt no pain. He expected to see blood gushing out of the wound but none came. He stared unbelievingly at the small slit the knife had made. Somehow, he thought, the enemy had made it impossible to kill himself this way. Had the so-called blood plasma they gave him in Peking been used to replace his blood so that he couldn't bleed any more?

Frantic that he was being cheated in his attempt to self-destruct, Barr became determined to win this last battle with his captors. He opened the window but saw that he was only on the second floor. If he jumped, he would probably only break his legs and wouldn't die from the fall. What other ways could he kill himself? There were no guns. Poisons would be locked up. Hanging? That was it. There was a light fixture in the ceiling? A chair. A rope. What could be used for a rope? A sheet? Too bulky. A belt? It had been taken away. Electrical cord? That was it, but where could he find one?

Barr looked up and down the hallway and in several deserted rooms. He found a room with a heat lamp. With the strength of a desperate man, he ripped the wire off, made a noose, wrapped it around the light fixture, positioned the chair underneath, placed his head in the loop, and kicked the chair away.

Barr's head snapped and the next few seconds were another nightmare. Huge sparks flew out of the ceiling. There was a crash of glass and metal. Barr crumpled to the floor with a thud that reverberated down the empty hallway to the medic's office downstairs. Orderlies rushed to his room as Barr screamed and struggled. They sedated him and placed him in a locked mental ward.

To Barr, the pattern was being repeated. He was again in a cell. There were no windows this time, no one to talk with, and nothing to do but pace the six-by-nine-foot room endlessly. The only difference between this cell and the one in China was that he was getting good food three times a day.

Since he was on a healthful diet, Barr regained strength gradually. He felt rational and was allowed to go into a ward with other patients. His spirits soared as he spoke with other men and was able to compare his experiences with theirs. But the strange saga of George Barr was to continue.

On November 9, without preliminary announcement, orderlies brought in straitjackets for the patients. To Barr's amazement, no one objected. He decided he wouldn't either. They were taken by bus to a railroad siding and boarded a Pullman car. Jackets were kept on and the shades pulled down. A doctor's report for Barr noted: "He will be started in restraint because of his suicidal outbursts. He will require maximum care en route, and unless he is observed he can be counted upon to injure himself."[5]

Barr didn't know it but he was being transported to a military hospital near Clinton, Iowa. Although he was actually from Yonkers, New York, he was sent to Iowa because he had enlisted as an aviation cadet from Northland College, Ashland, Wisconsin, and this was the nearest military hospital.

By the time the train pulled into Clinton, Barr's reasoning powers were about gone. The bad luck that had dogged him all his life and brought him to a hospital in a part of the country he had never seen before was being continued. Orphaned at the age of six months when his father disappeared while fishing off Long Island, he had been sent to foster homes at age nine when his mother found she could not raise him and his sister Grace any longer. Grace became the special charge of Mrs. Charles H. Towns, a social worker and wife of an executive with Pan American Airways. George was sent to a "home school" in Yonkers, where he stayed until he was eighteen. The Towns, themselves childless, adopted the Barr children in fact, but not legally.

The Towns were shocked to learn of George's capture and all

during the war had been the go-betweens for the families of the Raiders whose fate was unknown. When the announcement came that "their" George was one of the survivors, the Towns were elated. They received a single cryptic note from George written in China saying he would soon be home, but this was followed by weeks of silence. They contacted the Pentagon but no one could locate a Lt. George Barr. After days of frustration, it seemed to them that they were the only persons in the whole world who cared if he were ever found.

There was one person who cared mightily, however. That was the man who had led the epic raid against Japan. Mrs. Towns, her patience exhausted and angry at the army, wrote to the famed Jimmy Doolittle, now a three-star general, and asked for help. Doolittle dropped everything and started an official search. He wrote Mrs. Towns that "we who love George Barr will do everything we can for him. Our objective, however, is not to reform the Army but to find him and help him recover."[6]

But Barr was being kept incommunicado and was walking a mental tightrope. While Doolittle searched fo him through official channels, Mrs. Towns discovered his whereabouts on her own and notified George's sister, then pregnant with her first child and living in Milwaukee. Grace asked her husband, Bill Maas, to go to Clinton because she had been advised not to travel. Meanwhile, Mrs. Towns headed for Clinton.

When George was escorted by a medic to the visitor's lounge, he recognized his brother-in-law but he seemed much older than he remembered. Maas's face was now scarred from a motorcycle accident. As far as Barr was concerned, this could be another trick. It could be someone else and the Japanese had done plastic surgery on him to make him look somewhat like Maas. He could not believe that his sister would not travel the short distance from Milwaukee to see him.

When Mrs. Towns arrived, George was overjoyed to see her but she didn't look the same to him. She had aged too much, he thought, and he was suspicious of her. The brief visits did help his mental state, however, and he was transferred to an open ward. Yet, he still had not seen a doctor, had no money, no clothes, and no freedom. Although he felt better, he thought the Japanese were going to spring some kind of new surprise on him and he wondered when that would be.

One day in late November, there was a commotion outside the ward. Orderlies rushed in and hurriedly straightened up the ward.

"Lieutenant Barr, you've got a visitor," one of them said. "Better get cleaned up."

"Who is it?" Barr asked.

"General Doolittle. Says he knows you."

Barr's heart leaped and a surge of joy swept through him he had not known before. He trembled as he stood up and slid his feet into cloth slippers. The door opened and the man with one of the most famous grins in the world strode in briskly and made his way to Barr, hand outstretched.

"Hi, George! It's good to see you. How are you?"

The words to answer would not come. Tears welled up instead. Doolittle knew immediately that the last of his Raiders to return needed help urgently. He kept talking and invited George to go outside for a walk.

As the two men walked, George began to find the words that had been stored up inside so long. He answered Doolittle's kindly questions hesitantly at first, then more easily. The answers came as a shock to the man who had led the most renowned mission of the war. He found it difficult to believe that Barr had not seen a doctor, had no clothes, no money, and seemed to have lost all status as a human being.

Doolittle did not show the fury that was mounting within him but he could never stand incompetency nor tolerate injustice. He accompanied George back to the ward and headed for the hospital commander's office.

There is no official record of the conversation that ensued and Doolittle did not reveal what he said. What is known is that from that moment on, there was a definite turning point in the recovery of George Barr. He was suddenly outfitted in a new uniform, complete with ribbons and overseas stripes he never knew he had earned. He was retroactively promoted to first lieutenant and received a check for more than $7,000 in back pay. Best of all, he received the full attention of a psychiatrist who started him on the road to recovery.

Doolittle returned to see George the next day. "George, do you remember the promise I made the day before we left the

Hornet—that when we got to Chungking I'd throw you fellas the biggest party you ever had?"[7]

George nodded.

"Well, we never had that party because you and the other fellas couldn't make it. But I'm going to keep that promise now that the war is over. The whole gang is invited to be my guests in Miami on my birthday next month. I want you to come. I'll send an airplane for you."

The tall, smiling redhead needed no urging. This was the kind of medicine he needed. He attended the first reunion of Doolittle's Tokyo Raiders and began the difficult return to normalcy. In December 1946, he married Marcine Anderson, a warmhearted, understanding person who gave him the care and love that had been missing in his life. With her help and that of the Towns and Bob Hite over the next two years, he regained a balanced outlook on life.

Although George wanted to remain in the air force, he was retired for physical disability in September, 1947. He returned to college, earned two degrees, and became a management analyst for the U.S. Army. But the torture, imprisonment, and starvation diet eventually took their toll. He died of a heart attack in 1967 while attending a management course at Wright-Patterson Air Force Base, Dayton, Ohio.

Of the remaining three, Chase Nielsen was the only one to remain in the air force until retirement after twenty-two years of active duty. He became a civilian management engineer at Hill Air Force Base, Utah. Now retired, he enjoys the hunting and fishing he dreamed about while in solitary confinement. He lives in Brigham City, Utah.

Bob Hite remained in the air force for two years after World War II and returned to active duty in 1951 during the Korean War, serving for four more years. He later managed hotels in Memphis, Tennessee, and Camden, Arkansas, and is now retired in the latter city.

Jake DeShazer kept his vow to return to Japan as a missionary. He completed his seminary education at Seattle Pacific College in 1948 and went to Japan to preach the Gospel as a Free Methodist missionary. He remained there for many years until retirement, except for a brief period when he returned to the states on a sabbatical leave to earn a master's degree at Asbury Theological Seminary in 1958. He lives in Salem, Oregon.

One of the highlights of DeShazer's career was his conversion of Mitsuo Fuchida to Christianity in April 1950. Fuchida's acceptance of the Christian message received worldwide press attention for it was Fuchida who had led the "infamous" attack on Pearl Harbor on December 7, 1941. To DeShazer, his conversion was proof of the miracles promised in the Bible he had read so voraciously in prison. Fuchida made a lecture tour of the United States with DeShazer during which both told of their experiences and religious convictions. Fuchida died in 1980.

While DeShazer was the only one of the four survivors to enter the ministry, the others freely admitted that the message of the Bible they were given after Meder's death deeply affected them. They attributed their survival to the message of hope they found in its tattered pages. They harbor no resentment against their captors today and are grateful to God for their eventual release.

These men are also dedicated to the freedoms guaranteed by the U.S. Constitution. In an essay that earned them an award from the Freedoms Foundation in 1968, they said: "We have concluded that the concept of liberty—American liberty—is a religion. It is a thing of the spirit and exemplifies the highest ideals Man has ever expressed. Our buddies—Faktor, Dieter, Fitzmaurice, Spatz, Hallmark, Farrow and Meder—died to perpetuate those ideals. We do not think they died in vain."[8]

15

Justice the American Way

Jimmy Doolittle, newly promoted from lieutenant colonel to brigadier general, skipping the rank of colonel, received the Medal of Honor from President Roosevelt in the White House on May 19, 1942. The press was not invited to the brief ceremony and no details of the raid were made public. Although he was immediately put to work on other projects for General Arnold, including making speeches at war bond rallies and aircraft factories, he felt a deep obligation to the men who had followed him on their dangerous mission and whose physical condition and whereabouts were unknown. He tried to establish contact with the missing men through military, diplomatic, and International Red Cross channels but without success. He wrote personal letters to the next of kin of every man who had accompanied him and told what he knew about their loved ones.

When the majority of the men whose orders returned them to the States had arrived, an awards ceremony was held at Bolling Field in Washington, where they were presented with Distinguished Flying Crosses. The injured—Lieutenants McClure, Lawson, and Watson—received theirs at nearby Walter Reed Hospital.

The fate of the eight men captured by the Japanese worried Doolittle continually. Although he had arranged for ransom to be paid to the Japanese or Chinese guerrillas for their return, the gesture was fruitless. Nevertheless, Doolittle persisted and on August 15, he learned from the Swiss consulate general in Shanghai that the eight Americans were being held as prisoners at police headquarters—Bridge House—in the center of the city.

On October 19, 1942, the Japanese government announced that it had tried the members of two of Doolittle's crews and sentenced them to death. However, the report stated that while the death sentence had been commuted to life imprisonment for the larger number of them, it had already been carried out for certain of the accused. No names or other facts were given.

Secretary of State Cordell Hull contacted the Swiss minister to the United States and asked that his government inquire through their minister in Tokyo if the reports were true. On February 17, 1943, the Japanese stated that they intended to try all American prisoners of war before military tribunals and impose severe penalties upon them, including death. Hull conveyed this information to President Roosevelt, along with information received later, confirming that an unspecified number of the Doolittle raiders had been put to death. Hull proposed a long message to be sent to Tokyo via the American Legation in Bern, Switzerland, and recommended a public announcement to be issued shortly thereafter.[1]

Roosevelt was profoundly shocked and penned a reply to Hull on April 8, saying, "I am deeply stirred and horrified by the execution of American aviators by the Japanese Government." He approved the proposed message to the Japanese and added, "In view of the severe tone of this note and especially of the warning in the last paragraph that we propose to retaliate on Japanese prisoners in our hands, I can see no reason for delaying a public announcement."

The "severe" paragraph the president referred to was unprecedented in American history and presaged a new concept of international justice to be invoked at the end of the war. It said:

> The American Government also solemnly warns the Japanese Government that for any other violations of its undertakings as regards American prisoners of war or for any other acts of criminal barbarity inflicted upon American prisoners in violation of the rules of warfare accepted and practiced by civilized nations as military operations now in progress draw to their inexorable and inevitable conclusion, the American Government will visit upon the officers of the Japanese Government responsible for such uncivilized and inhuman acts the punishment they deserve.[2]

On April 21, 1943, President Roosevelt confirmed publicly what the news media had been speculating on for days:

It is with a feeling of the deepest horror, which I know will be shared by all civilized peoples, that I have to announce the barbarous execution by the Japanese Government of some of the members of this country's armed forces who fell into Japanese hands as an incident of warfare.

The press has just carried the details of the American bombing of Japan a year ago. The crews of two of the American bombers were captured by the Japanese. On October 19, 1942, this Government learned from Japanese radio broadcasts of the capture, trial, and severe punishment of those Americans. Continued endeavor was made to obtain confirmation of those reports from Tokyo. It was not until March 12, 1943, that the American Government received the communications given by the Japanese Government stating that these Americans had in fact been tried and that the death penalty had been pronounced against them. It was further stated that the death penalty was commuted for some but that the sentence of death had been applied to others.

This Government has vigorously condemned this act of barbarity in a formal communication sent to the Japanese Government. In that communication this Government has informed the Japanese Government that the American Government will hold personally and officially responsible for these diabolical crimes all of those officers of the Japanese Government who have participated therein and will in due course bring those officers to justice.

This recourse by our enemies to frightfulness is barbarous. The effort of the Japanese war lords thus to intimidate us will utterly fail. It will make the American people more determined than ever to blot out the shameless militarism of Japan.[3]

On many occasions after this announcement Roosevelt reiterated his determination that all Axis war criminals be brought to trial after the war. As soon as the Germans and Japanese surrendered, one of the first follow-up tasks for American troops was to search for evidence of war crimes committed and find those responsible. Top priority was given to finding any survivors of the Doolittle-led raid against Japan and accumulating evidence against those responsible for the execution of the others.

* * *

As soon as hostilities ceased in August 1945, American intelligence agents fanned out all over Japan and Japanese-occupied territory in China seeking information and evidence for the trial of individuals who had violated international law in the treatment of prisoners of war. Hundreds of Japanese were located who had been named by ex-prisoners as having been especially cruel or who had caused the death and torture of their comrades. Those who knew of the execution of three of Doolittle's crew members must have known they would be sought because a few days after the surrender, unknown Japanese came to the office of the International Funeral Directors in Shanghai to search for the urns containing the ashes of Lieutenants Hallmark and Farrow and Sergeant Spatz. They changed the names on the boxes from Hallmark to "J.C. Smith," from Farrow to "H.E. Gande," and from Spatz to "E.L. Brister" in order to confuse anyone attempting to learn the fate of these men. But American investigators soon uncovered the correct names from original records and the urns were properly identified.

Between August 1945 and the following February, a number of Japanese were named to be tried for the cruel and inhuman treatment of the Doolittle Raiders, but because many had died or were accused of more serious crimes, the list to be brought to trial before a military commission in China was narrowed to four: Lt. Gen. Shigeru Sawada, commander of the Imperial Thirteenth Expeditionary Army in China; Capt. Ryuhei Okada, a member of the mock court that tried the fliers; Lt. Yusei Wako, a lawyer from the tribunal during the mock trial; and Capt. Sotojiro Tatsuta, warden of Kiangwan Military Prison and official executioner. Two officers, Maj. Itsuro Hata, prosecutor for the trial court, and Lt. Col. Toyama Nakajo, presiding judge, had died. Gen. Shunroku Hata, commander of all Japanese forces in China, and Lt. Gen. Sadamu Shimomura, who had succeeded Sawada as commander of the Thirteenth Army and had signed the execution order, were held in Tokyo for the international war crimes trials. Their release to the military commission for this trial was refused.

Sawada, as commander of the Thirteenth Army, was charged with causing the eight captured Doolittle raiders to be tried and sentenced to death by a military tribunal on false and fraudulent charges, and with having the power to commute or revoke the sentences but failing to do so. He was also charged with responsibility for brutal atrocities against prisoners and for other offenses, including the denial of proper food, clothing, medical care, and shelter.

Tatsuta was charged with having executed an unlawful order of a military tribunal, which caused the death of the three fliers. As warden of Kiangwan Prison, he was also blamed for denying the prisoners adequate food, shelter, sanitary facilities, and medical care.

Okada and Wako were accused of unlawfully trying and judging the eight airmen under false and fraudulent charges without affording them a fair trial, interpretation of the proceedings, counsel, or an opportunity to defend themselves, and for sentencing them to death.

The charges against these men were forwarded to and approved by Gen. Albert C. Wedemeyer, commander of American forces in China. His staff judge advocate, in reviewing the charges, noted, "Here the test is international law, not the national law, civil or military, of any one nation, not the law of the United States nor of Japan, but the law of nations. Japan and the United States both were parties of the Hague Convention, and Japan agreed to abide by the provisions of the Geneva Prisoner of War Convention."[4]

The trial against the four was tentatively scheduled for early March 1946, and was to be held in the Ward Road Jail in Shanghai. The accused were assigned qualified defense counsel by the U.S. Army and three Japanese attorneys were added at the request of the accused. There was a marked contrast between the justice meted out to the Doolittle fliers and the American style of justice against the accused Japanese, where guilt must be proven without a shadow of a doubt and an accused is innocent until proven guilty. In this trial, the accused Japanese were allowed all the time they requested for the preparation of their defense. Their public trial lasted almost a month, and the entire proceedings were translated into Japanese and a verbatim record made in both languages. The accused were also provided free transportation to and from Japan for their witnesses and defense counsel.

At their arraignment it was made clear to the four accused

that the lawful maximum sentence that could be imposed for conviction of any war crime was death, although a lesser penalty could be assessed. The accused were now fighting for their lives, but they were made profoundly aware that their individual rights were going to be protected and that the trial was going to be as fair as the minds of free men could make it.

The trial began on March 18, after two postponements to allow the defense additional time for preparation. The first witness was Capt. Chase J. Nielsen, the only one of the four survivors who could return to the Far East to face those responsible for the death of the other four and for the torture and inhuman treatment of all of them. Nielsen, now fully recovered from his imprisonment, had sworn to himself early in captivity that he was going to survive and return to testify against his captors. Tough and resilient in captivity, he was the ideal one of the four survivors to give testimony on their behalf. He testified forcefully for the prosecution and held up strongly under cross-examination by the defense counsel, which was often severe.

Nielsen testified intensively for two days. After he left the stand, a forty-three-page deposition from George Barr and a joint statement by Bob Hite and Jacob DeShazer describing their capture, torture, and treatment were admitted in evidence. Other prosecution witnesses were introduced to substantiate the stories of the four survivors, including a Chinese named Teh Ling Chung, and Russians named Alexander Hindrava and Alexander Sterelny, who had been in the cell with Dean Hallmark in the Bridge House Jail. Other witnesses were Japanese guards who had been present at the execution of Hallmark, Farrow, and Spatz. Col. George E. Armstrong, an American physician, testified about the effects of beriberi, as it could have caused the death of Bob Meder.

On March 26, the commission members went to the cemetery where the executions were carried out. They also visited the cell block in Kiangwan Prison where the men had been kept.

Testimony was completed on April 9, 1946. Two days later, summations by both sides were heard, including an impassioned plea from Capt. Charles L. Fellows, one of the defense lawyers for the Japanese. In summing up the case for the defendants, he noted its importance as "the first attempt by an American Military Commission to review the acts of a tribunal of another nation, to review the laws, rules, and customs of another nation and to punish nationals of that nation who complied with those laws, rules, and judicial decisions of that nation. This function is usually performed by an International Commission of selected jurists."

Maj. Robert T. Dwyer summarized for the prosecution. Slowly and with careful legal precision over a two-hour period, he reviewed the testimony for the prosecution and attacked the defense's case on every point of substance. He then explained why the accused were brought to trial and why "we think they should pay the supreme penalty of the law, each and every one." Ending his argument, Dwyer said:

> I conclude by saying this: Four of these Doolittle fliers have paid the penalty with their lives when, as a matter of fact, both on the evidence before the tribunal of August 28, 1942, and upon the evidence of this commission, they were entitled rightfully and objectively and by every standard to the status of prisoners of war, and at no time did they get it, and four of them died for it, and four others, if not for the power of the United Nations, would still be paying for it. The evil began when these men were placed before a tribunal, a tribunal of any kind; and secondly, once they were placed before it they had no chance or opportunity of a fair and honest trial than I have with my right hand to stem the fall of Niagara's waters. . . .
>
> We have charged these men with the violations of the laws of custom and war. We have proven it by a wealth of evidence. We close by asking for the death penalty against all four of the accused.

On April 14, Col. Edwin R. McReynolds, head of the commission, reviewed the case and concluded:

> The offenses of each of the accused resulted largely from their obedience to the laws and instructions of their Government and their military superiors. They exercised no initiative to any marked degree. The preponderance of evidence

> shows beyond reasonable doubt that other officers, including high governmental and military officials, were responsible for the enactment of the Ex Post Facto "Enemy Airmen's Law" and the issuance of special instructions as to how these American prisoners were to be treated, tried, sentenced and punished.
>
> The circumstances set forth above do not entirely absolve the accused from guilt. However, they do compel unusually strong mitigating considerations, applicable to each accused in various degrees.

The four sad-faced Japanese were asked to stand and McReynolds announced the verdict of guilty against the defendants and then their sentences. To the surprise of all in the courtroom, including the accused, the sentences were relatively light. Sawada, Okada, and Tatsuta were each sentenced to five years confinement at hard labor. Wako, the lawyer, received a nine-year sentence, presumably because he was an attorney and knew that the Enemy Airmen's Act had been enacted after the Doolittle raid specifically to the detriment of the eight captured fliers.

The sentences, although criticized for being too light, were upheld by General Wedemeyer. The four Japanese were transferred to Sugamo Prison in Tokyo, where many other Japanese were to serve sentences handed down from the international war crimes trials. Three of the four (Sawada, Okada, and Tatsuta) served four years and three months of their five-year sentences. Wako, however, was subsequently tried on other charges developed as a result of activities later in the war and received an additional sentence of imprisonment at hard labor for life. He served thirteen years of his sentence. When released, he was extremely bitter and showed no remorse for his part in the mock trial and the deaths of Hallmark, Farrow, and Spatz.

When the news of the sentences was released to the world press, reaction in the United States was immediate. Parents and relatives of the executed men wrote indignant letters to the president and to their congressmen. Veterans' organizations protested vigorously about the leniency of the sentences. But the protests were academic. A fair trial had been held, the accused were judged fairly, based on legal evidence, and sentences were meted out that could not be increased according to the American system of law. Hallmark, Farrow, Meder, and Spatz had given their lives to help preserve that system.

16

The Judgment of History

Was the raid against Japan a success?

One point of view would be that it was a failure because all aircraft were lost to the American cause, three of the eighty crew members died, eight were captured by the enemy, and five were interned by a neutral nation. Several raiders were badly injured and one man had his leg amputated. Three navy airmen died during patrols after the bombers had departed and one lost an arm when the last aircraft took off. One C-39 transport had crashed while attempting to make preliminary arrangements to receive the group in China.

On the plus side, ten of the sixteen planes bombed their assigned primary targets and did varying amounts of damage to them. While failing to locate their designated targets, five others still bombed industrial installations on the Japanese mainland; only one plane had to jettison its bombs without hitting a target area. Since the principle of all military operations is the conservation of force so that the destruction to the enemy is greater than the loss to one's own forces, the raid in terms of damage inflicted on the Japanese, although never accurately ascertained, was many times greater than the estimated $3.2 million that the sixteen B-25 Mitchell bombers cost the United States to produce.

But the mission objective was more than damage to ground targets. In an intelligence report after the mission, Jimmy Doolittle spelled out what he understood the raid was to accomplish:

> It was hoped that the damage done would be both material and psychological. Material damage was to be the destruction of specific targets with ensuing confusion and retardation of production. The psychological results, it was hoped, would be the recalling of combat equipment from other theaters for

home defense, the development of a fear complex in Japan, improved relationships with our Allies, and a favorable reaction in the American people.[1]

Although the extent of the physical damage in the target areas was never completely reported, the psychological effect had been immediate, as Doolittle had hoped. Before the last bomber had finished its run, every level of Japanese officialdom was being besieged for information. The government moved almost immediately to screen off the effects of the attack from public view. In the first few hours, official control of information appears to have been lost as evidenced by some exaggerated statements, such as one heard over Tokyo Radio aboard the retreating *Hornet*, that large fleets of bombers had inflicted thousands of casualties in the four cities attacked. However, the official statements quickly downplayed the effects of the raid and became vague, misleading, and more often totally false. Embarrassed by the surprise raid, the government's official line quickly changed when the damage reports were analyzed: There had been little or no damage to industrial installations and the raiders had bombed only schools and hospitals.

Areas where the bomb damage had been significant were declared off limits to the general populace and put under guard until the damage had been repaired, and any evidence of the American attack had been obliterated. Various government officials at all levels issued continuous calming statements, such as Home Minister Yuzawa who said, "Although enemy planes were seen on 18 April in Tokyo and other areas, the damage was fortunately very slight and the people on the whole were not perturbed."[2]

As time passed, the exaggerations and false claims increased, proving the frustration and anger of the reigning military leaders that they had been upstaged and surprised by the Americans. This "loss of face" in the minds of the Japanese, was a fate worse than death. The issuance of the Enemy Airmen's Act, an ex post facto law enacted specifically to excuse the subsequent execution of three of the raiders and life sentences for the remaining five, was a desperate act of retribution against America for daring to attack the Japanese homeland in retaliation for the raid on Pearl Harbor.

* * *

Jimmy Doolittle and his raiders were unaware of these immediate reactions of the Japanese. For those who survived in the crash landing or bailout and were able to rendezvous in Chungking, the war was not over. Besides a bombing mission, it was also a ferry mission in that the aircraft were to be transferred to units in China that were just being organized. Many of Doolittle's crews volunteered to remain in the China–Burma–India theater and continue fighting the enemy; several died there. Others, including Jimmy Doolittle, were ordered home to new assignments, which for most of them meant returning to combat in North Africa, Europe, or the South Pacific. A few of these did not return and four of them became prisoners of the Germans.

To the people of the United States, the news of the raid was immediately stimulating and heartening. The Allied news media were unrestrained in their enthusiasm for the boldness exhibited by Doolittle's men in carrying the fight to the enemy. But as the war progressed, the raid seemed to pass into history as an interesting and courageous act of war that had only passing propaganda value. There was a minor note of discontent in the United States because the story of the raid was not fully told immediately after the raid and there were some expressions of doubt that the operation had really been a success. But any doubts were overcome months later by the official announcement that the Japanese had executed some of the captured airmen. A wave of rage swept over the country and the American people were stirred as they had not been since Pearl Harbor.

There was other proof of the effects of the Doolittle raid on the Japanese military psyche. The army and navy had been thoroughly imbued with the notion that it was their individual and collective duty to protect the emperor and his family from danger. It was considered a grave dereliction of duty to allow the emperor's life to be placed in jeopardy by even a single enemy raid on the capital city.

Although the primary responsibility for air defense of the home islands rested with the army, the fact that the bombers had come from an enemy naval task force made it a naval responsibility. Adm. Isoroku Yamamoto, commander-in-chief of the Japanese Combined Fleet, considered the Doolittle attack a personal affront to his military judgment and blamed himself for allowing the Americans to carry out a surprise attack from the sea precisely as his forces had done at Pearl Harbor. He vowed to take retaliatory action as soon as possible.

Within two weeks after Doolittle's planes had disappeared over the horizon, Yamamoto approved Operation MI, which had as its objective the occupying of Midway Island and the capture of certain positions along the Aleutian chain. It was an ambitious undertaking, with over 150 Japanese ships and five aircraft carriers sent into battle. In the ensuing fight on June 4–5, 1942, known as the Battle of Midway, American forces routed the enemy, sinking 4 carriers and a heavy cruiser and causing major damage to 6 other ships. An amazing total of 332 Japanese planes were destroyed or failed to return from their missions. The loss to American forces were only 1 aircraft carrier and 1 destroyer sunk, and 147 planes destroyed.

Historians now credit the Doolittle raid with luring the Japanese into the disastrous Midway defeat. Capt. Y. Watanabe, commander-in-chief of the Second Fleet at the Battle of Midway, was interrogated by U.S. Navy intelligence officers after the war. The following transcript, long buried in U.S. intelligence files, was made in Tokyo on October 15, 1945:

Q. What were the plans leading up to the attack [on Midway]?

A. We intended to capture Midway because on 18 April we were attacked in Tokyo for the first time. We thought the planes came from Midway.

Q. Did you believe that by taking Midway there would be no more raids on Tokyo?

A. Yes.

Q. Did you intend to go beyond Midway?

A. If we could, we wanted to go to Pearl Harbor but it was not authorized because it was too far. We intended to capture small islands between Midway and Pearl Harbor. If we captured these islands, the land-based planes could attack Pearl Harbor. We wanted to capture Pearl Harbor later.[3]

More curious evidence of the far-reaching impact of the raid, proving that it had fully justified its purpose, was discovered after the war. During the final stages of the war, the Japanese made a futile effort to attack the western portion of the United States by launching bomb-carrying free balloons from three sites near Tokyo. Carried by the prevailing westerly winds at high altitudes, they were calculated to descend over American territory. Over 6,000 balloons were released; 285 were identified as having landed in the lower United States, Alaska, and Canada between November 4, 1944, and August 8, 1945. Five children and a pregnant woman were killed by one while on a church picnic in southern Oregon on May 5, 1945.

After Japan's defeat, newsmen queried Japanese authorities about the reasons for the balloon attacks and learned that the balloon bomb "was Japan's V-1 weapon in efforts to get revenge for the Doolittle raid on Tokyo in April 1942."[4] The Tokyo raid had so angered Japanese military leaders that they were determined to get revenge, even in the waning days of the war. The balloons were made of large sheets of paper glued together in small family workshops. Two years of experimentation were required and the project was estimated to cost nine million yen (over $2 million at prewar exchange).

The 1942 raid on Japan had marked the end of five months devoid of good news for Americans. It signaled the beginning of the end of Japanese domination of the Far East and the Pacific, although many would die on both sides before the war was over. Although New Guinea and the Aleutians would still yield limited successes for the Japanese, there would be no more big victories. After the Doolittle raid came the U.S. Navy's victory in the Coral Sea, then the Battle of Midway, followed by the landings on Guadalcanal. Historians now concur that the many psychological aftereffects fully justify the risks taken by the eighty American airmen.

This story of an epic air raid demonstrated that seventy-nine brave Americans, led by a bold, imaginative leader, could change the course and outcome of a war. But it is the aftermath of Japanese terror and brutality, which has few equals in modern military history, that provides a reminder for all of man's capacity for cruelty to his fellow man.

Should the full story, with its unpleasant aftermath, be told now, nearly fifty years after the raid?

Perhaps Jimmy Doolittle himself provided the best answer. "I think it deserves to be told," he told the author, "not to open old wounds nor to condemn the Japanese. Rather, so that we will all remember what evils an uncontrolled militaristic government can bring to its people and to point up what the consequences can be of our own unpreparedness to meet aggression."[5]

Epilogue

On board the *Hornet* the day before takeoff on their mission, Jimmy Doolittle announced, "When we get to Chungking, I'll throw you fellows the biggest party you ever had." He couldn't keep that promise because he was ordered back to the States before his crews were collected in Chungking. However, he never forgot his vow. The comradeship and the voluntary sharing of a life-or-death mission meant more to him than anything else in his active military life. He had worked and trained beside them, then faced danger with them as he led them into battle. He loved them for their bravery and bravado. He respected them for their ingenuity and their individualism. He wanted them to stick together and keep in touch with him and one another.

On April 18, 1943, the first anniversary of the raid, Doolittle, then a major general, and a few of the officer veterans of the raid against Japan were in North Africa. A party was held in a small farmhouse to mark the anniversary, but it was not what Doolittle had in mind. He wanted all his Raiders to reunite and they were spread all over the globe. The fate of the eight men captured by the Japanese was unknown and five were still interned in Russia.

War correspondents on the scene in North Africa sent news and photos of the mini-reunion to the States but the Raiders didn't think much about it. Hank Potter, Doolittle's navigator on the raid, said he was more concerned about the war where they were then than the single mission he had flown a year before. The others felt the same way.

Informal reunions were held in 1944 and 1945 whenever several Raiders found themselves near enough to get together and could spare the time from their duties. In the fall of 1945, after the surrender of Japan, Doolittle located all of the surviving Raiders and passed the word that he wanted them to help him celebrate his forty-ninth birthday on December 14 by meeting him at the MacFadden Deauville Hotel in Miami. It cost Doolittle $2,000 of his own money to make good on the promise he had made aboard the *Hornet* but it was a vow he was determined to keep. Most of the Raiders who had survived the war were able to make the trip and had such a rousing good time that someone suggested, "Let's do this every year!" Doolittle replied, "I'd like that, fellas, but I'm afraid I couldn't afford it. From here on, it's up to you to carry the ball."[1]

No reunion was held in 1946 but Miami again echoed to the laughter of Jimmy Doolittle and his Raiders in 1947. With two years of postwar adjustments behind them, they relaxed completely, much to the chagrin of Tom Willemstyn, the hotel's night manager who wrote this report to his boss:

> The Doolittle boys added some gray hairs to my head. This has been the worst night since I worked here. They were completely out of my control.
>
> I let them make a lot of noise but when 15 of them went in the pool at 1:00 a.m. (including Doolittle) I told them there was no swimming allowed at night. They were in the pool until 2:30 a.m.
>
> I went up twice more without results. They were running, around in the halls in their bathing suits and were noisy up until 5:00 a.m. Yes, it was a rough night.[2]

The hotel manager was not upset when he read Willemstyn's report. He gave the report to Doolittle, saying that his boys had earned the right to make all the noise they wanted to in his hotel. He asked them to honor the occasion by autographing the report, which they did.

Each year since 1947 (except 1951 because of the Korean War and 1966 because of the Vietnam War), Doolittle and his Raiders have met in various cities as the guests of prominent members of the community, civic, and military organizations and industry. They have received mementoes of their visits including eighty silver goblets fitted into a beautiful display case by the City of Tucson in 1959, which are used by the men for an annual toast of their departed comrades. Between reunions, the goblets are on display at the Air Force Academy, Colorado Springs, Colorado. The North American Aviation Co. presented a B-25 Mitchell bomber to the group similar to the model they had all flown from the *Hornet*. It is on permanent display at the Air Force Museum, Wright-Patterson Air Force Base, Ohio.

The reunions are mostly three-day lighthearted affairs with much reminiscing. A press conference is held and a public banquet caps each reunion. The entertainment for the banquet is usually a celebrity who donates his time and talent in grateful appreciation to Doolittle and his Raiders. Bob Hope, Jimmy Stewart, Arthur Godfrey, Joe E. Brown, Bob Cummings, George Jessel, and other Hollywood stars have been among those who have attended, along with high-ranking army, navy, and air force personnel, senators, and congressmen.

The reunion held in Los Angeles in April 1955 was one that three of the Raiders will never forget. Col. Bill Bower, then commander of Dobbins Air Force Base, Georgia, Ed Horton, and Adam R. Williams were passengers on an air force C-47 en route to the West Coast. The plane departed Atlanta, where it had stopped for more passengers, and headed for Barksdale, Louisiana. A few minutes after takeoff, the propeller on the left engine began to surge out of control. The pilot, Capt. John England, turned back toward the nearest airfield but the overspeeding propeller could not be controlled and the plane rapidly began to lose speed and altitude.

The co-pilot, Capt. W. E. Brown, told the passengers to throw all their baggage overboard to lighten the load, then quickly told them they would have to bail out when the plane kept losing altitude. One by one, ten men bailed out, the last one about one thousand feet above the ground. Bill Bower elected to stay with the plane.

After the bailouts, the plane gained a little speed, managed to clear a ridge, and landed at the Fulton County Airport. When the crippled C-47 stopped, Bower leaped out and saw a helicopter warming up on the parking ramp. He quickly told the pilot what had happened and was soon back in the air searching for the ten men who had parachuted minutes before. All were found safe, although two were slightly injured. Ed Horton, the calm, efficient gunner on Dick Joyce's plane, suffered lacerations of an ear in this, his second jump. It was the fourth bailout for Adam Williams, his first being the night he jumped from his plane over China. Undaunted, the three Raiders proceeded to the reunion, but without their luggage, which had been strewn over the Georgia countryside and was not found until after their return.

The tone and tenor of the annual Doolittle Tokyo Raider reunions have changed over the years since Doolittle carried out his promise in 1945. The Raiders frankly admit they met at first solely for fun and fellowship. But as the years passed and their personal responsibilities grew, the original purpose enlarged and matured with them. Now they meet with three purposes in mind: to renew their long friendship, to honor the memory of those who have gone, and to participate in some activity that is of some benefit to the nation, the air force, and the community in which they meet.

Each year, the Raiders present a scholarship to a deserving young man or woman enrolled in an accredited university in the city in which they meet. The person chosen must be an outstanding student who intends to seek a career in aerospace science. The scholarship was established in 1963 by the Raiders in the name of General Doolittle because of deep respect and affection for his inspirational leadership.

Jimmy Doolittle and his men, now all past retirement age, will continue to meet each year as long as they live. They will always drink a toast to their fellow crew members who can no longer join them. The last two surviving members will open a special bottle of brandy and drink a final toast. When the inevitable day comes and the last man is gone, a glorious chapter in American military aviation history will close forever.

The epic deed Jimmy Doolittle and his raiders performed that eventful day in 1942 should not be forgotten. Our nation has been fortunate that it has always had men like Jimmy Doolittle and his intrepid airmen who have risen to the challenge and accepted the risk of certain death when our nation's life has been threatened.

May it always be so.

Acknowledgments

The author owes a debt of gratitude to many interested persons who willingly granted interviews or provided information about the 1942 raid on Japan and its aftermath. Special thanks are reserved for the numerous army, navy, air force, and Library of Congress information specialists, archivists, and historians for their knowledgable assistance. They not only gave access to significant, classified files and professional encouragement during the original research phase but provided important leads to people and incidental records that proved invaluable in being able to garner additional facts and eventually tell the whole story.

In addition to intelligence reports they filed in Chungking after their mission, the best sources of basic information proved to be the surviving members of Doolittle's Tokyo Raiders, who cooperated extensively by granting extended interviews and providing personal evidence of their experiences. Gen. James H. "Jimmy" Doolittle gave me unlimited access to his personal files on the mission and spent many hours answering my queries at annual Tokyo Raider reunions, during his visits to Washington, and, on one occasion, during his vacation at Cotuit, Massachusetts. Many elusive details, especially during the preparatory phase were known only to him. Without his personal interest and cooperation, many of the valuable human interest sidelights would never have been revealed.

I am especially indebted to Brig. Gen. Richard A. Knobloch, co-pilot on the thirteenth aircraft, who led me to the story of the raid while we were assigned to the Pentagon. We were pilots of a C-47 en route on official business to Colorado Springs, Colorado, when he suggested that we visit the Air Force Academy Museum nearby so he could see "our cups" on display. The "cups" were the silver goblets presented to Doolittle's Tokyo Raiders by the City of Tucson on which are inscribed the names of all eighty of the Tokyo Raiders. Some goblets are turned down signifying that those Raiders are "those who have gone." This poignant expression of fellowship and gratitude on display where future air force leaders are trained, was extremely moving and was the motivating factor that led me to this work. Some day, all those goblets will be turned down and it seemed that the story should be told while most of these courageous eighty airmen were still available as living witnesses to an outstanding and memorable event in aviation history.

The only previous book on this epochal air action when I began my research was *Thirty Seconds over Tokyo*. Published and made into a motion picture in 1943, it was only one man's experience, and the full story of the raid and its tragic aftermath was not known until long after the war. With the special encouragement of General Doolittle, I wrote the first definitive documentary of the raid under the title of *Doolittle's Tokyo Raiders*, first published in 1964. At his suggestion, I followed this in 1966 with a book entitled *Four Came Home* about the experiences of the eight men captured by the Japanese. Subsequent to the publication of both books, more information was obtained from readers with valuable first-hand accounts who were motivated to contact me and I am sincerely indebted to them. Other information arrived anonymously and mysteriously from Japanese sources. This book is, therefore, a result of more than twenty-five years of research and intensive effort to get all the facts and tell a story that has not been told in its entirety before.

Appendices

1. The Tokyo Raiders

(with Highest Ranks Held on Active Duty)

Bain, Edwin V., Master Sergeant
Born September 23, 1917, Greensboro, North Carolina. Killed in action July 19, 1943.

Barr, George, Captain
Born April 6, 1917, Brooklyn, New York. Died July 12, 1967.

Birch, William L., Second Lieutenant
Born September 7, 1917, Galexico, California.

Bissell, Wayne Max, First Lieutenant
Born October 22, 1921, Walker, Minnesota.

Bither, Waldo J., Major
Born October 31, 1906, Houlton, Maine. Died February 25, 1988.

Blanton, Thadd Harrison, Lieutenant Colonel
Born February 25, 1919, Archer City, Texas. Died September 27, 1961.

Bourgeois, Robert C., Flight Officer
Born September 28, 1917, Lecompte, Louisiana.

Bower, William M., Colonel
Born February 13, 1917, Ravenna, Ohio

Braemer, Fred Anthony, Captain
Born January 31, 1917, Seattle, Washington.

Campbell, Clayton J., Lieutenant Colonel
Born March 14, 1917, St. Maries, Idaho.

Clever, Robert Stevenson, First Lieutenant
Born May 22, 1914, Portland, Oregon. Died November 20, 1942.

Cole, Richard E., Colonel
Born September 7, 1915, Dayton, Ohio.

Crouch, Horace Ellis, Lieutenant Colonel
Born October 29, 1918, Columbia, South Carolina.

Davenport, Dean, Colonel
Born June 29, 1918, Spokane, Washington.

DeShazer, Jacob Daniel, Staff Sergeant
Born November 15, 1912, West Stayton, Oregon.

Dieter, William J., Staff Sergeant
Born October 5, 1912, Vail, Iowa. Died in action, April 18, 1942.

Doolittle, James Harold, Lieutenant General (promoted to General in 1985)
Born December 14, 1896, Alameda, California.

Duquette, Omer Adelard, Staff Sergeant
Born January 25, 1916, West Warwick, Rhode Island. Killed in action, June 3, 1942.

Eierman, Jacob, Major
Born February 2, 1913, Baltimore, Maryland.

Emmens, Robert G., Colonel
Born July 22, 1914, Medford, Oregon.

Faktor, Leland D., Corporal
Born May 17, 1921, Plymouth, Iowa. Killed in action, April 18, 1942.

Farrow, William G., First Lieutenant
Born September 24, 1918, Darlington, South Carolina. Executed by Japanese firing squad, October 15, 1942.

Fitzhugh, William N., Major
Born February 18, 1915, Temple, Texas. Died August 31, 1981.

Fitzmaurice, Donald E., Sergeant
Born March 13, 1919, Lincoln, Nebraska. Killed in action, April 18, 1942.

Gardner, Melvin J., Staff Sergeant
Born April 6, 1920, Mesa, Arizona. Killed in action, June 3, 1942.

Gray, Robert Manning, Captain
Born May 24, 1919, Killeen, Texas. Killed in action, October 18, 1942.

Greening, Charles Ross, Colonel
Born November 12, 1914, Carroll, Iowa. Died March 29, 1957.

Griffin, Thomas Carson, Major
Born July 10, 1917, Green Bay, Wisconsin.

Hallmark, Dean Edward, First Lieutenant
Born January 20, 1914, Robert Lee, Texas. Executed by Japanese firing squad, October 15, 1942.

Herndon, Nolan Anderson, Major
Born December 12, 1918, Greenville, Texas.

Hilger, John A., Brigadier General
Born January 11, 1909, Sherman, Texas. Died February 3, 1982.

Hite, Robert L., Lieutenant Colonel
Born March 3, 1920, Odell, Texas.

Holstrom, Everett W., Brigadier General
Born May 4, 1916, Cottage Grove, Oregon.

Hoover, Travis, Colonel
Born September 21, 1917, Melrose, New Mexico.

Horton, Edwin Weston, Jr., Master Sergeant
Born March 28, 1916, North Eastham, Massachusetts.

Jones, Aden Earl, Second Lieutenant
Born September 7, 1920, Flint, Michigan. Died March 9, 1983.

Jones, David M., Major General
Born December 18, 1913, Marshfield, Oregon.

Jordan, Bert M., Master Sergeant
Born September 3, 1919, Covington, Oklahoma.

Joyce, Richard Outcalt, Lieutenant Colonel
Born September 29, 1919, Lincoln, Nebraska. Died February 13, 1983.

Kappeler, Frank Albert, Lieutenant Colonel
Born January 2, 1914, San Francisco, California.

Knobloch, Richard A., Brigadier General
Born May 27, 1918, Milwaukee, Wisconsin.

Laban, Theodore H., Master Sergeant
Born July 13, 1914, Kenosha, Wisconsin. Died September 16, 1978.

Larkin, George Elmer, Jr., Staff Sergeant
Born November 26, 1918, New Haven, Kentucky. Killed in action, October 18, 1942.

Lawson, Ted W., Major
Born March 7, 1917, Fresno, California.

Lconard, Paul John, Master Sergeant
Born June 19, 1912, Roswell, New Mexico. Killed in action, January 5, 1943.

Macia, James Herbert, Colonel
Born April 10, 1916, Tombstone, Arizona.

Manch, Jacob Earle, Lieutenant Colonel
Born December 26, 1918, Staunton, Virginia. Died March 24, 1958.

Manske, Joseph W., Colonel
Born April 13, 1921, Gowanda, New York.

McClure, Charles L., Captain
Born October 4, 1916, St. Louis, Missouri.

McCool, Harry C., Lieutenant Colonel
Born April 19, 1918, La Junta, Colorado.

McElroy, Edgar E., Lieutenant Colonel
Born March 24, 1912, Ennis, Texas.

McGurl, Eugene Francis, First Lieutenant
Born February 8, 1917, Belmont, Massachusetts.

Meder, Robert John, First Lieutenant
Born August 23, 1917, Cleveland, Ohio. Died while prisoner of Japanese, December 1, 1943.

Miller, Richard Ewing, Captain
Born March 2, 1916, Fort Wayne, Indiana. Killed in action, January 22, 1943.

Nielsen, Chase Jay, Lieutenant Colonel
Born January 14, 1917, Hyrum, Utah.

Ozuk, Charles John, Captain
Born June 13, 1916, Vesta Heights, Pennsylvania.

Parker, James N., Major
Born February 4, 1920, Houston, Texas.

Pohl, David W., First Lieutenant
Born December 31, 1921, Boston, Massachusetts.

Potter, Henry A., Colonel
Born September 22, 1918, Pierre, South Dakota.

Pound, William R. Jr., Lieutenant Colonel
Born May 18, 1918, Milford, Utah. Died July 13, 1967.

Radney, Douglas V., Major
Born March 17, 1917, Mineola, Texas.

Reddy, Kenneth E., First Lieutenant
Born June 29, 1920, Bowie, Texas. Died September 3, 1942.

Saylor, Edward Joseph, Major
Born March 15, 1920, Brusett, Montana.

Scott, Eldred V., Lieutenant Colonel
Born September 29, 1907, Atlanta, Georgia. Died July 31, 1978.

Sessler, Howard Albert, Major
Born August 11, 1917, Boston, Massachusetts.

Sims, Jack A., Colonel
Born February 23, 1919, Kalamazoo, Michigan.

Smith, Donald G., Captain
Born January 15, 1918, Oldham, South Dakota. Killed in action, November 12, 1942.

Spatz, Harold A., Sergeant
Born July 14, 1921, Lebo, Kansas. Executed by Japanese firing squad, October 15, 1942.

Stephens, Robert J., Flight Officer
Born February 28, 1915, Hobart, Oklahoma. Died April 13, 1959.

Stork, J. Royden, Captain
Born December 11, 1916, Frost, Minnesota.

Thatcher, David J., Staff Sergeant
Born July 31, 1921, Bridger, Montana.

Truelove, Denver Vernon, Captain
Born November 10, 1919, Clermont, Georgia. Killed in action, April 5, 1943.

Watson, Harold Francis, Lieutenant Colonel
Born April 3, 1916, Buffalo, New York.

White, Thomas Robert, Major
Born March 29, 1909, Haiku, Hawaii.

Wilder, Ross R., Colonel
Born January 10, 1917, Taylor, Texas. Died June 7, 1964.

Wildner, Carl Richard, Lieutenant Colonel
Born May 18, 1915, Holyoke, Massachusetts.

Williams, Adam Ray, Master Sergeant
Born September 27, 1919, Gastonia, North Carolina.

Williams, Griffith Paul, Major
Born July 10, 1920, Chicago, Illinois.

York, Edward J., Colonel
Born August 16, 1912, Batavia, New York. Died August 31, 1984.

Youngblood, Lucian Nevelson, Major
Born May 26, 1918, Pampa, Texas. Died February 29, 1949.

2. Honorary Tokyo Raiders

(with Highest Ranks Held if in Military Service)

Bentz, Gerald E., Pharmacist Mate, First Class
Born January 25, 1922, Wisner, Nebraska.

Glines, Carroll V., Colonel
Born December 2, 1920, Baltimore, Maryland.

Graham, Charles J., Jr., First Lieutenant
Born February 21, 1923, Venice, California.

Leonard, Stephen
Born September 11, 1918, Kendallville, Indiana.

Liu, Tung-Sheng
Born December 3, 1917, Wei-Tying, Kiangsi, China.

Miller, Henry L., Rear Admiral, USN
Born July 18, 1912, Fairbanks, Alaska.

Pittenger, Richard M.
Born October 12, 1912, Pittsburgh, Pennsylvania.

3. Air Force Personnel Aboard Hornet But Not on Raid

Lt. James P. Bates, Pilot
Lt. James M. Belk, Bombardier
Lt. Warren A. Beth, Navigator
Lt. Wiley M. Bondurant, Navigator
Lt. Daniel W. Brown, Bombardier
Lt. Heston C. Daniel, Pilot
Lt. Robert M. Hackney, Co-Pilot
Lt. Bert H. Hartzell, Navigator
Lt. Harvey M. Hinman, Pilot
Lt. Harry Johnson, Jr., Liaison Officer
Lt. Louis E. Keller, Co-Pilot
Lt. Joseph R. Klein, Co-Pilot
Lt. Arvid E. Malmstrom, Co-Pilot
Lt. James D. Mathews, Navigator
Lt. Glen C. Roloson, Co-Pilot
Lt. Henry J. Sabotka, Co-Pilot
Capt. Vernon L. Stinzi, Pilot
Lt. Charles H. Sullenger, Navigator

Cpl. Donald H. Arbogast, Radio Maintenance, Gunner
Cpl. Louis H. Ahearn, Mechanic
Sgt. Joseph N. Baldwin, Maintenance
Sgt. William E. Batchelor, Mechanic
Sgt. Jess W. Brazell, Mechanic
S. Sgt. Albert S. Brisco, Mechanic
Sgt. Lilburn N. Cate, Mechanic
Sgt. Curtis L. Cloud, Maintenance
S. Sgt. Mike Coloff, Mechanic
Sgt. Harry W. Dullinger, Armament, Gunner
Sgt. Lowell J. Fichner, Mechanic
Sgt. Robert L. Habben, Mechanic
Sgt. Gordon B. Hansen, Mechanic
Sgt. Leonard N. Hanten, Maintenance
Sgt. James F. Hattan, Mechanic
Sgt. Thomas W. Hill, Clerk
Cpl. Maurice J. Hilton, Radio Maintenance
T. Sgt. Wendell C. Horne, Bombardier, Gunner
Cpl. Foster S. Johnson, Radio Maintenance
S. Sgt. Raymond K. Johnson, Mechanic
Cpl. Laurell E. Julius, Mechanic
S. Sgt. Harrison D. Lacquey, Armament
Pfc. Wayne H. Lash, Armament, Gunner
Sgt. Francis M. Lee, Mechanic
T. Sgt. Joseph A. Lopez, Armament, Gunner
T. Sgt. Wilson L. Minich, Mechanic, Gunner
Sgt. James B. Murphy, Mechanic
Sgt. Charles E. Reed, Maintenance
Cp. Richard L. Schwartz, Mechanic
S. Sgt. Douglas P. Smith, Mechanic
Cpl. Leslie A. Sucker, Armament
S. Sgt. Roy R. Sweigard, Maintenance
Cpl. Charles T. Treadwell, Armament
S. Sgt. Lawerence E. Wikoff, Armament

Chapter Notes

1. The Day of Infamy

1. John Toland, *The Rising Sun* (New York: Random House, 1970), p. 151.
2. Stanley Ulanoff, *Bombs Away!* (New York: Doubleday & Co., 1970), p. 314.
3. *Ibid.* pp. 328–329.
4. *Ibid.* p. 338.

2. A Concept Is Born

1. Memorandum of White House Meeting, January 4, 1942. Gen. Henry H. Arnold files, Library of Congress.
2. Memorandum to Maj. Gen. Edwin M. Watson, January 7, 1942. General Arnold files, Library of Congress.
3. Interview with Adm. Francis S. Low, San Francisco, Calif., September 12, 1962.

3. The B-25B Special Project

1. Henry H. Arnold, *Global Mission* (New York: Harper and Brothers, 1949), p. 299.
2. *Ibid.*
3. *Ibid.*
4. Based on interviews conducted at Seattle, Wash., April 16, 1963; Washington, D.C., June 25–26, 1963 and October 5, 1963; Cotuit, Mass., August 5–6, 1963, and letter to the author dated February 1, 1963.
5. *Ibid.*
6. *Ibid.*
7. From interview at Las Vegas, Nev., April 10, 1986.
8. Arnold, *Global Mission*, *op. cit.*, p. 289.
9. Interview, May 1, 1963.
10. This document is the only known record of the planning phases of the mission against Japan at this point. Undated, it was believed written during the first week of February, 1942, but it was never actually sent to General Arnold. When shown a copy of the document, Doolittle said, "It is definitely in my handwriting but I do not recall preparing this letter. It may have been done at the request of General Arnold, or it is

possible I may have jotted some of my ideas down in letter form to clarify my thinking in connection with the various phases of the project."

4. "Tell Jimmy to Get on His Horse"

1. Unpublished, undated manuscript by Rear Adm. Henry L. Miller, forwarded by letter dated January 7, 1963, p. 3.
2. Based on interviews with Doolittle and crew members between April, 1962 and December, 1963.
3. Miller manuscript, *op. cit.*, p. 4.
4. Col. Charles R. Greening, "The First Joint Action," prepared for the Armed Forces Staff College, Norfolk, Va., December 21, 1948.
5. Interview, Albuquerque, N. M., April 16, 1985.
6. Interview, Randolph AFB, Tex., May 30, 1963.
7. Interview, Santa Monica, Calif., April 19, 1962, and letter dated June 13, 1962.
8. Interview, Cortuit, Mass., August 5, 1963.
9. *Ibid.* He told the author, "I'll have to admit that I really counted on leading the mission from the moment I first heard about it. My only problem was how to approach Hap so he would say 'Yes.' " Further proof of this is his plan reported in Chapter 3.
10. *Ibid.*

5. "This Force Is Bound for Tokyo!"

1. John Toland, *op. cit.*, p. 287.
2. William F. Halsey and J. Bryan, III, *Admiral Halsey's Story*. (New York: McGraw-Hill Book Co., 1947), p. 32.
3. Interview, Cotuit, Mass., August 5, 1963.
4. Ted W. Lawson, *Thirty Seconds Over Tokyo*. (New York: Random House, 1943), p. 32.
5. Interview, Washington, D.C., October 5, 1963.
6. *Ibid.*
7. Halsey and Bryan, *op. cit.*, p. 104.
8. Interview, Randolph AFB, Tex., May 30, 1963.
9. *Ibid.*
10. Miller unpublished manuscript, *op.cit.*
11. Message No. 284, Ulio, Adjutant General, U.S. Army to AMMISCA, Chungking, March 16, 1942.
12. Message No. 391, Stilwell to Arnold, March 29, 1942.
13. Message No. 371, Arnold to Chungking, March 31, 1942.

14. Doolittle interview, Washington, D.C., October 5, 1963.
15. *Ibid.*
16. Knobloch interview, Seattle, Wash., April 17, 1963.
17. Interviews with General and Mrs. Doolittle, Cotuit, Mass., August 5, 1963.
18. Radiograms, Gen. Henry H. Arnold, Headquarters, Army Air Forces, and Gen. George C. Marshall, Chief of Staff, U.S. Army, Washington, D.C. to Lt. Col. J. H. Doolittle, March 31, 1942.
19. Radiogram, Adm. Ernest J. King, Chief of Naval Operations, Washington, D.C. to Capt. Marc A. Mitscher, USS *Hornet*, March 31, 1942.
20. Interview, Cotuit, Mass., August 5, 1963.
21. Capt. Frederick L. Reifkohl, USN, post-mission interview with intelligence officers, U.S. Navy file, April, 1942.
22. Capt. Marc A. Mitscher, USN, "Commanding Officer's Report of Action," to Commander-in-Chief, U.S. Pacific Fleet, April 28, 1942.
23. Miller unpublished manuscript, *op. cit.*
24. Interview, Washington, D.C., June 25, 1963.
25. Robert G. Emmens, response to questionnaire, Air Force Office of Information, March 28, 1957.
26. J. Royden Stork, response to questionnaire, Air Force Office of Information, March 28, 1957.
27. From interviews conducted by the CBS Television Network for "The Doolittle Raid," produced by the Public Affairs Department of CBS News.
28. From statements made in Washington, D.C., December 26, 1945. Because of the limited damage that could be inflicted by the B-25s, Doolittle wanted the raiders to concentrate on military targets only. The Imperial Palace was not considered a military target. It was believed that the Japanese would retaliate harshly against any Americans captured who had bombed the palace.
29. Interview, Santa Monica, April 19, 1962.
30. From CBS interviews, *op. cit.*
31. Interview, Washington, D.C., June 25, 1963.
32. Message No. 464, Marshall to AMMISCA, Chungking, April 12, 1942.
33. Message No. 519, Chungking to AGWAR for AMMISCA, April 14, 1942.
34. Message No. 479, Marshall to AMMISCA, Chungking, April 15, 1942.

35. Message No. 501, Marshall to AMMISCA, Chungking, April 18, 1942.
36. Operation Plan No. 20-42, United States Pacific Fleet, April 7, 1942.

6. The Enemy Is Alerted: The Mission Begins

1. Extract from "Homeland Air Defense Operations Record," undated, Japanese Monograph No. 157, Headquarters, USAFFE and Eighth Army, Tokyo.
2. An anonymous military historian, *Yomiuri Shimbun*, March 25, 1950, p. 2.
3. Tokyo Radio broadcast, April 15, 1942 as reported to Task Force 16.
4. Doolittle interview, Cotuit, Mass., August 5, 1963.
5. *Ibid.*
6. *Ibid.*
7. Miller manuscript, *op. cit.*
8. *Ibid.*
9. Letter to the author, March 6, 1965.
10. Navy Department, Office of Naval History: CINCPAC Report, May 4, 1942.
11. Halsey and Bryan, *Admiral Halsey's Story*, p. 105.
12. *Ibid.*
13. Doolittle interview, Cotuit, Mass., August 5, 1963.
14. *Record of Sea Battles: Diary of the Late Vice Admiral Matome Ugaki*, War History Office, Japan Defense Agency, Tokyo. Entry for April 18, 1942.
15. Diplomats remained at the American and British embassies until June, 1942 when they were exchanged for Japanese diplomats in Washington.

7. ". . . Believe All Planes Wrecked"

1. Headquarters, American Army Forces, China, Burma, and India. Mission report filed by Doolittle in Chungking, April 30, 1942.
2. *Ibid.*
3. *Ibid.*
4. Richard E. Cole, response to questionnaire, Air Force Office of Information, March 28, 1957.
5. Interview, Seattle, Wash., April 18, 1963.
6. Interview, Washington, D.C., October 5, 1963.
7. *Ibid.*

8. William M. Bower, personal diary, entry for April 30, 1942.
9. *Ibid.*, entry for May 9, 1942.

8. Takeoff into History

1. Lt. Travis Hoover, *Personal Report*, Chungking, China, May 15, 1942.
2. *Ibid.*
3. *Ibid.*
4. S. Sgt. Douglas V. Radney, *Personal Report*, Chungking, China, May 14, 1942.
5. Hoover, *Personal Report*, *op. cit.*
6. *Ibid.*
7. Lt. Richard E. Miller, *Personal Report*, Chungking, China, May 14, 1942.
8. Chuchow and Chuhsien are used interchangeably because the city was known by both names on old maps used by the raiders.
9. Miller, *Personal Report*, *op. cit.*
10. Hoover, *Personal Report*, *op. cit.*
11. Jacob E. Manch, response to questionnaire from Air Force Office of Information, March 28, 1957.
12. *Ibid.*
13. *Ibid.*
14. *Ibid.*
15. *Ibid.*
16. *Ibid.*
17. Lt. Everett W. Holstrom, *Personal Report*, Chungking, China, May 14, 1942.
18. It is believed that the aircraft sighted by the B-25 crews were Type 97 fighter planes used to defend the home islands. Built in the late 1930s, they could not match the speed of the B-25s at full throttle.
19. Bert M. Jordan, response to questionnaire from Air Force Office of Information, March 28, 1957.
20. Report of interview with Lt. H. C. McCool by Capt. J. McGhee, Washington, D.C., August 23, 1942.
21. Col. E. W. Holstrom, letter to the author, January 28, 1963.
22. Joseph W. Manske, response to questionnaire from Air Force Office of Information, March 28, 1957.
23. Capt. David M. Jones, *Narrative Report*, Chungking, China, May 18, 1942.

24. *Ibid.*
25. Manske response to questionnaire, *op. cit.*
26. Jones, *op. cit.*
27. *Ibid.*
28. Ross R. Wilder, response to questionnaire, Air Force Office of Information, March 27, 1957.
29. Jones, *op. cit.*
30. Lt. Denver V. Truelove, *Personal Report*, Chungking, China, May 18, 1942.
31. From undated manuscript furnished by Chase J. Nielsen.
32. *Ibid.*
33. *Ibid.*
34. *Ibid.*
35. Ted W. Lawson, response to questionnaire, Air Force Office of Information, March 28, 1957.
36. Dean Davenport, response to questionnaire, Air Force Office of Information, March 28, 1957.
37. Corp. David J. Thatcher, *Personal Report*, Chungking, China, May 15, 1942.
38. *Ibid.*
39. *Ibid.*
40. *Ibid.*
41. Edward J. York, response to questionnaire, Air Force Office of Information, March 28, 1957.
42. Robert G. Emmens, *Guests of the Kremlin* (New York: The Macmillan Co. 1949), p. 6.
43. York response to questionnaire, *op. cit.*
44. *Ibid.*
45. Emmens, *Guests of the Kremlin*, pp. 16–17.
46. *Ibid.*, p. 18.
47. Emmens, letter to the author, May 3, 1963.
48. Harold F. Watson, response to questionnaire, Air Force Office of Information, March 28, 1957.
49. *Ibid.*
50. Thomas C. Griffin, response to questionnaire, Air Force Office of Information, March 27, 1957.
51. *Ibid.*
52. *Ibid.*
53. James M. Parker, response to questionnaire, Air Force Office of Information, March 27, 1957.
54. *Ibid.*
55. Griffin, response to questionnaire.
56. Parker, response to questionnaire.

57. Richard O. Joyce, *Mission Report*, Chungking, China, May 5, 1942.
58. *Ibid.*
59. *Ibid.*
60. Richard O. Joyce, interview, Santa Monica, Calif., April 18, 1962.
61. J. Royden Stork, response to questionnaire, Air Force Office of Information, March 27, 1957.
62. Richard O. Joyce, *Mission Report*, *op. cit.*
63. Frank A. Kappeler, response to questionnaire, Air Force Office of Information, March 27, 1957.
64. William L. Birch, response to questionnaire, Air Force Office of Information, March 27, 1957.
65. As related by Frank A. Kappeler, April 19, 1963.
66. William R. Pound, Jr., response to questionnaire, Air Force Office of Information, March 27, 1957.
67. Report of interview with Capt. J. Pinkney, Headquarters, Army Air Forces, Washington, D.C., June 15, 1942.
68. Pound, response to questionnaire, *op. cit.*
69. Waldo J. Bither, response to questionnaire, March 27, 1957. Bither had helped around the parachute shops where he had repacked tow targets many times before; he felt reasonably sure the packing principles were the same. He told the author, "I *knew* it would work. In fact, I felt a lot better about it after I repacked it than I had before."
70. *Ibid.*
71. Bither interview, Seattle, Wash., April 19, 1963.
72. Adam R. Williams, response to questionnaire, Air Force Office of Information, March 27, 1957.
73. Richard A. Knobloch, unpublished manuscript dated November 22, 1963.
74. *Ibid.*
75. Sgt. Robert C. Bourgeois, *Personal Report*, Chungking, China, May 5, 1942.
76. Clayton J. Campbell, telephone interview, December 2, 1987.
77. Knobloch manuscript, *op. cit.*
78. Lt. James H. Macia, *Personal Report*, Chungking, China, May 5, 1942.
79. John A. Hilger, personal diary, entry for April 18, 1942.
80. *Ibid.*
81. Jack A. Sims, response to questionnaire, Air Force Office of Information, March 27, 1957.

82. Hilger diary, entry for April 19, 1942.
83. *Ibid.*, entry for April 20, 1942.
84. Lt. Donald G. Smith, *Personal Report*, Chungking, China, May 14, 1942.
85. *Ibid.*
86. Lt. (Dr.) T. Robert White, personal diary, entry for April 18, 1942.
87. *Ibid.*, entry for April 19, 1942.
88. *Ibid.*, entry for April 20, 1942.
89. Interview, Cotuit, Mass., August 5, 1963,.
90. White diary, entries April 24 through May 9, 1942.
91. A PBY amphibian was requested from the Philippines but the request could not be honored. Corregidor surrendered on May 6, 1942.
92. Dr. White was the donor this time. Lawson's leg had to be amputated because gangrene had begun to set in before White arrived. Dave Thatcher had kept a tourniquet on Lawson's leg and released it periodically as required but Lawson ordered him to stop, thus possibly aggravating the infection. "I wanted to save the leg if I could," White told the author, "but it had gotten to the point where it was his leg or his neck so I took his leg."
93. Interview, McLean, Va., June 30, 1965.
95. *Ibid.*
96. *Ibid.*

9. A Psychological Blow to the Japanese

1. *Record of Sea Battles: Diary of the Late Vice Admiral Matome Ugaki*, War History Office, *op. cit.*, entry for April 18, 1942.
2. *Ibid.*, entry for April 19, 1942.
3. *Ibid.*
4. Undated statement made to intelligence officers, Army Air Forces files, 1943.
5. Joseph C. Grew, *Ten Years in Japan* (New York: Simon and Schuster, 1944), p. 526.
6. Otto D. Tolischus, *Tokyo Record* (New York: Harcourt, Brace & World, 1943), p. 268.
7. Interview, Arlington, Va., November 20, 1962. Now wife of John Toland, noted for his many outstanding books, including *But Not in Shame* and *The Rising Sun.*
8. *Asahi Shimbun*, April 19, 1942.
9. *Ibid.*, April 21, 1942.

10. *Shashin Shuho*, April 29, 1942.
11. Otto P. Tolischus, *Tokyo Record*, *op. cit.*, p. 269.
12. From interview reported in *New York Times*, April 25, 1943.

10. The Chinese Pay with Their Lives

1. Message from Commander-in-Chief, China Expeditionary Forces, Shanghai, April 20, 1942.
2. Cable to United States Government, April 30, 1942.
3. Claire L. Chennault, *Way of a Fighter* (New York: G.P. Putnam's Sons, 1949), p. 168.
4. From records of War Crimes Trials, Shanghai, China, 1946.
5. Interview reported in *New York Times*, November 21, 1943.
6. *Ibid.*
7. Letter to Bishop Paul Yu Pin, Nanking, 1942.
8. From "The Doolittle Air Raid on Japan Known as First Aviation Project" by Col. Merion C. Cooper, Chungking, China, June 22, 1942 and letter dated January 11, 1963.
9. *Ibid.*
10. Interview, Cotuit, Mass., August 5, 1963.
11. Filed with Cooper report. *op. cit.*
12. Chennault, *Way of a Fighter*, *op. cit.*, p. 168.

11. Guests of the Kremlin

1. Years later, some would accuse York of having been directed by unnamed intelligence sources to fly deliberately to the Soviet Union, thus forcing it into the war against Japan. York and Emmens have emphatically denied this and say it was a matter of life or death for their crew. With the fuel consumption they experienced, they would have gone down in the China Sea about three hundred miles from the coast with little hope of survival in the stormy, shark-infested sea.
2. Report entitled "Interview with B-25 Crew that Bombed Tokyo and Was Interned by the Russians," Assistant Chief of Air Staff, Intelligence, Headquarters, Army Air Forces, Washington, D.C., June 3, 1943.
3. Emmens, *Guests of the Kremlin*, *op. cit.*, p. 39.
4. York, *op. cit.*
5. Message, Ambassador Standley to State Department, April 22, 1942.

6. Message, Michela to American Embassy, Moscow, May 25, 1942.
7. Message from Maj. Gen. Follett Bradley, Moscow, to Chief of Air Staff, Headquarters, Army Air Forces, Washington, D.C., November 6, 1942.
8. Emmens, *Guests of the Kremlin*, *op cit.*, p. 212.
9. *Ibid.*, p. 240.
10. *Ibid.*, p. 252.
11. *Ibid.*, p. 276.
12. *Ibid.*, p. 278
13. *Ibid.*, p. 280.
14. Letter to the author, September 12, 1987.
15. *Ibid.*
16. Emmens, *Guests of the Kremlin*, *op. cit.*, p. 291.

12. Forty Months of Hell

1. Unpublished manuscript, Chase J. Nielsen.
2. *Ibid.*
3. *Ibid.*
4. From evidence presented at War Crimes Trials, Shanghai, China, 1946.
5. Undated deposition by Robert L. Hite and Jacob D. DeShazer taken in Washington, D.C.
6. *Ibid.*
7. Interview, Ft. Worth, Tex., April 17, 1964.
8. From documents introduced during War Crimes Trials, Shanghai, China, 1946.
9. *Ibid.*
10. *Ibid.*
11. *Ibid.*
12. The Japanese did not turn over these letters to the International Red Cross. They were translated into Japanese and the originals lost or destroyed. The translations were discovered after the war in the files of the War Ministry in Tokyo. The condemned men wrote twelve letters but only three were introduced as evidence.
13. Testimony at War Crimes Trials.
14. Deposition made at Schick General Hospital, Clinton, Iowa, December 30, 1945.
15. Document presented at War Crimes Trials.
16. Interview, Ft. Worth, Tex., April 19, 1964.
17. C. Hoyt Watson, *The Amazing Story of Sergeant Jacob*

DeShazer. (Winona Lake, Indiana: Life and Light Press, 1950), pp. 120–121.

18. Unpublished manuscript by Jacob DeShazer.

13. "Four Doolittle Raiders Located"

1. Letter to the author from Richard S. Hamada, August 11, 1964.
2. Letter to the author from Dr. F. G. Jarman, Jr., April 19, 1965.
3. *Ibid.*
4. *Ibid.*
5. *Ibid.*
6. *Ibid.*
7. Letter to the author from Hilaire du Berrier, March 8, 1965.

14. Last to Return

1. Based on a series of interviews and letters between April 19, 1964, and July 31, 1965.
2. Clinical Record Brief of Lt. George Barr (NMI). Diagnosis: Beri-beri, psychosis, paranoid condition.
3. Letters to the author dated May 31 and June 16, 1964, from Ernest W. Manley, medical orderly assigned to monitor Barr's condition at Kunming.
4. This information is derived from an unpublished manuscript by George Barr written as therapy during convalescence in 1946; also interviews with Barr in 1965.
5. Handwritten medical report by Capt. (Dr.) S. H. Green, Letterman General Hospital, October 17, 1945.
6. As related by Mrs. Charles H. Towns, Manchester, N.H., August 3, 1965.
7. Interview, Cotuit, Mass. August 5, 1963.
8. Carroll V. Glines, *Four Came Home* (Princeton, New Jersey: Van Nostrand, 1966), p. 223.

15. Justice the American Way

1. Letter from Secretary of State to the President, March 15, 1943.
2. Letter to Secretary of State, White House, April 8, 1943.
3. White House press release, April 21, 1943.
4. All statements are from transcripts of the War Crimes Trials conducted in Shanghai, China, in 1946.

16. The Judgment of History

1. Report by Lt. Gen. James H. Doolittle, June 25, 1945.
2. *Asahi Shimbun*, April 19, 1942.
3. U.S. Army Air Forces, *Mission Accomplished: Interrogations of Japanese Industrial, Military and Civil Leaders of World War II* (1946).
4. *Ibid.*
5. Interview, Cotuit, Mass., August 6, 1963.

Epilogue

1. Interview, Santa Monica, Calif., April 19, 1962.
2. Note to hotel manager, April 20, 1947.

Bibliography

Arnold, Henry H. *Global Mission.* New York: Harper & Bros., 1949.

Craven, Wesley F., and Cate, James L. (eds.) *The Army Air Forces in World War II*, Vol. I. Chicago: The University of Chicago Press, 1948.

Emmens, Robert G. *Guests of the Kremlin.* New York: The Macmillan Co., 1949.

Fuchida, Mitsuo, and Masatake Okumiya. *Midway: The Battle that Doomed Japan.* Annapolis, Md.: Naval Institute Press, 1955.

Glines, Carroll V. *The Compact History of the United States Air Force.* New York: Hawthorn Books, 1963, 1973.

———. *Doolittle's Tokyo Raiders.* New York: Van Nostrand Reinhold, 1964, 1981.

———. *Jimmy Doolittle, Master of the Calculated Risk.* New York: The Macmillan Co., 1972; Van Nostrand Reinhold, 1980.

———. *Four Came Home.* New York: Van Nostrand Reinhold, 1966, 1981.

Halsey, William F., and Bryan, J. *Admiral Halsey's Story.* New York: McGraw-Hill Book Co., 1947.

Karig, Walter, and Kelley, Welbourn. *Battle Report: Pearl Harbor to the Coral Sea.* New York: Rinehart and Co., 1944.

King, Ernest J., and Whitehill, Walter Muir. *Fleet Admiral King: A Naval Record.* New York: W.W. Norton, 1952.

Lawson, Ted W. *Thirty Seconds over Tokyo*, ed. Robert Considine. New York: Random House, Inc., 1943.

Morison, Samuel Eliot. *The Rising Sun in the Pacific, 1931–April 1942.* Boston: Little, Brown and Co., 1948.

Reynolds, Quentin. *The Amazing Mr. Doolittle.* New York: Appleton-Century-Crofts, Inc., 1953.

Smith, S. E., ed. *The United States Navy in World War II.* New York: William Morrow & Co., 1966.

Taylor, Theodore. *The Magnificent Mitscher.* New York: W.W. Norton Co., 1954.

Toland, John. *But Not in Shame.* New York: Random House, Inc., 1961.

———. *The Rising Sun.* New York: Random House, Inc. 1970.

Ulanoff, Stanley M., ed. *Bombs Away!* New York: Doubleday & Co., Inc., 1971.

Watson, C. Hoyt. *The Amazing Story of Sergeant Jacob De Shazer*. Winona Lake, Indiana: Life and Life Press, 1950.

INDEX